STOCKWELL STORY

BOOK ONE OF THE REDEYE SERIES

STOCKWELL STORY

RICHARD WHITTLESEY

CONTENTS

Chapter 1 1
Chapter 2 11
Chapter 3 19
Chapter 4 25
Chapter 5 34
Chapter 6 39
Chapter 7 46
Chapter 8 56
Chapter 9 70
Chapter 10 78
Chapter 11 87
Chapter 12 100
Chapter 13 106
Chapter 14 117
Chapter 15 125
Chapter 16 133
Chapter 17 140
Chapter 18 149
Chapter 19 158
Chapter 20 166
Chapter 21 173
Chapter 22 184
Chapter 23 190
Chapter 24 198
Chapter 25 207
Chapter 26 217
Chapter 27 227
Chapter 28 245
Chapter 29 261
Chapter 30 274
Chapter 31 280
Chapter 32 288
Chapter 33 298

Chapter 1

I've got a bad feeling about this fight, and guess what? I'm never wrong when it comes to feelings. Dubs is his usual, relaxed self before a tear up, but that's down to the fact he never loses. The thing is, none of us knew fuck all about this mysterious French bod he's up against until a few days ago. In other words, we ain't got half a clue what he's capable of; just know his name is Norbert. We've called him Napoleon Stretch as he is so fuckin' tall. Skinny bastard with the longest arms you've ever seen. Picture a six foot four, shaved sloth with a centre parting, and you'll get some idea what this fella looks like.

When the bell rings for the first round, Stretch comes out like a possessed praying mantis on speed. His combinations are a blur, but so is Dubs's bobbing and weaving. A crunching body shot by Dubs has Napoleon in trouble two seconds before the end of the first round, clearly about to fold. In round two, the slippery Frenchman brings his dirty, little trick into play, sharpened nails like scalpels on each pinky. The crafty cunt punches with a clenched fist, but leaves the little finger slightly loose; flicking them out with lightning speed and accuracy, aiming just above the eyes. For the entire round Dubs gets sliced to fuck above both eyebrows and sustains a three-inch gash to the right cheek; looks a complete mess at the end of

1

three minutes. It's pretty much the same story for the next two rounds as well. Dubs is having problems getting close enough because of Stretch's long reach that is now aiming for the eyeball itself. Whenever Dubs takes a step forward, he risks permanent blindness. At range, Napoleon is landing every slice from his nails exactly where he wants, always in the same spot as the last cut, making it deeper every time. He then lands a punch on the cut to open it up. That is his signature piece, the nails. Like Dubs has his famous Panther Punch. It wouldn't surprise me if Stretch had won all his fights with that naughty technique, it's pretty effective. I've never seen Dubs get into this kind of trouble before. Normally he gives the crowd their money's worth then ends the fight when he's ready. This is slightly different though.

The fight was being held at a scrapyard just off the Wandsworth Road in South London. The ring was a sixteen-foot square made up of clapped-out, rusty old bangers that wouldn't look out of place in a Mad Max movie. A deafening crack of thunder is soon followed by a heavy downpour that reduces the yard to a swamp in a matter of minutes. There are no seats of any sort available, only standing space. People have been funnelled in to maximum capacity, jostling for space that doesn't exist.

I'm sitting by Dubs's corner and have a very good view of what's unfolding. The problem's simple; Napoleon is a straight-up freak of nature. He's got no devastating knockout punch to speak of, so that instantly neutralises Dubs's counter 'Panther Punch' which pretty much puts an end to most of his fights. Then there's the weapons on this fella's little fingers; what the fuck is that all about? Somebody needs to blow the dust off the rule book sharpish, or somewhere down the line a fighter will have a signature move simply called 'The kick up the bollocks'.

Napoleon's weak-arse punches wouldn't normally faze Dubs, on any other day he'd simply stroll right through them while winking at girls in the crowd. Today is another story, there's a mutant, maniac insecto-sloth in front of him, hell-bent on trying to pluck his eyes out, which when you think about it, tends to dampen the fun a touch. It must have taken Stretch years to perfect his technique, but then again Dubs trained for five solid years to get his titanium knuckles, so maybe that also makes him a freak. Let me just quickly fill you in on the Panther Punch before the next round starts.

This punch took Dubs five years to develop, and I seriously can't remember a single day during that time I ever saw him without his hands wrapped in blood-soaked bandages. For the first two years he conditioned his knuckles on a leather punchbag filled with gravel. For the next three years he would constantly punch a concrete wall from a distance of four inches for two hours a day, every day without fail. This process blessed him with knuckles that were as hard as stone, and the Panther Punch was born. The way he'd pull it off was to wait for just the right moment when his opponent would throw his most brutal knockout punch. Then, with unbelievable timing and accuracy, Dubs would deliver his own devastating punch, coupled with knuckles made from solid granite, that would intercept the incoming fist, smashing it to pieces. As all fights were bare knuckle, the end result would be an opponent with a totally destroyed hand that could no longer continue, and the fight would be over. That punch alone has made Dubs a bit of a star in the underground fight scene. I'm not kidding when I say his fans will travel miles to watch any fight he's in, just for that special punch, and they go fuckin' insane when it's delivered. They also call him the Black Panther, and to be honest, it suits him bang on. Dubs is of Nigerian descent, but born and raised in Stockwell. A sharp dresser with a cheeky cockney accent the girls go totally nuts over. Quite a fanatic about his training and diet, he never carries an ounce of fat on his six-foot frame. He's got one of those physiques that looks like it's carved from solid ebony, and shoulders like fuckin' cannonballs; a graceful fighter that would stalk his opponent in the ring, waiting to pounce with that crazy punch. Whenever Dubs knocked a bloke down, he always gave him plenty of time to get back on his feet, rather than smash the fuck out of him on the floor, so he's well liked inside and out the ring.

Dubs was losing, and going into the fifth round he's a crimson mess. I can count five cuts that'll stay with him forever; two on the right cheek, one over the left eye and two really deep ones over the right. How the fuck he was getting through each round I don't know. The blood pouring into his eyes and down his face was immense, blurring his vision so he couldn't see the fierce body shots in time to block them.

Fights are beginning to erupt in the crowd as pissed off punters await an upset. Security, with American pit bulls, is called in to calm the matter, which the dogs ignore, preferring to fight each other instead. After two minutes, twelve seconds of the sixth round, something takes place that will haunt me forever. I turn away from the fight to pick up a bottle of water and miss what people far and wide are hailing as the 'knockout of knockouts'; the most incredible punch known to man. This punch started off in Nigeria, came up through Libya, smashed its way through Italy without even stopping for a cappuccino. By the time it got to France it was moving so fast you might as well call it a blur. French air traffic control picked the punch up on radar with shouts of 'Mon Dieu!'

Across the Chanel with hypersonic speed the punch

reaches its destination; Napoleon's chin. At the point of impact, everything goes into slow motion. The sweat spray from Napoleon's face freezes mid-air, as the uppercut connects, in an exact copy of the rings of Saturn. Dubs lifts a finger, reassuring his fans he's still number one, as Norbert crumples to the canvas. That's what I'm told anyway; like I said, I missed it. Last thing I saw was Dubs on the ropes, blind, taking an absolute pounding.

Napoleon is still asleep ten minutes after the fight, with his people darting about clueless as to what to do with him. I don't think they expected him to get horizontal; they definitely weren't prepared for it that's for sure. The crowd's going nuts. More fighting breaks out, then sure enough the police come, fuckin' hundreds of them. The police dogs let loose are instantly taken down by the pit bulls, giving people that extra second or two to split. Full-on chaos is now at maximum flow, as somebody slings a smoke grenade bang centre of the commotion. The police are using their batons on anyone within range.

We've gotta get out of here; we both have a lot to lose if we get nicked. The smoke, rain and churning up mud makes the yard look like a battered war zone. We slip our way through the madness and climb up over a pile of old bangers hoping to find the street on the other side empty. Luck's with us, and we jump down onto the roof of a parked car and make our way through a very convenient alley. Police sirens blazing from every direction force us over a wall into someone's back garden. My car's parked just around the next corner, though getting Dubs there, looking the way he does, in broad daylight, without being seen, is another story. The cuts on his face need sorting, but he agrees they can wait until things die down. We glance across the garden towards a house, there are no lights on; maybe nobody's home. We chance a sneaky tiptoe over to an old, green wooden shed tucked away at the far end of the garden, hidden from view of the house by brambles and a large holly bush. It doesn't seem like the shed's been used in years going by the collection of spiderwebs and dusty crap all over the place, but as the rain turns into hail, it's a cushy little hideout all the same.

Dubs grabs a pair of dungarees that are draped over a rusty lawnmower and puts them on over his blood-soaked boxing shorts. They come halfway up his shins and look fuckin' hilarious. Why on earth did I leave my phone in the car? Could of just called a pal to drive round and pick us up. Still, there's no point moaning about it. I roll a spliff that hits the spot and chase it with two more that gets us nicely baked.

"What happened to Posh Mark, blud? I thought you was meeting him at the fight for business. Did you see him?" asks Dubs.

"Yeah, he took a hundred bits off me while you was getting in the ring. Fuck knows what happened to him after, he was coked out of his nut, mate. I had to fuck off. He had all that white shit in the corner of his mouth from non-stop talking bollocks. I can't have it with that; makes me fuckin' ill."

"What's he taking that for? I never knew he was into lemon."

"They all are Dubs, mate."

"Psst."

"And I'll tell ya something else."

"Oi, psst!"

"What the fuck is that noise?"

"Open the door, blud. Have a look."

Very quietly, I open the creakiest door in London. If I really wanted to make this much noise I would have brought my trumpet.

"Over here, in the bushes."

"What the fuck are you doing in the bushes?"

"The same as you innit, hiding."

"So why didn't you take the shed? It's pissing down."

"I didn't see it, bruv."

"Who are ya anyway?"

"It's me Span, Pete."

"Pete who?"

"Pete Pete."

"Mate, I know quite a few Petes. Unless you stick your boat out of them bushes you're gonna remain a mystery, and keep your voice down."

"It is down, I'm whisper shouting. You're louder than me."

"Oi, bumbaclart, just tell us which fuckin' Pete you are before I throw this lawnmower in them bushes."

"Dubs? Is that you? Fuckin' hell! Who else is in there with ya? It's Dingo's brother Pete."

"Dingo's brother Pete? Blimey."

"Yeah man. I knew I could hear your voice Span. I'm coming over."

Pete is a character and a half, funny as fuck and a massive stoner. His mum ran off with the gardener when he was a kid, leaving the old man to bring him up, if you can call it that. He was too busy running his very successful property business to get involved with Pete and Dingo, so money done the raising. Whatever they wanted the old man would give it to them. He owned quite a few acres of land across Kent which he left to Pete and his brother when he died. Dingo sold his bit and fucked off to Australia with a dream in mind. I suppose I lost touch with Pete around the time he got all loved-up with some nutty sort from Peckham, preferring to permanently stay indoors high as a kite, getting his dick sucked while playing video games and eating Pot Noodles.

"Fuckin' hell, Pete, you're looking slim, mate. How've ya been?"

"I've been a lot drier, bruv, that's for sure."

"How long have you been in those bushes?"

"A couple of minutes before you two showed up, but I didn't know it was you until I heard your voice."

"I take it you watched the fight then?"

"Sure did."

"What did you think?"

"I think Dubs got his arse kicked then landed a very lucky punch. Look at the state of him; he looks like he's been run over by a combine harvester."

"Hold my dungarees, dread."

"What for?"

"I'm not even gonna ask him to step outside, I'm gonna bash him up here in the shed."

"Fair comment."

"Oh come on, Dubs, have you seen yourself, bruv?"

"Listen, that fight went according to plan, and the plan was to win, alright?"

"Exactly, you tell him, Dubs. Bloody cheek. You've got some nerve coming into our shed with that attitude."

"I'm just telling ya what I saw."

"You must have been watching a different fight then Pete, because I easily won that one."

"Yeah, Pete, he easily won that fight. What's the matter with you?"

"Oh, of course, I forgot. Silly me. It's only been a couple of years since I last saw ya. I should've remembered."

"Remembered what?"

"You two. You always agree with him and he always agrees with you, Dubs."

"I don't agree with that. What do you reckon Span?"

"Not at all, mate. I definitely don't agree with that. I think you're making things up Pete. Am I right Dubs?"

"All day long, dread. Pete always makes things up."

"See what I mean? You two will never change, man."

It's now dark outside, so us three musketeers decide to move. Over a wall we stumble, jogging through what seems to be a never-ending alley to the road I'm parked on. I have no idea how Dubs managed to squeeze himself into the boot of my Stag, but that's what happened next. All's quiet, so time to visit the Rabbi's place, for a fix up, just off the Edgware Road. I call the man to make an immediate appointment and all is kosher.

The Rabbi was the man to see if you had any injuries brought on by criminal activities or illegal fights, such as our current situation. Fucking expensive practice he had going on, but what are you gonna do? First place the Old Bill will come looking will certainly be the hospital, so that's a no go. He's a proper rabbi too, and a doctor, or so he told us. Always immaculately clad in a black suit, hat, side-curls and long, grey beard, he certainly looks the part and seems to know his trade. As for him being a full-on, kosher rabbi though, that I'm not so sure. I'll tell ya a funny, little story that happened a couple of years ago, and see what you reckon.

So there I am, sitting round the Rabbi's place one afternoon waiting to have a cut stitched over my right eye. The Rabbi had just worked on some fella for two hours who'd caught part of a shotgun blast to the shoulder, apparently aimed at a person standing next to him. The Rabbi asks for his payment which is normally made up front, it's then given to a runner who disappears with it. On this occasion though, the guy tells the Rabbi his friend is en route with the rest of the money and only pays half. The Rabbi finishes mending the bloke and is then told to go fuck himself for the rest of the cash. Then like magic, a Desert Eagle handgun manifests from under the table which the Rabbi very calmly puts to the gentleman's balls, holding his other hand out for the rest of the money that also mysteriously manifests pretty fuckin' lively. With the little misunderstanding sorted, the guy leaves the premises looking like a cunt but with his balls intact. The Rabbi doesn't bat an eyelid, he's back to business sewing up the next fella in line, who just so happens to have the full payment in hand.

Chapter 2

It's been a few days since the fight; we've been lying slightly low for obvious reasons. I spoke to Dubs a couple of times over the blower, and he tells me he's healing up nicely, but his face hurts whenever he smiles, so he ain't been smiling.

The thing I really fuckin' hate about those underground fights is you're always gonna see cunts you've fallen out with, and that's without fail. You can't avoid them – well I can't anyway – envious, angry eyes everywhere. Not because I've done anybody any harm, it's just that being two steps ahead in my business doesn't sit well with those who do a similar thing but get caught doing it. They go to prison and want you to get the same treatment... Fuck that. It's a simple formula, two steps ahead is all you need to be. That's why I don't get caught, and have never been caught, because I run my business in a professional manner; it's why you buy your drugs from me and not them dodgy fuckers. It's all down to trust, which is the most valuable thing in my trade. You can't put a price on it. It can take forever and a day for me to let you into my bubble, and a second for you to pop it. Pretty much most of those bods watching the fight at some point in time were friends of mine, but guess what? Jealousy always comes knocking when you're on form. Even your pals can be infected by the green-eyed monster; prime example being a certain bod called Ratboy.

Not that I let it haunt me, but roughly around five months, one week, three days and seven hours ago, that rodent-faced cunt set me up to get robbed by the most murderous gang in South London, which just so happens to be his old man's firm. To cut a long story short, the Rat's father is the boss of a psychotic bunch of wrong'uns that go about dressed up as the police to rob drug dealers; you can see where I'm going with this can't ya? So yeah, he set me up alright. The mob that came round had killed numerous people, by the way, it was a well-known fact. They burst into my flat shouting "DRUG SQUAD!" and cable tied my hands behind my back. They done the same to my girlfriend, another girl, her boyfriend and two other mates that just happened to be in the wrong place at the wrong time. There were seven robbers in total, all in their late thirties, early forties, white and fuckin' huge. Two were outside the door standing guard with seal bats (huge bats used to club baby seals with). As they were bending over to put the cable ties on the other people, I noticed three of them had pistols. One had a gun tucked down the back of his strides and the other two wore shoulder holsters. They put everybody else in the front room and took me into the kitchen with an enormous monster of a man while the others ransacked every room, putting anything of value into bin liners. Meanwhile, I'm standing in my kitchen with both hands cable tied behind my back having my Rolex cut off my wrist with a pair of pliers. They done a cracking job cleaning me out too, even took my full set of Luis Vuitton cases. When I say they cleaned me out, I really mean it, left me with 50p to my name.

So then the biggest of these gorillas now wanted me to tell him who my supplier was. He was towering over me, sweat dripping onto my face; fuckin' massive, probably the biggest cunt I'd ever seen. Don't get me wrong, I'm only five foot nine but as strong as an ox. This guy seemed like he was around six eight, he had to duck his head and turn sideways to come through the doorway. In a one-on-one scrap with this bloke I would fancy my chances. He was carrying a lot of fat and breathing hard just standing there. I'd snap his knee with a kick and destroy him on the floor where we're the same height.

This geezer knew I was never gonna tell him fuck all, so he casually opened my kitchen drawer to find a suitable knife to stab me in the head with, twice. I could feel the warm blood as it poured down the side of my face, then I saw him pull his arm back to lunge again for a third time. He focused on my throat, smiling. This maniac wanted to kill me for the fun of it. In a split second I decided to collapse on the floor and fake that I was bang in trouble from the two previous stabs to the head. The angle I was lying made the blood flow down my face and into the side of my mouth. I positioned my tongue in a way that the blood ran out the other side, for added effect, while keeping my eyes open but deadly still. Trying not to blink for so long hurt more than the fuckin' wounds, believe me. I twitched a couple of times, then stayed as still as I could, my life depended on my newly discovered acting skills... and it worked.

The psycho shouted out to the others standing in the passageway and they made a run for it. Soon as they left, I burst into the front room to see the horror and relief on the faces of the other captives who thought I'd been killed. As we were helping each other out of the cable ties there's a buzz on the intercom and surprise, surprise it's the Rat that stitched me up; said he was just passing by and fancied scoring a bit of smoke. It's as clear as day he was waiting in a hole somewhere and was told to go see if I had died. My plan was to keep cool and not let him think that I knew he was part of what had happened. I'd never seen any of the fellas that robbed me before, but I knew they were part of his old man's mob, the Rat obviously didn't know that. The day before I was robbed, Ratboy came round my place moaning on about how broke he was. He kept going on about how much he wanted to go to Africa to see crocodiles in the wild. He'd got a strange obsession with them, even used to strut about in a pair of crocodile skin cowboy boots thinking he looked all dapper. I told him I had a job the following day where I was picking up a new kind of designer drug called Fantasia, and stood to earn around £80,000 if all went well. I was gonna surprise him with an all-inclusive couple of weeks safari to Kenya, where he could see his beloved crocodiles in the wild. As it was a close friend that set me up, the robbers knew exactly where all my drugs and cash were stashed. It may sound stupid for me to let even my close mates know where I kept my stuff, but sometimes it's wise to let one or two good friends know in case you're stopped while out on a mission and arrested. I would have pals call my mobile if they hadn't heard from me while I was out and about by a certain time, so that if I was in the shit they could go to my place and clear out everything incriminating.

Rather than go to the Rabbi for stitches, on this occasion I went to the hospital purely because I wanted an X-ray just to be sure. I was told by the doctor my skull was chipped in two places, and was lucky I had an unusually thick skull or I would've been dead or suffered brain damage.

The girl I was seeing at the time, that experienced all that, for some strange reason fucked off afterwards; could never understand why, probably got something to do with me always leaving the toilet seat up.

Anyway, changing the subject, I've got a strange feeling today is gonna be a good day, and my feelings are usually quite accurate. Business has been slow recently, so the unexpected call I got this morning was a right touch. I've gotta drop a parcel off to a friend of a friend. Nothing major, just a thousand Ecstasy pills and a kilo of Northern Lights skunk, which so happens to be under my bed; naughty I know. Before that though, I'm gonna treat myself to some grub from one of the finest restaurants on the Wandsworth Road.

"Ah, Anthony my good man, what's the special of the day?"

"Same as what it is every day."

"Excellent. In that case, I'll have two of your finest pies with double mash and a generous helping of liquor. And what vintage is the Lilt?"

"Two pies, double mash and liquor... and a can of Lilt. Eat in or take away?"

"Eat in, of course... As much as I've tried in the past, it's never the same taking it away. I reckon it's got something to do with your uplifting charisma that keeps me and everyone else here coming back for the sole purpose of eating in. Hang on a second... I think I've got a better word for how you make us all feel... Euphoric...! Am I right everybody?"

Everybody that knows what euphoric means nods.

"How the fuck are you always so chirpy Span?"

"It's your pies, Tone, they make me happy."

Next stop is Clapham North to pick my car up. It's had an alarm fitted by a dodgy-looking Indian fella with a squint. I head back home and stash the pills I was talking about up inside the passenger seat, the weed in the boot and set off for the drop.

Did I mention earlier on something about today being a good day? Yeah well, that didn't quite happen, nearly but not quite. You see I'm only a young fella, in me early twenties, and here I am, in the armpit of London, stuck in the traffic jam from hell. I'm sitting in a nice motor I probably look like I've stolen, carrying goods that could get me into a fair bit of trouble. That's pretty fuckin' stressful on its own, but that's not enough for me. No, what's missing in my life, at this precise moment in time, is a car alarm that decides now is a great time to come on, in all its glory, and stay on. Not just stay on though, that's still nowhere near enough. It needs to sound like a cross between a World War II air raid siren and a drowning ambulance. Also, as a bonus, I'd like it to burst my fucking eardrums and make every single light on the car flash like I'm sending out Morse code to some cunt on the moon. Everybody's pointing, even people up in Scotland, but what can I do? There's a jam both ways. A U-turn is out of the question, and why would I want to anyway? I'm having a fantastic time sitting here thinking that any minute now the police are gonna show up and drag me out the car by my chin. Exactly thirty-eight minutes later, I reach a turning I can take. I sling a left and a right, drive all the way back to the alarm shop wearing the biggest happy hat you've ever seen, blaring away like a beatboxing ice cream van. On arrival, a necessary decision is made to slightly strangle the gentleman with the squint until I get my money back. The drop's been rescheduled for another day, so I head back home to get stoned and call it a day.

OK, today is definitely gonna be a good day. Why? Because it's gotta be better than yesterday, that's for sure. It took just one soppy cunt to completely fuck everything up, so I've taken it upon myself to create a very special day, 'Spaniard's avoid soppy cunts day'. I'm going straight down the gym to catch up with Dubs, as soon as I finish this spliff that is. Getting stoned is a very important part of the 'special day' process. You see being baked is a great way to avoid people; all people. You just say "Sorry mate, I'm caned. I'll catch up with ya another time" – job done. Nobody questions you when you're mashed.

My drive to Brixton is a success, no soppy cunts encountered. The heavy sound of reggae rumbles the windows as I stand outside a tired, old gym that has seen better days, decorated with graffiti and bullet holes that pepper the walls and ceiling the entire length of the gym, ending with a single shotgun blast in the backdoor as a full stop. Despite its appearance, it always feels like a comfortable place to be, just like your battered, old favourite slippers. I place my palms on the door to absorb the bass vibrating through and can't help but crack a grin. The smell of sweat and leather fill my nostrils as I enter, immediately followed by a sea of smiles, nods and winks.

Dubs is working the heavy bag with a vengeance, while a pretty, oriental girl dressed all in black sits by with a British bulldog at her feet.

"How's it going Dubs?"

"Always good, blud, always good."

"Cuts still look nasty, mate. Beautiful stitches though."

"Cheers."

"How long have you been on the bag?"

"Two hours!" replies the unimpressed girl.

"Oh yeah, I don't suppose you've seen Chinese George about? That's his sister sitting there with the dog. I'm keeping that dog hostage until he turns up."

"Nah, mate, I ain't seen him in ages. What's he done now?"

"He sold me a parcel of car alarms, and guess what? They're all fucked."

"Car alarms?"

"Yes, blud, thirty broken car alarms."

"What a cunt. Have you still got them?"

"No, I sold them to some dodgy Indian fella up Clapham North who Raj put me on to."

Chapter 3

Lucky thing, bumping into Pete like that the other day. He still lives in his huge mansion left by the old man, or should I say, he lives in the main front room, the rest of the twelve bedrooms are busy collecting dust.

He's invited me and Dubs round for hot dogs and what he calls a sci-fiathon. Basically, he's got a shitload of science fiction videos for us to tuck into while we fill our bellies with hot dogs. Pete's got himself one of those hot dog machines you see in the cinema, like the one you normally find by the popcorn section. Not sure it looks right in the front room, but that's a typical Pete thing to do.

"*Barbarella*? Nice choice, Pete. Have you seen this Dubs?"

"What's that, blud? Nah mate, but she looks fit on the cover."

"That's Jane Fonda."

"Does she get her tits out?"

"I think she does, as it happens."

"Hot dogs are ready you two."

"Sweet, I'm fuckin' starving, dread."

"Do you want onions Span?"

"Nope."

"How about some mustard?"

"Fuck off, Pete."

"Only asking."

"But I will have some ketchup, mate. Where is it?"

"In the fridge."

"Where's the fridge?"

"Behind the sofa."

"And which sofa would that be, Peter? I can see eight chesterfields in this room, including that one right over there. That's easily a fuckin' cab ride, mate."

"Behind the one we're sitting on, but then again, I can see how you two could miss that massive, white box standing up against the dark, green wallpaper."

"Of course, where else would it be, you mad bastard? Why didn't you just say the ketchup is in the fridge behind us? Oh, and by the way Pete, since we're chatting, every other cunt keeps the fridge in the kitchen, not the front room."

"Bruv, have you got any idea how far the kitchen is from here? It's way over in the east wing, man."

"The east wing? Oh, I know how you feel now; I've got exactly the same problem. Are you listening to him Dubs?"

"I see you sure like your *Star Trek* videos, Pete."

"I love my *Star Trek*, Dubs. Don't take the piss, man."

"How is that taking the piss? I'm just saying."

"Oi, Dubs, have a look, mate. Oi, Pete, what the fuck do you call this?"

"It's a bottle of ketchup Span, what do you think it is?"

"I'm talking about the top, what's all that?"

"It's only dry ketchup, it won't kill ya."

"It looks like a tramp's arsehole, ya cunt."

"Fuckin' hell Pete, have you never thought of giving that a wipe, dread?"

"Why would I?"

"Hygiene comes to mind, and when was the last time you

opened the curtains?"

"I don't open the curtains, because I've got a twenty-foot ceiling innit, which means long, heavy fuckin' curtains, bruv. You try getting stoned and moving them bastards about, it ain't happening. And what's with all the questions? Can't you see I'm caned?"

"Do you ever leave this room Pete? I know it's the size of my flat, but for all you know there could be half a dozen squatters living in this house."

"And that's how I get my exercise. I walk the whole house every day, visiting every single room. Do you wanna come and see my footprints in the dust? I'm serious, they're there."

"No thanks, we believe ya, but is there any chance we could have some ketchup in a little bowl with maybe a spoon, because Dubs is itching to see Jane Fonda's tits?"

I'm losing count of how many hot dogs I've had; eight I think, or was it six? I'm not sure, I'm a bit mangled. Or maybe my head's in warp drive from so much *Star Trek*. Did I mention Pete knows the Klingon language? Yeah, really. The three of us smoke some more until the inevitable conversation.

"Pete, has Spock ever banged any alien sorts?"

"Not that I know of Dubs."

"Not with them fuckin' ears, mate. Imagine never being able to wear a hat with a brim, tragic."

"Well he could cut holes in either side, innit, so his ears fit through."

"But then he's gonna look like a right cunt, Pete. He'll never get a bird that way."

"Why would he wanna wear a hat anyway, bruv?"

"In case he transports to the Wild West or somewhere they wear hats."

"Yeah, Pete, how the fuck is he gonna wear a cowboy hat,

dread?"

"Or even a bowler hat."

"Blud, he'll never get away with a bowler hat and them ears."

"So I take it there aren't many hat shops in Vulcan land then?"

"It's the planet Vulcan, Span. I knew you'd take the piss, man."

"I'm joking, Pete, put another one on. I think watching five hours' worth is just a warm up, mate. It's such a shame we can't watch it all in Klingon so you can translate it to us."

"It's true, dread, put something else on. Do you have any more films like that Barbara one where we get to see titties in space?"

"*Barbarella*? No Dubs, no more titties in space, but I do have *Aliens*."

"*Aliens*? Now that's a fuckin' good film Dubs, mate, I've seen it."

"What's it about?"

"Well, without giving too much away, it's about aliens with heads like knobs having a row with some soldiers. Loads of shooting, explosions, pretty much everyone except Ripley and Newt dies. That Sigourney Reaver sort is in it from the first movie."

"Weaver, bruv."

"Who?"

"Her name is Sigourney Weaver."

"That's what I said Pete."

"Do they fuck any birds with them knobheads, blud?"

"They're called Xenomorphs, and no, Dubs, they don't, but they do fuck people up."

"Stick that bad boy in the player then, Rasta, I'll have

some of that."

Two hours and five joints later...

"So tell me Pete, and don't fuck about man, be honest, can Spock do one of them aliens in a fight? And I mean without using his special powers."

"What special powers? He ain't got special powers Dubs."

"So what the fuck is that neck pinch then? Or is it on the shoulder he does it? Are you telling me that ain't a special power?"

We took our choice from eight sofas to crash on. As I woke up the next day my blurry vision slowly regained focus on the ring-piece of a basset hound, four inches from my face.

"Wow...! What the fuck...? Pete...! Pete, wake up you cunt!"

"What?"

"Where'd this dog come from? Its bollocks and starfish are in me boat. Are you fuckin' sure, mate?"

"That's Wilson. He's alright, Span. You're on his sofa. Relax, bruv, just push him off."

"Push him off? Have a look at how he's lying. One false move my end and I'm getting full-on teabagged. Sort it out, Pete, because his arsehole is winking at me, and I've got a feeling he's about to blow a parting in me hair."

"Honestly, he's sweet as a nut Span. Chill, bruv."

"No Pete, I'm not fuckin' chillin' mate, because if he follows through my boat's getting pebble-dashed, so liven up, my arms are trapped."

Talk about a touch, my phone rang and freaked Wilson out which made him fuck off to another sofa.

"Hello?"

"Hello Spaniard."

"Who's that? Is that you Mark?"

"It is indeed."

"What's up, fella?"

"Oh, I just thought I'd give you a call to thank you for the disco biscuits. Didn't really get time to chat at the boxing event, what with all the commotion. Did you get away OK?"

"Yeah, mate. You?"

"Yes, thank God. Ended up getting a lift from somebody that says he knows you."

"If he wasn't with me then he probably fuckin' hates me. You wanna mind how you go with some of them people, Mark. They can get you into a lot of trouble before you know it. Can you remember his name?"

"No, and I don't think there's any danger of that. I can't see me being a regular at that vicinity."

"You'll miss it, you wait and see."

"Oh, before I forget, I have some business for you."

"Go on."

"Write this number down and give her a call... Her name is Amber."

"Got it. What is she after...? Hello...? Are you still there, Mark?"

I swear I'm gonna end up throwing this fuckin' phone in the Thames. This cunt drops calls more than it hangs on to them. Three attempts to call Mark back gets me nowhere, so I sit down with Wilson and rewind *Barbarella*.

Chapter 4

Dubs has decided to stay at Pete's for a few days. He reckons the slow pace there will help his face heal; you gotta love him.

I need to venture out and earn some pennies. I'm meeting a new contact today, a guy from Amsterdam who so happens to make pure MDMA tablets. I'm always a bit edgy meeting new bods for business; like to stay with trusted people I know and have made a few deals with in the past. My number one rule whenever I meet a new contact is to listen to my gut. If it tells me there's something not right on the first encounter, I'll go through the motions of a pleasant meeting, so as not to cause a scene of any sort, then when the time is right I'll casually slip off. It's also a very good idea to bring along an extra potent, ready-rolled zoot to break the ice, plus it doubles up nicely when the time is right to vanish in a puff of smoke, so to speak.

I drive to London Bridge and park by a flower stall. Ten minutes later, a silver Audi with foreign plates pulls up in front. A tall, blonde guy, wearing a black mac and Wayfarers, gets out. I flash my lights, as he gives me a nod.

"Hi, you must be Spaniard? It's great to meet you. I'm Dutch," he says stepping into my car.

"Nice to meet ya, Dutch. Sorry for staring, mate, but has anyone ever told you you're the double of Sting?"

"Yes of course, Sting from The Police? All the time, my friend."

"It's fuckin' uncanny, mate, you look more like Sting than he does. In fact, I reckon you're the real Sting. What made you wanna knock the music business on the head and become a drug dealer? And whatever happened to those other two cunts from the band? Do you still keep in touch with them?"

"I assure you I'm not Sting, but I am the real Dutch."

"If you say so Sting… I mean Dutch… I mean Sting… See, now I'm fuckin' confused."

"You're a funny guy Spaniard, but what I can tell you for sure is, my merchandise will have you 'Walking On The Moon'."

"Brilliant, I see what you done there, Dutch."

He wants £7 a pill on a thousand, I tell him I'll give him £6 on five thousand which he agrees to. We arrange a time and place for another day, as he hands me six samples of what I can expect. Dutch pops one himself then gives me a wink, as he says goodbye. It's a rare touch getting those pills for £6. I must be the only person in London with this sort of quality, and that's without even trying them first. I just know these are gonna be pukka; pure white burgers, not a speckle in sight. Even if I sold the whole parcel at £7 a tab, in one go, it'll still be a nice day's wage, and Dutch reckons he can get them all day long because he makes them all day long, exactly what I like to hear.

Curiosity gets the better of me while I'm sitting in a traffic jam, so I call the number Posh Mark gave me and arrange a meet for eight tonight on the Kings Road with this Amber sort, who also happens to be rather posh.

I pop home for a shower, then cook one of my famous omelettes for a quick snack. As always, just as I sit down to tuck in, I get a call from a friend asking me if I've heard the news?

The local old people's home got broken into last night and an old girl of eighty-four had been murdered, strangled apparently. The bloke who's called me is going slightly nuts because his nan stayed at the very same home. Her room was two away from where it happened, so she's now moved in with him.

On a brighter note, my omelette came out fuckin' perfect, no burn marks whatsoever. The secret is to first base your pan with olive oil, then gently pour your ready-mixed eggs evenly. Always remember to flip the omelette with your wrist, not your whole fuckin' arm. You want it on your plate, not your neighbour's lap. Washed down with a perfect cup of tea, it's a beautiful thing. It's also kinda funny, now I think about it stoned, because I forgot to mention to ya that I'm made with Spanish and English ingredients, and my favourite little munch when I'm caned is an omelette with a cup of tea. How Spanish and English can you get?

Don't you just hate people being late? Yeah, me too.

I make a call and a well-spoken girl whispers, "Hello."

I ask her if she remembers anything about meeting a fella on the Kings Road at 8 p.m.

"FUCK!" She shatters my eardrum. "I'm so sorry. I had a terrible migraine and had to have a lie down, must have dozed off. Can we still meet? Can you come to my place?"

As a rule, I don't normally go to a new client's place on a first visit for various reasons, but as I'm not holding anything other than a bit of percy and have no cash on me to bother about walking into a trap with, I agree.

Amber is a good-looking girl in her mid twenties, tidy

dresser with a lot of panache. Judging by her shoes, bag and dress, Chanel was her flavour. From the way she first looked at me to the way she shook my hand, I knew I'd be knee-deep in her before sunrise, or at least down to the second knuckle.

Her apartment overlooked the River Thames on the Battersea side, a beautiful home that must have cost Daddy a fair few quid; far too neat and tidy though, not a thing out of place, like a show home for the upper crust. We move out onto the balcony to get to know each other, illuminated by a handful of scented candles. She asks if I want a drink, I tell her I'd rather skin up, as I place two of the sample pills Dutch gave me on the table. Without any hesitation she immediately puts one in her mouth then looks at me puzzled as to why I've not done the same.

"I didn't expect to be dropping on this meet, to be honest. I was just gonna leave them for you to try some other day," I tell her.

"Oh, I see. Sorry, I didn't know that. As you can probably tell, I'm new to this. Will you take the other one with me? If I'm going to be buying any of your tablets, and I'm talking about potentially a lot of business here, then at least have the decency to get to know me, Mr Spaniard."

"Just Spaniard will be fine, Miss Amber. It's not the way I normally do things, but no problem; I'll drop one with ya."

I check my supplies: king-size skins, 20 Marlboro Lights, Clipper lighter, eighth of green, four more samples plugged away in me sock plus one on the table. Not much of a head-scratching decision to make here, she was already looking tasty, and I hadn't even taken the tab yet. I know full well that if I'm taking Ecstasy at a pretty girl's place, just the pair of us, things can get messy, especially if the pills are as kick-arse as Dutch says they are, and I believe him.

"Down the hatch," I say, placing the tablet on my tongue.

It's 10.30 in the evening, and things are as busy outside as you'd expect on a warm, Friday night in this part of town. We stand looking over the balcony at the nightlife down below waiting for the pills to kick in. Half an hour passes, then we're both hit at the same time with a tidal wave of a monstrous rush, dripping with euphoria.

"Oh my word, wow! I can't stop smiling. I feel incredible. How about you Spaniard?"

"Fuckin' hell yeah, they're proper strong," is all I can manage.

"I think some music is in order. What kind of sounds are you into?"

"If I'm buzzing, Amber, I like house, but put whatever you want on, I'm easy."

"Are you now? I like the sound of that."

I knew it. I said so didn't I? Knee-deep before sunrise.

Man these pills are fierce, I'm feeling nice, really fuckin' nice. Amber comes back with a jug of iced water that she places on the table and takes a seat next to me on the lounger. The air is filled with Sueño Latino as she takes my hand and places it over her heart.

"Feel how fast my heart's thumping," says a wide-eyed Amber.

Yeah, her heart is indeed ticking along as it normally does when you're rushing off your nut on Ecstasy. I'm more aware of the fact my hand is cupping one of her tits and I have half a thick'un. She backs off and starts dancing on the spot slowly, and in my state, quite erotic.

"These are bloody amazing Spaniard. I want three thousand. How much are you asking?"

"Three thousand? Don't you mean three hundred?"

"No, I mean three thousand. Who said anything about three hundred?"

"Are you on drugs or something? OK, don't answer that. I came here thinking you wanted maybe fifty at a push. Three thousand little fellas for a first-time order doesn't happen that often, you know what I mean?"

"No, I don't. I was under the impression any amount wouldn't be a problem. I heard you was the man who can, if you know what I mean?"

"Heard from who?"

"That's not important, and nothing for you to worry about. I'm not a dealer, Spaniard. I plan to buy and sell as a one-off business deal to an individual I know who'll take them off me at a worthwhile profit."

"Calm down… You can't blame me for being a touch suspicious. If you take three thousand off me you can have them for £8 a tab. Tell that somebody you know, in Ibiza these go for £25 a pop, and they're £15 in the clubs over here."

I assure her that all my goods are returnable at the cost of what the buyer pays minus whatever is missing from the parcel. As we shake on it she leans forward and kisses my hand.

"Do you have any more samples with you?"

"Yeah, four more. Why? You wanna get proper wasted?"

Hiding a fiendish grin with my cloak, I place the four remaining Es on the table in front of Amber. She flicks one down and places another in my mouth. I'm starting to like her, she's tidy, shiny and pretty, but most importantly likes getting really out of it. I feel comfortable with her lying alongside me on the lounger, she smells good too. Maybe I'm reading too much into this, we are pretty fucked up after all. Stay cool and see how it pans out is the way I'm gonna play it. One of these pills is easily twice as strong as what's going about at the moment; I'm genuinely blown away by how clean they feel.

Just as the second E is coming up, Amber jumps to her feet recommending we be devils and do another.

I'm surfing on a comet faster than the speed of light through a supernova. Far away in another galaxy, I hear the faint echo of Amber's voice, like a whisper getting louder by the second, pulling me back to earth. She's flapping her gums telling me all sorts of random bollocks, like stuff from her childhood at school to her family and friends. Her high-paid job as an estate agent in Mayfair is especially hard work to listen to. Even her horse got a shout out for fuck's sake. I'm starting to fear for my buzz, she's killing it. Then it's time for her to rattle on about her father, for nearly thirty fuckin' minutes. Apparently, he's some important bod up in the City that would send her off to a finishing school in Antarctica if he ever found out about her rebellious ways.

Her granddad though, he was fuckin' special. He had his very own space on the wall all to himself; a Spitfire pilot with the RAF during World War II and took part in the Battle of Britain. I couldn't help chuckle looking at the old photos of him standing by his plane looking all dashing and proud, seemed like a top bloke to me.

Amber is standing bent over, with her palms on her knees, blowing hard. Her jaw looks like it's about to do an Elvis and leave the building. As for her eyes, they're on their way to Ibiza.

"I'm super fucked!" is what I think she says. Then looks at me, smiles and says, "Back in a minute."

I'm also having a bit of a moment. This MDMA is so fucking strong, that for a few seconds, I lose the plot completely and don't know what country I'm in; absolute total confusion.

I even think to myself that if Amber comes back all tackled up wanting a stiff one, I'll have to tell her to fuck off because I'm too wasted. After what seemed like hours, Amber strolls in wearing a long T-shirt and shorts.

"How are you feeling, Spaniard?"

I struggle to open an eye and focus on her.

"Fuckin' missing, and by the way, I hope you know I'm not going home in this state."

"Of course not, silly. There are some new toothbrushes in the bathroom. Help yourself to whatever you need, but let's take those last Es shall we? The night is still young."

She's a full-on pill monster this one, but then so am I; a pretty dangerous combination. A nice, cool shower later, and I'm ready for the last E. Amber quickly drops it in my mouth and the other in hers. She staggers off into another room that has me wondering whether I'm expected to follow. I didn't see her look round indicating for me to join her. She didn't even say she was off to bed. She also knows I've just got out the shower, and I'm sitting here like a cunt with just a towel around me. A fuckin' quilt would be handy, at least. Then again, I'm too hot anyway. I'll just mind me own business here on the sofa all nice and comfy. Don't really fancy moving anyway as it goes. I'm gonna close my eyes for a minute, stretch out and maybe drift off.

Rush after rush hits me hard. I'm blowing like there's a birthday cake with candles in front of me. Really fancy a joint, but can't see fuck all. It's pitch-black in here, and I'm far too caned to be bothered to look for the light switch. I'm so relaxed. Am I falling asleep? I think so. Deeper and deeper I go. I imagine slowly floating back first down a well, with the little circle of light getting smaller and smaller until blackness.

My cock feels rock hard, feels like it's moving.

Am I asleep?

Am I awake?

Is this a fuckin' dream?

I open my eyes but can't see a thing, it's too dark. Is that heavy breathing I can hear? As I lift my head, the lights from a passing car trickle across the room and settle on a naked girl sitting on top of me, or should I say riding me? Don't have any idea how long she's been in the saddle, didn't even feel her slide on. I go to ask her, but she puts a finger across my lips as if to hush me. She's on the final furlong and thrusting hard. Faster and faster she rides. There's no holding this girl down, as she senses the finish line approaching. Closer and closer to victory, she gives it her all, dismounts, then vanishes.

I hear the door to Amber's bedroom close, she doesn't say a word. I shout to see if everything is OK, but get no reply. I'm starting to think she took a bit of a liberty really. Rumps me while I'm missing and half a kip, has an orgasm, then fucks right off without a word, leaving me here with a lonely boner. Confusion and paranoia start messing with my canister. Is Amber a nutter? If she can get my Hampton hard enough to slide onto while I'm pretty much asleep and not know about it, I'm sure she could easily sneak up and stick a blade in me. Then again, with a bit of luck she might come out for part two. Where the fuck are my skins anyway? I'm gonna roll a spliff in the dark, and if she doesn't appear by the time I've finished smoking it then I'm gonna jet, simple as that; it's goodnight from me.

Chapter 5

Well I've smoked that joint and she hasn't come back out... fuckin' weirdo.

I shoot off home and have one of the best sleeps I can remember. I'm meeting Terry Taxi this afternoon for a little chat at his office, or should I say the pie mash shop. The thing about meeting Terry Taxi is you always know what to expect. What I mean by that is if he says he'll be alone, then that means he has some serious, confidential info just for your ears only. If he says he'll be with such-and-such, then that means he still has juicy info, but not as confidential.

You see with Terry it's all about information. His dad is the same, also drives a black cab and has always got some news you never knew. Terry is your typical London cab driver, flat cap, diamond jumper and loves to talk. He's never touched a drug in his life but is a cracking geezer all the same. As I walk into the pie shop he's there, alone but smiling. Thank fuck for that, must be good news then.

"Terrence, mate, good to see you smiling. How's things?"

"I'm good, Span. You know me, busy, busy, busy."

"Yeah, Tel, you need to slow down my friend, take a vacation once in a while."

"Can't do that, fella, too many interesting things on the horizon."

"Oh really? Tell me about the horizon. Am I gonna need a telescope?"

"No mate, it's pretty much on your doorstep."

"Go on."

"What if I said to you crocodile boots? Ring any bells?"

"Crocodile boots? No bells rung, Tel."

"Ratboy?"

"Say that again."

"Ratboy."

"One more time, Tel, just to make sure."

"Ratboy."

"Fuckin' hell, really? Where? When? How?"

"I knew you'd be interested. He's been seen, and I'm on it. Apparently he visits a pet centre up in Kent somewhere, and get this Span, the horrible cunt has got a caiman, you know? It's like a little crocodile."

"Yeah, I know what a caiman is Tel."

"Well, he feeds it a live kitten every month as a treat. Gets all his pals round to watch."

"Charming, I'd love to feed him to that fuckin' caiman. Last I heard, he was dabbling in a spot of human trafficking; something about a long-distance lorry driver bringing Eastern European girls over. He gets them bang on the brown gear and brasses them out."

"Yeah, apparently he's been doing that for a while, and from what I hear does quite well out of it too."

"Really? I don't suppose you know where he lives by any chance?"

"No, but I do know where he drinks."

"How do you know all this, Terrence?"

"You know me, confidential, but I'll fill you in as I get it. Are you on the same number?"

"Always."

I certainly didn't see that coming. Well, well, well, the Rat has finally surfaced, and I was only just telling you about the horrible cunt a little while ago. How weird is that?

The info Terry Taxi has given me has stirred up some dormant emotions, mainly anger and hate. Let's not forget something important here, Ratboy sent killers to my flat that still wanted to kill me after they'd cleaned me out. He's now out of his hole, and I want revenge, big time.

Strolling through the streets of Stockwell, my head is filled with all kinds of torture devices, from the Spanish Inquisition to Spaniard's imagination. Mine ain't so elaborate, mine are very simple. Like bury Ratboy up to his neck with his head covered in jam and see how long it takes for insects to eat his face, that sort of thing. It's tricky though, as much as I'd like to deal with the Rat head-on, and believe me that would be simple, his old man would have me and my family killed in a heartbeat if he knew it was me that ghosted his son. I need to think of something on another level here, but fuck knows what.

When you hear on the news that some poor, peaceful place has been hit by a tsunami it always makes me think that shit should happen to Stockwell; wash it away down a huge plughole. Just going about doing your normal day-to-day stuff is pretty fucking grim, like popping down the shop for bread and milk is a depressing chore on its own. Long, miserable, grey faces with hollow eyes stare back at you with a look that says 'My life was over years ago. I'm just waiting to die'. Teenage sluts pushing fully loaded, double buggy pushchairs patrol the streets in groups of five, scoping to find another witless sperm donor to bump up their child support. The mental thing is, they also have a fifteen-year-old sister who does exactly the same thing, and so do all her pals. It's so grim around here that whenever I leave South London, don't matter where I'm going, could be just an hour's drive away, but it always feels like a vacation.

The constant ringing from my mobile snaps me out of a dreamlike state. I swear I've been staring at these traffic lights for hours waiting for them to turn green.

"Hey Spaniard, it's Dutch. Are you set, amigo?"

"Yeah, Dutch, I'm set. Look out for a black cab parked outside Westminster Cathedral. Jump in, and he'll take you to where I am, down the road a bit. Don't worry he's a friend of mine. I've told him to look out for Sting, so he's got an idea what you look like."

I'm parked across the road from the taxi waiting to see Dutch get in and drive off. I want to see if he's followed, or if I've been lured in to be robbed. Ever since that time I was set up by the Rat, I've stepped up my game when it comes to my well-being, always analysing my chances. My mind drifts back to Ratboy again.

Is it wrong for me to wanna take his soul? That human trafficking thing that's been floating about needs looking at closer. Word has it these young Eastern European girls are tempted over on the promise of well-paid cleaning jobs in fancy offices. He drugs them up, then pimps them out to weirdos that fuck them up the arse and smack them about a bit, probably at the same time. The Rat gets £100 per girl which he keeps £90, giving the girl £10 for her nightmares. If it's true, surely that alone justifies ending Ratboy? I bet those girls would agree with me.

All looks good, Dutch ain't been followed. I tail the taxi to where it stops by Pimlico School and jump in. I don't like to hang about for more than a couple of minutes in situations like this, so I keep it short.

"It's all there, Dutch."

I hand over £15,000 and he gives me a Holland & Barrett plastic carrier bag containing two emptied out bodybuilding protein tubs with the pills plugged inside. The tubs are passed to Terry Taxi who puts them in a hidden compartment under his seat. Dutch then jumps into my motor and we follow Terry back to Victoria where Dutch says goodbye. I transfer one tub from the taxi to my car, the other tub I leave with Terry for later on. That way, if something goes tits up, I'll still have a tub to play with. Now I need to get something out of the way; a call to Amber.

Chapter 6

"Hi, Spaniard. Before you say anything, I'm so sorry about the other night. Are we still friends?"

"Yeah, don't worry about it, we're still friends. But what the hell was that all about; violating me while I'm mangled?"

"I know, I know, please don't remind me. I'm so embarrassed. I was mangled too, you know?"

"Anyway, forget about it, that's not why I'm calling. Those spare parts are ready when you are."

"The what?"

"The little fellas."

"I'm sorry?"

"Fuckin' hell. The things we dropped at yours that night which turned you into a sex maniac."

"Oh, excellent. Can you bring them tonight? I'll cook you a nice dinner if you do."

Not one to turn down a home-cooked meal, I agree to be round her place for eight. All I'm gonna do is have a spot of dinner and leave twenty-one grand richer. I'm growing to like this girl a lot. Yeah, she's pretty and petite, knows how to dress and is a touch loopy, but there's something else about that whole first encounter that's stayed with me. Maybe it's because I was so blitzed that night that it all feels like some kind of erotic dream I wanna return to.

I deliberately haven't eaten a thing all day, I'm absolutely starving. Hope she's cooking up something substantial, not some petite nouvelle cuisine shit with a little camp twist on top. I like to feel like I've actually eaten something, not imagined it. I want something that's gonna spend a bit of time in my mouth being chewed, otherwise what's the point? You may as well just have a drink.

I climb the stairs to her apartment with nothing but food on my mind, cursing the growls coming from my belly. Amber opens the door, and is just about to greet me with a kiss on the cheek, when my stomach lets out a sound I can only describe as a puma getting its bollocks waxed.

"Hungry are we?" she laughs. "Take a seat. It'll be ready in a minute. But first things first, I have a gift for you."

She brings out a spanking new Louis Vuitton suitcase with £21,000 inside. I was expecting maybe a couple of cheques plus cash, but am nowhere near disappointed.

"I bought you the case because I remember you telling me you lost your Louis and loved to travel. So now you can travel in style again," she says with a wink.

Now don't get me wrong, even though the case she's got me is flash as fuck, what with it being logo city, personally I'm not into labels much, especially on the outside. I find it all a bit brash and pretentious, but there you go. I know that makes me sound like a bit of a hypocrite after telling ya about those robbers taking my full set of Louis luggage, but technically that doesn't count, because those cases didn't really belong to me in the first place. A couple of my pals found them in the back of a Mercedes estate parked outside Harrods one afternoon, that somehow ended up in my flat, for three hundred quid and an ounce of green.

The notes inside the case Amber gives me are crisp and

new; just how I like my money.

"Blimey, do you work in a bank or something?"

"No, as far as I'm aware I still work as an estate agent in Mayfair, but I know somebody who does." She giggles her way back to the kitchen. "Hope you like Chinese food, I've made us sweet and sour chicken with some beautiful, fluffy rice. My rice is normally a disaster, so trust me, I'm chuffed to bits, and you better like it, mister."

Thank fuck for that, can't stand anything green and leafy on my plate. I'm more of a meat and potatoes sort of bloke, easy to please when it comes to grub. Just keep it simple. I'll eat most things, as long as any sort of salad isn't happening. Just doesn't seem like food to me. I've tried chewing lettuce in the past but end up gagging it back up. Can't for the life of me keep it down. My eyes water like fuck, and just like a cow, it comes back up for a second chew. On a normal day, I'll munch every three hours, between five and six small meals all containing meat or fish. Two of those would often be a high-protein meal replacement shake, depending on how hard I've hit the gym. On my off day I'm a pie and mash monster.

I hand the pills to Amber and sit down for a nice, relaxing meal. She tells me she's gonna want ten thousand tabs every month; something about a geezer in the music business wants them, but his name is confidential. I swear blind Amber said she wasn't a dealer that night we dropped the pills. Didn't she say something about a one-off deal to some fella? Do you remember? Maybe I imagined it. Anyway, she asks if there'll be a problem with that amount and can she have them cheaper. I tell her no and no. I'm in this game to make as much money as possible in the shortest time possible. I'm sure the bloke who wants the ten thousand will have a bunch of bods knocking them out top whack at raves and festivals all day and night long. He's gonna earn well, so I ain't budging from my price even if she sucks me gristle.

"If you want cheaper pills, Amber, I can get them for ya. They'll be good, but not as good as the ones sitting in front of you. They're the same as what we done that night; that was the point of the samples, remember? How did you feel the day after?"

"Surprisingly good as far as the tablets are concerned, but mortified about the other thing that happened... Spaniard, I really am sorry. Believe me, as you get to know me you'll see that jumping on somebody I've just met is so far from what I'm about, you have no idea. I've never ever done anything like that before, and sure as hell never had a one-night stand. That's what's so bloody crazy about it all, it just isn't me. I honestly can't explain it. All I remember about the incident was lying on my bed buzzing off my tits, the next thing I'm on top of you."

"You ain't kidding you was on top of me. Violating me is what you was doing. In fact, I'm so traumatised by the whole experience, I don't think I'll ever be able to trust a woman again."

"Oh come on Spaniard, we were both really gone that night. Can we just put it down to the tablets and forget about it?"

"You do know I'm only joking around with ya? Of course it was the pills, but do me a favour, next time you fancy having any more of those saucy ideas, wake me up before the action starts so I can actually feel like I'm taking part."

Amber gets a call that produces a frown.

"Sorry, I need to take this." She leaves the room, then comes back ten seconds later with, "So sorry, Spaniard, I need to quickly pop out. My friend has split from her boyfriend.

She's in a terrible state and really needs me."

I fuck off home to a grim, grey street, find a place to park, and as I'm about to reverse into a space, I look over my shoulder and everything instantly goes into slow motion, including my heartbeat. My eyes fix on a police car cruising by, then lock on to the eyes of the person sitting in the back. It's Ratboy.

Did I just have an LSD flashback? I've done a fair bit of acid in my time so it's possible. The car slowly passes and keeps going, leaving me with a hundred questions I want instant answers to. Has the Rat been nicked? Was that a fake police car the Rat was in, and were the other cunts in it the bods that robbed and tried to kill me? Was it a real police car and Ratboy was there to point me out as a dealer?

I'd probably still be sitting there thinking about the other ninety-odd reasons if it wasn't for someone tooting their horn reminding me to finish parking. Apparently other people wanna use the road too, and sitting there with the arse of your car in a space while the front is sticking out in the road with you staring wide-eyed out of the side window at nothing seems to be a problem for some people. I climb the stairs to my flat, put the key in the door and decide to head over to Pete's instead.

"Hello, Pete. I tried to call ya, but my phone is playing up again. Is Dubs here?"

"Safe, bruv. Yeah, he's out the back walking Wilson. Come in, man."

"What a fuckin' thing I just saw, me head's all over the shop."

"What's that then?"

"I'll tell ya when Dubs gets back. Fuckin' hell that was good timing, Dubs mate, listen to this."

A few minutes later.

"Blud, you know I can get some Yardies to deal with him. Trust me, nobody will know we're connected to it."

"Cheers Dubs, but I'm thinking more along the lines of an accident. I don't want it to be a hit."

"Cool, dread, I'm feeling that. Good idea."

"Yeah, but for the time being, I wanna be able to protect myself in case Ratboy sends them fellas back."

"Leave that to me, blud. I've got something at home you can hold on to, it's loaded and ready to go."

"Nice one. Cheers Dubs, I'll take that."

"Not a problem. You can take this spliff too, man."

"If you need weapons, bruv, I've got something in the cellar you can use, innit. Maybe keep it in your car for emergencies. This shit will end any ideas someone's got of fuckin' with ya while you're out and about. Let me go get it. Wait here a second."

"Pete, I'm alright when I'm out. It's for when I'm home, mate, and Dubs has sorted it."

Twenty minutes goes by when a very dusty-looking Pete comes back with what looks like something wrapped in ancient rags.

"Pete, you do realise your head is covered in cobwebs?"

"It's all good, bruv. Check this out."

So, according to Pete, a medieval mace and chain is the way to go. Keep that in the car he said, and he had a serious face. I'm not kidding, he actually fuckin' meant it.

"So what will I tell the Old Bill if I'm pulled over with that then, Pete? I play conkers with it? Because I'm struggling to find any other reason you could say that thing is used for other than caving in skulls, mate."

"Just tell them it ain't yours, innit."

"But it's in my car, ya cunt. Pete, what planet do you live on?"

"Yeah, Pete, you bumbaclart from another planet. Skin up man, it's your turn."

"Skin up? Dubs there's already two joints going around, bruv."

"And there's three of us, dread, so what are you saying? Span ain't got one."

I leave Pete's at 3 a.m. and take the long way home, stopping off by Victoria Embankment for a stroll along the Thames; it's how I like to gather my thoughts. The slight drizzle doesn't bother me. In fact I don't even notice it until I light my joint. I think of how my life is going, where I've been and where I could end up. I could fuck it all off and maybe move in with Amber. It's not too soon. I reckon she'd be up for it too if I was to unleash the full power of my charm. My rainy day money I've got plugged away in the bank is enough to set myself up a little business and go legit; not bad for someone my age. I look across the river at an old boat chugging by, belching out pollution high into the night sky. I remember I used to fish here as a kid. I'd catch eels and sell them live to the pie shop. Which reminds me, I need to talk to Terry. If there's anything hovering around that I should know about, he'll know for sure.

Chapter 7

I've turned my spare room into an artist's studio, so if the police decide they wanna pay me a visit, it looks like I'm working on a painting or doing some other sort of artwork for a client. The good thing about original art is you can charge whatever the fuck you like for it. I normally airbrush an abstract piece on canvas and finish it by hand with a brush. My paintings are hung all around my flat, in expensive frames, hopefully creating the illusion of a half decent gallery. I've taken the piss even further by setting up three easels with unfinished work on each one. The main point of that is so I've got a great on-the-spot argument if I do happen to get raided. Those unfinished pieces are for clients that have already paid for them. A bulging portfolio of my work rests against the wall to complete the lie that I'm a busy, successful artist. To back up my bullshit, I've given out a lot of my artwork to friends and their families with the understanding that if I'm in trouble they'll happily say they bought them from me and paid top dollar for the privilege.

I mentioned to Amber that if she can sell any of my paintings she'd get a handsome commission, doing me a big favour in more ways than one. Maybe I should actually do this for a living instead of ducking and diving for a crust. I mean, I've genuinely sold my paintings before, so I know they're saleable.

Meeting Amber has the possibility of opening up spanking new opportunities for me, as her upper-class contacts are way outside my circle. Most of her pals she's spoken about seem to come across as those star fucker 'It girls' that do nish for a living but show up at important events, looking clueless and glammed up, hoping to get an invite to a celebrity party where the possibility of having a photo snapped with somebody famous is all that matters. None of them need to work, as their fathers seem to have unlimited cash ready to splash.

Speaking of cash, business my end seems to be picking up nicely; to a point I can sit back these days and pay a little team of trusted bods to do my dirty work for me. Problem is, they're so efficient; my bank and building society accounts are starting to fill up at a rate that has me a little uneasy. I need somewhere else to plug my money, somewhere super secret to hoard my filthy earnings. Over the past few days, and especially after seeing Ratboy, I've been rattling a sneaky, little idea about that I wanna run by Pete. Speaking of Pete, Dubs is on the blower.

"Yo, Span, what network are you with?"

"Cellnet."

"And what's your phone?"

"NEC 9A."

"Sweet."

"Why?"

"Pete's telling me he can get phones cheap, but he's trying to sell me what he's got."

"What's he got?"

"Hang on, let me ask him… What phone you got Pete…? He said it's a Motorola 8500x, any good?"

"Homosexuals love 'em. Apparently it's got something to do with the antenna being fixed rigid. Whereas on the NEC it slides straight down into the phone if you put any pressure on it, eliminating all possibilities for anal plunging."

"Pete, why are you trying to sell me a batty man's phone? I thought we were bonding and shit. Now I've gotta set your own bloodclart dog on you... WILSON, SEIZE HIM...! KILL...! UNGAWA...! What's the secret attack word Pete...? ROSEBUD!"

"Man, you two are wasted. To be honest with ya though, Dubs, both phones do the same thing so it's gonna be down to looks."

"Blud, they're both big-arse bricks. Don't they sell anything smaller that I can put in my pocket?"

"If they did I'd have one, mate."

"Anyway, Span, your phone cuts out all the time. You said yourself the phone's pony."

"That's only because I bounced it down the stairs a couple of times. It was pukka before that."

"Oh, and check this out, dread. You see this joker standing next to me?"

"No, but yeah."

"He's rolling spliff after spliff, trying to get me mashed up, so I tell him all my secrets on how I get the ladies. What do you reckon, Span, should I tell him? We're trying to negotiate a deal in between the phone thing, but I'm not sure he can be trusted."

"What else is he bringing to the table?"

"Hot dogs. Three a day, no questions asked."

"What brand?"

"Hang on... Pete what brand are the hot dogs...? He said they're Princes. What are they saying Span?"

"A bit touch and go, mate, it's your call. Personally, I think he's holding out on ya. This is what I would do, Dubs, are you listening?"

"I'm here, dread."

"Ask him about the Herta frankfurters. Keep eye contact at all times, and if he looks away then you know he's got a hidden stash plugged away somewhere, probably under the floorboards knowing Pete. Go for the four-a-day deal and push for quarter toasted buns."

"Gotcha."

"I'm on my way round if you need backup. Should be there in twenty minutes. Do you need anything?"

"Yeah, an orange Tango, and Pete wants a Dr Pepper."

What was I saying? Oh yeah, about plugging up my cash. Now that Dutch is on the scene and I can get my hands on a constant supply of outstanding tablets, it's very possible for me to speed up my early retirement, and the idea of burying it in a secluded, private forest is becoming quite appealing to me. Over time I could make a tidy little fortune for myself, like a million notes, who knows? You see, we're rapidly coming to the end of 1989, and I'm taking it upon myself that 1990 is gonna be a life changer for me; things are gonna happen. I'll take it easy and bury my cash in Pete's land. He's got fuckin' acres of it; woods and fields that go on forever. He does fuck all with it anyway, plus it's mostly overgrown, probably never even been stepped on. Pete knows a lot of people too, like your student types. He can sell a constant shitload of pills to them and plug the cash with mine. With the right amount of patience, we could be talking skies and limits all day long. Need to take it nice and easy though, rushing things always creates fuck-ups down the line. Stay focused and two steps ahead is the way I'm gonna play it out. I'm not up for being a greedy cunt that doesn't know when to stop.

I wanna tiptoe through this quietly while making me, Dubs and Pete millionaires, then I'll think about when to stop... sort of... maybe.

While I'm bouncing all that around my mind, a quick peep at my rear-view mirror tells me that black 7 Series has been with me for the past twenty minutes, or am I being a bit paranoid – which, let's face it, ain't a bad thing in my trade. I flick the indicator stalk to turn left into a Shell garage and watch the BMW cruise by. I style it out by casually grabbing pump number three and begin filling my car. I'm a couple of minutes into it, when coming up behind me to my right, I hear my name.

"Span? Fuckin' hell, it's been a while, brother. See you've still got the Stag then."

I didn't even have to turn around, I could see in the corner of my eye who it was... Ratboy. Play it cool, my son, he has no idea you know it was him that set you up to get robbed and almost killed, is on constant loop in my head.

"Yeah, still got it. It's been really reliable. It's one of those things you can trust won't let ya down." Calm the fuck down will ya, Span. He's gonna know that was aimed at him.

"Span, mate, it wasn't me that went around saying you was making deals with the Old Bill and that's the reason you've never been nicked. Honestly, you got it all wrong."

He is such a cunt.

"Well, what's done is done. It's water under the bridge. You're now doing your thing and I'm doing mine, so all's good."

"Yeah, I suppose, but I'm really here about the other day."

"What about the other day?"

"The day you saw me in the back of that police car."

"Oh, was that you? I had no idea. It did make me

wonder why they drove so slowly past me though, almost like somebody was pointing me out to them." Easy does it, Span. For fuck's sake, don't be too obvious.

"No listen, brother."

Brother? This cunt's got some front.

"I got nicked on your road, that's why you saw me in the car. I just wanted to clear that up with ya. I knew you'd think something suspicious otherwise, like I'm grassing you up or something."

How fuckin' nice of him, such a thoughtful chap.

"There's nothing to grass me up over, knocked everything on the head a while ago. What did you get nicked for anyway?"

"They found a gram of charlie on me."

I could ask Ratboy how they found a gram of charlie on him, and what was he doing on my road in the first place when nobody around there likes him. I mean, did the Old Bill just randomly happen to stop him and decide a search was in order for no apparent reason? But I can't be bothered, I don't believe a word he says so what's the point.

"A gram of charlie? That's not so bad. Sounds like you had a right touch there."

"Yeah, boy, you know that."

Boy? I'm looking at his lipless mouth thinking how easy it would be to slam my elbow into his jaw, when I notice the 7 Series slowly pull up behind him. I can't see who's in it, the windows are blacked out.

"Is that motor anything to do with you?" I ask, knowing it is.

"Yeah, that's me old man. He said to say hello, by the way."

And that's when he slipped up. As soon as he mentioned his old man, he cracked a crooked smile but kept his eyes serious; a look filled with absolute hate and envy.

"Tell him I said hello."

And also while you're at it, tell him I'm thinking about murdering you, you lipless, bug-eyed cunt. Maybe I should ask him about the girls he's brassin' out; that should cheer me up.

"So, I hear you're getting yourself a purple Cadillac and leopard-skin hat and suit?"

"What do you mean?"

"I hear you're a pimp."

"Span, if you wanna call it that, it's all good, brother. There's no business like ho business. Which brings me to something I wanna put to ya."

"Oh yeah? What's that then?"

"I wanna expand, Spaniard... I wanna stretch out. You know what I mean?"

Here it comes.

"In what way?"

"Well, in a way that your flat would be the perfect place to expand to, do you get me? I mean look at the location, it's perfect. You're ten minutes away from Piccadilly, and we all know how busy Piccadilly is. I've been thinking to myself for a little while now. I know we ain't seen eye to eye in the past, but I thought we could put that shit behind us and move on; just like the old days."

"So, what are you saying? You want my flat to pimp out from?"

"Well, my old man said to just take it... but I said, Dad that's not necessary. Spaniard is a reasonable bloke. When I tell him how much money he could make I'm sure he'll jump on board. Not to mention all the free pussy you can handle."

"I'm alright there, thanks."

"Well, when I say handle, I mean you can do whatever you want with the little sluts. Half the time they don't know what's going on anyway; it's fuckin' hilarious."

"Yeah, I've heard they're all wasted; pretty much comatose central."

"It's funny you should say that. I was banging one once, thinking she was out of it, and found out after she was dead. Can you believe that? I was fucking a corpse for ten minutes."

"You fucked a corpse?"

"Well, I didn't know she was dead at the time. I thought she was fucked up on the gear. It turned out sweet anyway; she was small enough to fit inside a suitcase."

Why is he telling me all this for Christ's sake?

"Why are you telling me all this? Somehow I don't think I really wanna know."

He's not finished yet.

"I'm just letting you know how easy it is, Spaniard me old pal. We folded that girl into a suitcase with a dumb-bell for company; she's now at the bottom of the Thames. You'll like this bit though, I cut a hole this big in the case," he joins his thumbs and fingers to form a circle, "just big enough for eels to get in. It won't take long for them to leave nothing but bones. Luckily for me, the girl was sixteen and small enough to fit in the case. A larger person would be a bit messier, but still easy to get rid of without a trace. We'd have to chop the body up and go with two suitcases."

OK, that was definitely aimed at me.

What he's just come out and told me must be bollocks, it's gotta be or Terry Taxi would've heard about it. He's obviously telling me that he wants my flat and how easy it is to kill and dispose of a body, meaning me. Fucking a corpse though? No, that can't be right. He's just trying to freak me out, I'm sure, but he did look serious when he said it, plus he is the sort of horrible cunt to do such a thing. What he's not aware of, however, is Spaniard's superhero-type ability to think of a credible lie in an instant.

"As for my flat, I knocked serving up from there because of the copper living on the floor below me. He moved in about five months ago, so I now pretty much stay at me bird's place. The flat is my studio where I create my art these days. It's far too hot to do anything there after what happened."

"What happened?"

"Didn't you hear?"

"No."

"Well basically, one night while I was over at my girl's place, one of me pals was staying at the flat with some sort for the night, and arranged for a parcel of charlie to be dropped round there that he had a buyer coming to pick up. Anyway, to cut a long story short, the copper living downstairs could hear everything being said from my flat through the ceiling. At night that place is bollocks for acoustics, you can hear everything. Anyway, at the end of the day my pal ends up getting nicked and a five stretch."

That wasn't too bad considering I kept eye contact all the way through.

"Who was that then?"

This is a bit trickier, as he knows all my friends.

"One of my mates I met through the missus."

I'm on fire, he doesn't know my missus. Hang about; did I just call Amber my missus? Steady on, Span.

"So you say you don't serve up anymore? I've been hearing different, like you're getting hold of some pukka Es."

"Pukka Es? Nah, mate, I don't know where you got that from."

54

"You know how it is, word gets around."

There's that fuckin' look again with the crooked smile.

"No, like I said, I dropped all that out a while ago. I've been selling my paintings these days. In fact, I've got some in the boot for sale if you fancy bringing some colour into your life."

I haven't, but as I can sense the Rat is about to leave, I know he ain't got time for that and won't ask to look.

"Maybe another time, Span. I've gotta split, you know how it is. Things to do and people to see... I'll catch ya later."

No you won't, and another thing, when he turned to get into the BMW he repeated 'People to see'. What the fuck does he mean by that? What people to see?

Chapter 8

I need a holiday, and sharpish. This whole area is becoming too fuckin' depressing for words. Now that Ratboy is scurrying about, everybody is bang on, super alert; me more than anyone. I don't know if I'm on for a raid from the police, or the fake police that'll fancy having another crack at trying to murder me. I just can't seem to settle, I'm on edge day and night. I feel like a right greedy cunt with all these problems. I wish I could share them out, but somehow I think I'd be told to keep them. I don't have all the problems though, there's still the odd one about that's nothing to do with me, like last night for instance.

On the estate next to mine another old lady was killed, found by a kind neighbour who normally brings her shopping. The neighbour noticed the old girl's bedroom window was unusually wide open for so early in the morning. After knocking a few times without an answer, the neighbour let herself in with a spare key she had for emergencies and found her friend dead. She was strangled like the last one, only this time, the killer punched her face in until she was an unrecognisable mess. The neighbour let out a scream that a bunch of young kids outside playing heard, who ran in to witness the gruesome sight.

The local newspaper printed a brief article about the

murder, but seemed to play it down a touch. Not a lot of details were given, just some pictures of antique jewellery that was taken from the home. The victim was Agnes Pope. She was eighty-six years old.

Leaving my block of flats, I've just noticed something that's got me in meerkat mode. I'm looking left and right, up and down, you name it I've looked at it. There's a car parked opposite me. It was there yesterday too. Can't see who's in it without being too obvious, but I've scoped a couple of bods sitting in the front. They could be on to me, but it could also be the most innocent thing in the world. There's never any flow of punters coming to my front door to score making me look like a dealer. I'm always super strict on that rule, so who the fuck are they?

The thought of a vacation is rapidly making a lot of sense. I'll shoot off over to Spain for a couple of weeks to see my family. Yeah, that's a good idea, nice and simple. Two weeks of dunking churros in chocolate is just what I need.

I head back over to Pete's, which is now pretty much our HQ, to tell the boys I'm jetting off to Spain.

"Why go to Spain, bruv? You've been a million times already. We should all go to Dahab, innit."

"Dahab?"

"Yeah Span, Dahab, in Egypt. I used to go there to chill out once in a while. We could all go; the three of us."

"And what about Wilson?"

"No he can't go, bruv, it'll be too hot for him."

"No, I mean who'll look after him, you cunt."

"Oh right, yeah. No, that's sorted. I normally leave him with the lady in the baker's whenever I go away, Doris; she fuckin' loves him. Not a problem, Span, trust me. He likes her more than he likes me."

"You mean he likes all the free cakes."

"So are we settled, gentleman? Dahab? Dubs? Span? Come on, man, it'll be sick, and I'll arrange it all, innit. I take it you've both got passports?"

"Yeah, I have. What about you Dubs?"

"Of course, blud, but please tell him to stop saying innit."

"That's it then, I'll sort it for next week and you can pay me later innit... sweet?"

"How much are we talking here Pete? Just out of curiosity."

"Cheap, man. Call it three hundred quid there and back. Your accommodation is pence, literally pence, and that's no joke."

I need to pick the right time to put my idea to Pete, but things are looking good. As we chat about this and that, he tells me the inheritance money left by his old man is rapidly drying up, and he's been thinking of ways to earn a crust without actually working for it.

The thing is, Pete's a massive stoner, and being a stoner he's always too mangled to get off his lazy arse and do something about it. It's like I've always said, puffing kills your ambition. When you wrap your head around it, Pete's in a rather funny old situation. I mean, he lives alone in a twelve-bedroomed house for fuck's sake. Why not sell it and buy something smaller? He'd probably never have to worry about his inheritance money drying up. The catch to living in a beautiful, listed building like Pete's family house is that he's not allowed to sell it. It needs to stay in the family, which is him or Dingo. Pete promised his old man on his deathbed he'd live there until he croaks, just like his dad did who was also born there, and the same for his grandfather. So that gives ya some idea how long that drum has been in the family.

"So whatever happened to that bird of yours Pete, the one with the big tits that was always round here? Dark-haired, spotty sort with a fat arse."

"Who Brenda? I ain't seen her for ages, man. Fuckin' girl is off her head, I'm telling ya. Last time I saw her was when she woke me up one morning sucking my dick, then turned around and said she was leaving me and left, just like that, bruv. I'm not even kidding when I say, to this day, I still ain't got a clue what happened. Fuckin' madness, man."

"Sounds like maybe some narcotics were being used Peter, am I right?"

"Only puff and the odd trip; nothing really heavy. You know what I'm like."

"The odd trip? Mate, acid can be really fuckin' odd, especially if your mind's not with it. I've lost the plot more than once tripping. It happens, Pete."

"Yeah, true. I suppose you're right... Never really thought about it before... Anyway, whatever bruv, it was a long time ago. I'm over it."

"That's the spirit, my son. Now skin up, Pete, for fuck's sake. I rolled the last two joints, you joker smoker."

The moment seems right, so I bring up the crafty idea that I've been keeping under me hat the past few days and drop it right on his toes.

"Fuckin' sick idea, Span man. I can sell untold pills for ya. Let's go, bruv, I'm ready."

Well that was easy.

"Yeah, but the thing is I don't know your land, Pete. That's your job, mate. It needs to be super secret; we're talking about our life savings here."

"Leave it to me, Span. I'm on it, bruv. I think I know just

the perfect place. I can also probably get you a good deal on some Es, if you want? I know some bloke in Orpington. He's got the sickest rhubarb and custard caps."

"I'm sorted there, as it goes. I've got this new contact, a Dutch fella, who funny enough is called Dutch. Anyway, I'm not joking, but this geezer makes the bits himself, in a labotory... a labaratory... in a fuckin' lab, mate. I'm talking white coat and rubber gloves, Pete."

"Really, bruv? So they must be good then?"

"You ain't kidding. I got on three with Amber at her place one night. We got proper messed up. No complaints and super clean; the cleanest I've had, to be honest."

"Wicked, man. I can't wait to try them bad boys. What the fuck is this mad shit we're smoking here anyway, Span? It's messing with my vision."

"That's a bit of Silver Haze, but this red and purple one I've got here in my pocket, if I can find it... Fuck, I've lost it...! Oh, here it is. Check this out, Pete. That there, my friend, is Dark Devil."

This weed, by the way if you're wondering, is red and purple. No colour green anywhere to be seen whatsoever. The aroma is kinda fruity, like a peachy passion fruit mixed with orchids, and really sticky.

"Fucking hell, Span, that's insane. I've never seen weed like this before. That's some mad-looking, alien shit, bruv. I bet it's lethal too, innit?"

"Nah, mate. That's the thing with this gear; it's different to what you've ever smoked before. You get stoned but can function. On my life, Pete, last Tuesday I smoked some of this, got well and truly caned, then went for a two-hour workout, I kid you not. Fuckin' amazing stuff."

"That's nuts, man, but I can believe it. I'm telling ya, Span, we gotta thank them aliens for the gift of weed, bruv."

"Aliens? What are you going on about now?"

"Span man, I believe in that shit, you know? About aliens leaving cannabis seeds with the first humans? Weed is an all-in-one cure for the human race, innit. Think about it. There are no fossil records of any cannabis plants before humans turned up, and that's a fact, because I read it in a proper book. So how did weed get here? Can't you see, bruv? It all fits together."

"Not really Pete, but go on."

"Well, you know about that mad evolutionary jump, how us humans came to be?"

"Nope."

"Well check this out, Span man. One minute we've only just come down from the trees, then there's a good few thousand fuckin' years' gap from the apes, the Neanderthals, Cro-Magnon man, and the rest I can't remember. Then the next thing you know, bosh bruv, we're wearing slippers, reading newspapers and sipping cappuccinos. It's the alien DNA, I'm telling ya. The aliens needed drones they could control, so they spliced some alien DNA with caveman DNA and we turned up, humans. That's how they built the Pyramids, trust me, with human drones controlled by aliens."

"That's pretty fuckin' deep, Pete, I've gotta tell ya."

"That's what I'm saying, bruv, and that's where the ganja comes in. The oil from cannabis can cure pretty much every fucking thing that humans get wrong with them. I'm not talking about the oil you smoked back in the day, spread on the outside of a cigarette, I'm talking about medicinal oil, CBD oil. Put that goodness inside you and that shit will cure cancer. The government know all about it, believe me, which is why it ain't legalised, and how could they legalise it? If they make weed legal the government won't earn fuck all, because people will be sitting at home curing cancer themselves for free."

"Pete... not being funny, mate... but all that you just said was a noise. Here smoke some more of this and pass us those Jaffa cakes."

"That's what I've been thinking of doing, Span man."

"What? Passing me those Jaffa cakes?"

"Nah man, oil. Manufacture medicinal cannabis oil in capsules. I've been thinking about it for a while now, it's a quality idea. People can take one a day and never get ill, man. Here's the thing though, and check this out for a bastard, it's illegal to grow the plant, but legal to have the seeds and oil. You need to grow the fuckin' plant to get the oil, that's where they've got you by the bollocks."

"That is a bit weird, as it goes... So why don't you manufacture the oil in another country?"

"I'm thinking about it, Span, but..."

"But you're always too stoned Pete?"

"Nah man, it's just, well it's fuckin' huge, bruv, you know? I'd rather do that shit with a partner. Why don't you think about it, Span? It'd be an epic adventure."

"Mate, I know fuck all about medicinal oil, that's your department. It's food for thought, all the same, though."

"That's what I wanna do, CBD, man."

"Well, you seem to know your stuff, Pete, that's for sure, and it is really interesting, I must say, but at the end of the day it boils down to one thing. Are you listening Pete, because it's important?"

"I'm listening, bruv."

"OK... See that fuckin' box of Jaffa cakes? Slide that cunt down the table towards me or we're gonna have a bit of a fall out."

I leave it up to Pete to get back to me when he has a strong idea about where on his land we can safely bury the money and head off back home.

My phone wakes me stretched out on the sofa snatching some afternoon shut-eye; it's Amber. She wants to treat me to dinner at a posh restaurant in Piccadilly. She'll pick me up at half eight this evening, which gives me loads more time to sleep. I tell her how great that sounds, lie about the battery on my phone about to die, and grab more zeds.

Time flies by, when my eyes spring open to the sound of a car tooting outside. A silver Karmann Ghia, double-parked down below, has got to be Amber. She said something earlier on about picking up her baby; thank fuck it was a motor.

"Do you like it?" she asks, looking like an excited kid on Christmas day.

"Yeah, it's beautiful. Really suits ya." And it does. Amber is dressed in a short, black summer dress with silver flowers embroidered down one side. Her blonde hair, slight tan, emerald green eyes and peach lipstick, all framed by the black leather interior of the Karmann Ghia, were somehow all meant to come together at this precise moment in time. I'm sure it's got something to do with the universe or stars lining up perfectly, but whatever way you look at it, she looks fuckin' stunning.

Pulling up outside the swanky restaurant, the thought of feeling a little underdressed comes over me. I'm not a lover of these kind of places; bunch of snobby, inbred Ruperts looking down their nose at ya. Gaff looks like a fuckin' palace, with chandeliers and silver candelabras all over, and I'm the only plum not wearing a suit and tie. I notice people being turned away at the door for not being appropriately suited and booted, yet for me wearing jeans and a shirt not a word is said. I'm starting to think Amber or her old man carry a bit more weight than she's letting on.

As much as I normally avoid these places, one thing you can count on is being made to feel special, which let's face it, is always a nice touch. We're shown to a table for two where the fastest waiter in the West brings us a couple of menus. I peep over the top, as I'm reading, at all the quiet chitter-chatter going on around us from plastic-looking people that resemble mannequins from a shop window. Almost like loud whispers they sound, or like a distant swarm of bees. Can't make heads or tails of this damn menu, and it's doing my nut in, which I feel needs pointing out to Amber.

"This menu is all in French."

"That's because it's a French restaurant, Spaniard sweetie."

"But we ain't in France, so why the fuck not have it in English too?"

That's the way I see it, anyway, so I'll leave it down to her. She can order for both of us, which she does, two lots of something in French, that when it turns up at the table I think for a second we're gonna play KerPlunk. A cute little smile breaks across Amber's face, as she can clearly see I'm a fish out of water. Have I mentioned how stunning she looks tonight? I'm sure I did when she picked me up earlier on. You know them sort of girls that no matter how much they scrub up and dress up, they still seem to look a touch unkept? You could have them professionally painted by a top make-up artist and it still wouldn't matter, they're always missing that shiny girl mineral. Amber, however, has that shiny girl mineral with a flawless complexion and always so immaculate. I'll tell ya something else I've noticed about shiny girls like Amber, their make-up is always flawless but not obvious, if that makes any sense. I mean, take now for instance. I'm looking at Amber across the table and her make-up is so on point that it looks like she naturally looks that way stepping out of the shower. Do you know what's really funny about shiny girls though? And this is just an observation. I've stayed round Amber's place for a whole weekend and not once did I notice her go to use the toilet. It's like they have some kind of cloaking device whenever it's time to slip off for a dump. I personally don't have a problem saying 'See ya in a while, I need to crimp one off', but with shiny girls it's all really taboo. Don't get me wrong, I'm not into girls and toilets in a weird way. I'm just saying it's strange that Amber and quite a few other shiny girls I know do the same thing, and that's to never let you know when they've been to the khazi.

While I've been explaining that interesting little chestnut for ya, this waiter, who looks a bit like an eighteen-year-old Starsky from *Starsky & Hutch*, has been hovering around our table constantly gazing at Amber's cleavage, which to be fair, she has got a decent pair on her. Amber looks longingly over at me. I can tell by her candyfloss gaze that romance is on her mind. Just as she gently, and I mean so delicately gently, leans across to say something so romantically sweet that it would make a flower instantly bloom, this huge booming voice smashes a clean path to us from six tables away.

"Fuckin' hell, fancy seeing you here Spaniard, you sly old cunt," comes the voice completely out of the blue, like *The Beast from 20,000 Fathoms*.

I look round to see an old acquaintance of mine, Tommy the Cannon, a mad, bald bastard that loved to headbutt people and bite noses off. He's also got more scars on his boat than Dubs, and that's saying something. He's a giant of a man, six foot six and muscle-bound, well into steroids and constantly sticking needles in his arse. Thing about Tommy is his volume, which is stuck on maximum plus a bit more; an ear-rupturing, loud bastard you'd never visit a library with.

"Hello, Tommy. How ya doing?" Probably the worst thing to say to him in a posh restaurant like this, should of just acknowledged him with a nod and kept me head down.

"I'm alright, Spaniard. Ain't seen you about for fuckin' ages. Is that your missus? Very nice, son, very fuckin' nice."

"Cheers, Tommy. We're just friends, mate, out having a munch."

"Fuckin' good choice of place, the grub here is handsome, brother."

Hang about… How the fuck did he order, anyway? As if this cunt can speak French.

"It's my first time here, Tom. Just about to get stuck in, mate. I'll let you know how I get on. Enjoy the rest of your night. Good seeing ya."

My feeble attempt at swerving Tommy doesn't work. He needs to get something off his chest.

"Did you hear what happened to me last Friday? No? Span, you ain't gonna fuckin' believe this. You know what I'm like with the birds? I like to have a good time. So I go to a club over in New Cross, charlied up off me fuckin' nut, looking for one of those gothic sorts. You know the ones I'm talking about? I fancied something different for a change. So I meet this bird at the bar who's full-on. She's got the eyes done all black, big fuckin' army boots, long, black coat, black nails and lips, the works. We're getting it on sweet as a nut, doing the sniff, knocking back shorts; we're rotten as ya like by the time we get back to my place. She was gagging for it, mate, but like a cunt I'd done so much lemon, getting a stiff one was a fuckin' nightmare, brother, you know what I'm saying?"

At this point, Tommy looks around at the other diners sitting at their tables pretending to be invisible.

"These cunts know what I'm talking about, especially him down the end there with the syrup. I still managed to wreck her bottle though, proper smashed it, mate. Anyway, you'll love this bit. In the morning, I wake up, flat on me back, looking up at the ceiling, and all I can smell is shit. As I lift me head, and I swear on my little boy's life this is gospel, I look down to see this huge, fuckin' turd curled up on me chest, no joke. Filthy cunt shit on me chest, mate! There I am out cold, while she squats over me to curl one off; fuckin' disgusting. What is the world coming to, I ask ya? And to make matters worse, listen to this, she fuckin' robs me, takes a hundred and eighty quid from me wallet, and my last wrap of charlie, the old shitcunt."

I glance over at the people sitting in complete silence, looking down at their desserts wondering what to do with them, especially the fella that ordered the chocolate gateau. For the first time all evening you can hear a pin drop, and the silence is fuckin' golden.

"That's not good, Tommy. You wanna pick a better class of girl, mate," I tell him as if I'm his dad. Funny thing is Tommy has just said all that while sitting there with another girl he's out on a date with who couldn't care less. She's far too busy tucking into a banana split with a mountain of ice cream that's obviously way more important than any conversation. Poor Amber, on the other hand, is now the fish out of water. She somehow can't quite get her head around what's just been said. By the time Tommy gets up to leave and says "See ya later", Amber can only muster a muffled squeak. The second Tommy has left the restaurant, the waiter glides over to apologise to everyone, for some reason or another, but also to look down Amber's top again. She tells me the waiter is starting to freak her out because of the attention he's giving her, which makes me laugh. I tell her, he's only a young kid that's just added her to his wank bank and to take it as a compliment. I get a giggle, the first all night, so I take a chance purely in the name of fun.

"Take off your knickers."

"Excuse me…? Why?"

"Because I'm gonna tip that waiter your drawers. Come on, it'll make his day, and let's face it, because of you he didn't hang about with our order, whatever the fuck it was. He's been a champion all night, like a fuckin' blur."

By the look on Amber's face I can see she still thinks I'm joking, looking a bit confused, taking in what I've just asked her.

"You're serious?" she whispers.

I nod, as she looks around quick time, nobody but the waiter is taking any notice of us. I never thought she'd do it, but in one slick motion, Amber slips off her panties and passes them to me under the table. She leaves £110 for the meal, calmly gets up and makes for the exit. I neatly place the black silkies on top of the bill and cash, with an extra tenner thrown in, covered by the menu. As I reach the exit Amber is already outside. Starsky is now at our table looking rather happy with himself. He swiftly plugs the knickers in his pocket, giving me a nod of approval. Amber is at the window blushing a few shades of red, as we set off to her place.

"I can't believe I just done that," is the first thing she says getting in the car.

"It's only a bit of fun, Amber. It's not like you're gonna see him again."

"I know that, because now I can't go back there."

"Don't worry about it. I'll introduce you to a beautiful pie and mash shop I know, but don't tell all your mates."

I like to create memories that people are gonna remember. That young waiter now has a cool little campfire story to tell and edit to suit himself. I can imagine him telling all his pals later.

"So I go over to take this cracking looking bird's order, who's definitely on me case, when all of a sudden she slips her knickers into me pocket. I'm thinking hold up, what the fuck is going on here? As I come back to put her food on the table, I swear on my mother's life, she gets up, grabs me by the tie and drags me outside to her Roller where she sucks me cock dry on the back seat. Begging me to bang her she was. Mate, I came sixteen times, no lie."

Chapter 9

I've gotta tell ya a little something. It's not the most interesting thing you're gonna hear today, but waking up round Amber's place is such a fuckin' treat. I mean, no cunt knows where I am, other than Dubs and Pete of course. When I'm at my flat, I sleep with one eye open and my feet in the starting blocks. Anybody walking into my block creates an echo that in the early hours travels up to my landing where I can hear, and pretty clear too. Only problem is you don't know who's outside. Could be Old Bill about to grace my front door with a hydraulic ram, or it could be my next-door neighbour shooting off for a few laps in his milk float at five in the morning. So you could say my sleep situation is slightly fucked, and more so now the Rat's in town. I'm gonna be even more tightly coiled in bed than I normally am, ready to spring like a gazelle with its arse on fire at a moment's notice. Here at Amber's apartment it's the polar opposite, everything is violins and poetry. I woke up today to harp music. I don't mean Amber was playing the harp by any stretch, it was a tape or CD, but still a fuckin' harp.

"What do you have planned for today, sweetie?"

"Nothing much, to be honest, just getting some last bits together for tomorrow."

"Why, what's tomorrow?"

"I'm off to Wales, remember? I told ya the other day."

Or should I say Dahab? No, better not.

"Wales, Spaniard?"

"Yeah. I said me and Dubs were going with Pete, something to do with his family. It's all a bit heavy… inheritance thing… His grandmother… She's not very well, Amber. Pete really needs us there for support."

She can't say fuck all about that, and I'm certainly not being out of order. Remember when her pal called that time? Amber said her friend needed her, and put a stop to our night point-blank so she could be a shoulder to cry on. It's exactly the same only mine's a lie… She won't find out about Dahab anyway, unless you tell her, which I know you won't do because you're coming with us.

"Oh… I don't remember you saying anything about Wales. Is Peter Welsh? He doesn't sound Welsh."

"No, he's from London, but he's got family up there… So I'm gonna grab something to eat and get cracking with me packing."

Maybe I should be a rapper? There's defiantly something there.

"I can cook you a meal here. It's no trouble, Spaniard."

Man, I feel bad doing this to her; it actually hurts my fuckin' stomach. She looks like a lost kitten, but I can't let her know about Dahab, I don't know why.

"No, don't worry about it, Amber. I'll grab something to eat on the way home."

"Will you go to the pie and mashed potato place?"

"The pie and mashed potato place? You mean the pie and mash shop? Or if you're a pro, you drop the 'and'… it's the pie mash shop."

"Listen mister, you've explained to me in great detail what

71

it is, and however way you want to say it, it's pie with mashed potato… so there."

"I won't argue with that."

Amber is starting to take up a lot of my headspace, and I think I like it. They say opposites attract, and in this case it's bang on. I'm not sure I really need it at the moment if I'm being completely upfront with ya. I've got the Ratboy thing going on, not to mention the dealings with Dutch. Do you see what I mean? There's shit going on at the moment, and the thought of bringing a delicate little flower like Amber into my world is a little worrying. What's more worrying, is why the fuck is she in my head so much? Maybe what my brain needs right now is some fuel for clearer thinking.

"Ah, Tony my good man, how the devil are you today? It's absolutely wonderful to see you as always. If you'd be so kind, I'd be rather interested in purchasing two of your magnificent pies, with two glorious helpings of mashed potato por favor."

"With liquor?"

"Well, why the bloody hell not Anthony? That's a grand idea."

I swear he fuckin' hates me. If it wasn't for the fact the pies are cooked downstairs by someone else, then brought up on a tray and handed to him, for all to see, I'd probably not eat here, and you know very well why I wouldn't. Mallet-head Tony would be downstairs in a shot wiping his gristle all over my pies, or emptying his sack in me mash. Where I've had the result though is that Tony can't leave that spot, he just serves the grub, and that's right in front of ya.

"Thank you so much, Anthony, you're very kind."

I can't help it though, he's such a miserable cunt. I've been coming here for years, and I swear to God I've never seen him smile, not even once. He kinda laughed one time, I think it was back in '86 if I'm not mistaken. I'm not a hundred per cent on the year; I'd have to check the archives. Anyway, I bowled up to the counter like a usually do, and Tony is standing there reading a comic. Not a Marvel kind of comic, more like a *Beano*. So, as I'm waiting for him to serve me, he's obviously seen something in those pages that's tickled him. He drops the comic then produces a foghorn-type sound which is clearly his laugh. His whole face is totally serious, but his mouth couldn't get any wider. The shoulders are doing their bit, so you know he's definitely laughing, but it's mental on another level. In conclusion, he's one weird Boris Karloff-looking cunt that needs to go spend a bit more time staring at himself in the mirror. Not because he's as ugly as sin, that goes without saying – his head looks like a Ford Granada doing a handstand – I'm saying he needs to have a long, good look at his aura, if he's got one.

"Hello, Tel, fancy seeing you here… Jellied eels? Blimey."

"They're beautiful, Span. Wanna try some?"

"I'd rather lick me own piss off a stinging nettle thanks."

"You don't know what you're missing."

"I do… Them bastards you're eating… fuckin' hell, Tel, they stink, mate."

"Handsome."

"Certainly doesn't look it."

"Put hairs on your chest, son."

"I've got hairs on me chest, Tel, and on me Niagaras, but that what you're eating there smells like Sally from the alley's drawers, mate."

"Well, you fucked her, you'd know."

"Did I bollocks."

"That's what I heard, Span, that you and Dubs went through her."

"Mate, you do know she's a brass don't ya?"

"I didn't know that."

"Yeah, she knocks about with Trappy… I ain't knobbed her and neither has Dubs. That's a scandalous thing to say, Terrence, hope you choke on your eels, which by the way, that bit on your spoon, looks like snot mixed with bird shit."

"Tastes even better now you've given me that image."

"So what's the apple then, Terrence? Anything new? Come on, fella, spill the beans. You know I'm always in here on Thursday at this time, or is it just coincidence?"

"You know me too well, Span."

"I certainly do, Tel."

"It could be nothing."

"Or it could be something."

"Well, I'm not so sure, but as I live round the corner from you and have to pass your flat ten times a day, I've seen a car about that I'd rather have not, you know?"

"Go on."

"Well, the reason I'm not a hundred per cent is because I'm always driving and never get a proper look, but I could swear I've seen Ratboy's old man's motor parked up outside your block a couple of times last week, around two in the morning."

"A black 7 Series?"

"That's it, with blacked-out windows."

"Couldn't be more of a cunt could he?"

"What do you mean?"

"A black BMW with blacked-out windows? Is he fuckin' sure?"

"I'd have it."

"Behave, Tel."

"So, what do you think?"

"I dunno... Hopefully it's nothing. There's a couple of little things Ratboy said to me the other day when I saw him at the garage that kinda bugs me though."

"What's than then?"

"He mentioned something about me getting hold of some pukka pills, which I denied of course. So is he setting me up to get robbed again? Or do they want me completely out of the way so the Rat can take over what I've built up? Maybe his old man thinks I can lead him to my supplier through torture. The other thing he said I'd rather wait until you've got a mouthful of eels before I tell ya."

"Hold up... Go on then."

"There's no need to slurp it, Tel."

"It's the only way to do it. I like to savour the flavour."

"You're an animal, but anyway, he said he fucked a corpse."

"Who fucked a corpse?"

"Ratboy, then put the body in a suitcase and dumped it in the Thames. How's those eels?"

"Beautiful."

"He said he cut a hole in the case so eels could get in to eat the body. How's those eels now?"

"Still beautiful."

"Fuckin' hell, Terrence, I might end up at the bottom of the Thames; food for them eels you're eating."

"Not these ones, these are going in my belly."

"Cheers... Mind out they don't make you sick, you're taking us to the airport tomorrow."

"Don't make much sense though does it, Span?"

"What's that?"

"I mean, why fuck a corpse when he's got other girls at that place that are breathing?"

"Well, he said he didn't know she was dead while he was banging her. He reckons he thought she was out of it from the gear."

"So do you believe him? About dumping the body in the Thames?"

"Tel, chew with your mouth closed for fuck's sake, you're doing it on purpose."

"I need to open my mouth to speak, Span, that's normally how it works."

"You know what you're doing, it's fuckin' horrible, and that's why you're laughing."

"Is that better for ya?"

"Only a little bit. I don't know if I believe him though, I was gonna ask if you've heard anything about a body of a young girl being found in a case dumped in the Thames."

"Bodies are found in the Thames all the time, Span."

"Yeah, but in a suitcase?"

"Fuck knows, mate, I ain't heard anything."

"Mind you, he said he stuck a dumb-bell in the case, so it's probably at the bottom of the river anyway, if he's telling the truth."

"One of those things we'll never know, Span."

Terry ain't bothered about anything, he's the most composed cunt I've ever met. Surely he must get problems like the rest of us? And even more so what with the amount of eels he shovels down.

"Tel, while I'm away, can you do me a favour and keep your ear to the ground?"

"I'm not a Cherokee Indian, Span, I'm a taxi driver that drives a black cab for a living. What you're asking me to do is not something I fancy getting involved in. I like to keep myself to myself."

"Oh fuck off, Tel. You're not just a black cab driver, you're Terry Taxi. I'm not asking ya to be a Cherokee Indian, just to keep an eye on the ranch while I'm away."

"Relax, Span, I'm winding you up, mate. You know I will."

And he's right, I knew he would.

Chapter 10

I never thought he'd actually do it, book the holiday I mean. How he went about it is a complete mystery to me, what with him always being so stoned and rooted to the sofa. Pete has done just like he said he would and sorted our little vacation to Dahab. Today is the day, and I can't fuckin' wait to be on that plane out of here. Fair play to the man for proving me wrong. He's also in tour guide mode level pro. Terry Taxi managed to survive the night and is in a surprisingly good mood. Judging by the speed he's going, he can't wait to get rid of us, must be Pete's enthusiasm.

"Terry, have I told you that Dahab is situated on the south-east coast of the Sinai Peninsula?"

"No, Pete, you haven't mentioned that before, mate. I should imagine it would be very interesting to someone who cares."

"Yeah, it's a Bedouin village, just a stone's throw from Sharm el-Sheikh."

"That's amazing. I hope you don't think I'm driving you there if that's what you're getting at."

"Have you told Amber where you're going Span?" asks Dubs.

"Nope, she thinks I'm going to Wales with you and Pete. We ain't serious enough yet for her to know my ins and outs.

She's cool, but I don't know. When we get back I'll see how it goes with her."

"Smart move, blud. Don't be an open book so soon, dread."

"Exactly."

The thing is I've already been an open book with her.

Meanwhile, Terry Taxi has somehow used reverse psychology on Pete, and for the time being has nudged him out of tour guide mode.

"So I saw your ex in Sainsbury's Pete. Brenda is it? Seems like such a nice girl."

"Man that's spooky, I was just telling Spaniard about her the other day. She's double mental, Tel, trust me."

"You was with her for a while, so she couldn't have been that bad, surely? I actually thought you'd have kids by now Pete."

"Who, with Brenda? Nah, man, I never used to really bang her, blow jobs only, innit."

"Really? How does that work then?" I have to ask.

"Span man, you'll take the piss if I tell ya, and then Dubs will take the piss for the whole holiday, so I'm not saying."

"Fair enough."

"No, I'm serious, you wouldn't understand."

"OK Pete, it's not a problem."

"You know I'd tell you lot if I could, but I can't."

"Yeah, we get it, mate. Forget about it."

"Oh fuck it, her hole was too big."

"Blimey, Peter, are you sure, mate? That's a bit out of order... How big are we talking here, anyway?"

"Bruv, I couldn't touch the sides, had to go in at an angle to get any friction; made me feel like I had a micro cock."

"I know how you feel, dread, I've been in the same place,

man. Span, you remember Shantel?"

"How could I forget, Dubs?"

"Blud, I'm telling ya, she was like a fuckin' horse's collar."

"Probably because she shat out three kids, Dubs. I mean look at the size of their heads for Christ's sake."

"True."

"Mate, what about that bird Sandra from Kennington I was seeing? She had zero kids whatsoever, and I could still fly a fuckin' hang-glider in there."

"Really, blud? Damn I remember her. You tried to set me up with her sister."

"Yeah, that's the one."

"Fuck, she had a tight body too. Wasn't she a fitness girl from the gym or something?"

"Sure was, and I kid you not Dubs, I could wear her as a hat; absolutely shocking, mate. I had to hire a St Bernard to sit in the bedroom every time we had a bunk-up; cost me a fuckin' fortune in brandy. First time I knobbed her, I dropped me phone in there and had to bungee down to get it."

"Gentlemen, we are here. Have a great holiday, boys, and mind how you go. I'm not gonna hang about because I need to fuck off, I'm playing golf."

More like he's got the shits from those eels yesterday.

"Cheers, Terence. See you when we get back," we almost said all together; trust Pete to be late.

The flight to Egypt was pretty much the same as any other cheap economy flight, cramped and fucking horrible. Don't even get me started on the food. Then it was time for a little coach ride; twelve hours' worth on a rickety old bastard with no windows. It had holes where the windows were meant to be, but shy of any glass. The carpet nailed to the dashboard was a nice touch though; my nan had the exact same one in her hallway. There's eight passengers on board including us three, the other five are girls from all over; one Italian, one French, an Aussie and two Americans, all in their twenties, that seem to know each other very well.

An hour into the drive, I pick up the sweet smell of ganja drifting between the girls. We're heading deep into the desert and the only vehicle for miles around. It's pitch-black outside, with the stars way up high winking down at me, which I take as a good sign. Within no time at all me, Dubs and Pete are passing joints up and down the coach quicker than the British Olympic relay team.

The twelve-hour drive flew by in a flash, and before we knew it we'd arrived at Dahab on a beautiful, sunny morning. The first thing that hits you is the overbearing smell of camels' piss, which I suppose is expected, as everywhere you look there are camels and more camels. I walk up to a group of six that are lounging on the beach to get a closer look at the necklaces they are wearing. Black, shiny pearls that glisten in the sunlight hang like grapes around each camel's neck. On close inspection, I realise they aren't wearing a necklace at all, but each camel has hundreds of blood-sucking ticks around its neck; bugs as big as your thumbnail bloated to the max, really fucking nasty.

Our accommodation is a row of tiny, windowless huts on the beach made from breeze blocks, with a corrugated sheet metal roof and just sand on the floor, or should I say the beach was the floor. Oh and there's also a bicycle padlock from the seventies for security, which has me slightly teary-eyed daydreaming about my old Raleigh Chopper from back in the day. The only thing inside the hut is a two-inch-thick mattress on the ground. The cost for this fancy, little set-up is twelve pence a night. Not a bad deal when you think about it, as I'm only gonna be sleeping in there, the rest of the time I'll be on the beach or splashing about in the water.

After the long hours of travelling we've just been through, I'm ready to get my head down for some proper shut-eye, but first I desperately need a shower, as I'm sweating like a cunt and my armpits are seriously chucking up. I sling my gear in the corner of the hut and take a shower on the beach which is pretty much just outside my door. The girls decide to look somewhere else along the beach for better accommodation because they're girls, and Dubs goes along with them because he's Dubs.

"Is Dubs coming back here, Span, or is he staying with them birds?"

"I ain't got a clue, mate, I've been under the shower on the beach. Only just got back. Don't tell me you miss him already Pete? That's really touching."

"Hell no, but if he's making moves on the girls I wanna be there, innit. One out of five must like me, and I'm feeling lucky, bruv. Here, take this water, I'm gonna catch them up."

"That's a block of ice, Pete, inside an Evian bottle. Where the fuck did you get it?"

"Just over there by the trees. Some bloke's got a freezer plotted on the sand."

"Ain't he got anything drinkable, or is it all like this?"

"All frozen, I checked, but this one is sweet anyway, look it's melting."

A couple of sips of frozen water is all my teeth can take, but it hits the spot all the same; time for some shut-eye. As well as having no windows, there's also no electricity in the hut. The only light available is from the sun piercing through the cracks in the old, wooden door. I wanna nut out as quickly as possible, because the heat in here is beginning to get a little uncomfortable for me. Too hot and sleeping will be impossible. The last thought I have is that I'd rather take my chances outside with the mosquitoes.

I wake up three hours later with a pain in my gut I can only describe as somebody going to town on my stomach with a Kango hammer drill. I desperately try to sit up, but it is as though my shoulders are pinned to the floor, all I can move are my eyes. The heat is fucking unbearable; I'm slowly being cooked alive in here. It takes all my strength to lift my head from the mattress. The sweat that pours from me as I sit up is as though I'd just stepped out of the shower. My stomach is in knots and my arse feels like it is gonna explode. It can't be anything I've eaten, because I haven't eaten. I must have swallowed some water from the shower earlier on, something they tell you to triple make sure you never do. On very shaky legs, I set off to find a toilet, seriously dizzy and weak. My head is thumping and my fucking arse is pouting. I'm praying for a khazi, and there in front of me, as I turn a corner, my prayers are answered – a wooden shed that looks like it's been built by a chimp using driftwood found washed up on the beach. As I glance up at the word TOILET badly scrawled in red paint, I swear I can hear angels singing. I open the door to park my arse and I'm greeted by a toilet sitting on the sand, not piped in, just sitting on the sand; no water, no plumbing, no flushing. People have been taking a dump in it all day long and the shit is piled way above the rim; kudos going out to some pretty impressive aiming skills, creating a mountainous peak resembling Everest.

The smell must have come from hell itself, so must the job the poor cunt has at the end of the day scooping all that crap out getting it ready for the next day. It's party time for the flies and everyone was invited. There are fuckin' thousands of them buzzing around in this tiny, confined space. The only thing stopping me puking up is the thought of them flying into my mouth.

I apologise to my arse for the inconvenience and continue onwards with my quest, bent over clutching my guts looking for somewhere to unleash the demons within. I'm not normally a religious person, but I'd be lying if I said I wasn't praying for real in the hope of finding a shithouse very soon. I tell God I'll change my ways and go to church every Sunday without fail, but the man upstairs isn't listening. I'm flushing hot and cold, trembling and weak, you name it, and I guarantee it is all happening inside me. I'm beginning to think that maybe my arse needs a priest to perform an exorcism. Everyone around me stands and stares, but no cunt bothers helping me. I'm clearly in a bad way and in desperate need of some help, which never comes. All the people I approach to ask directions for a toilet don't speak English, or don't want to. My attempt at some sort of international sign language for 'Where the fuck is the toilet?' to passers-by must just look like some drugged up, crazy freakazoid body-popping. I swear to Jehovah, if nobody would've been around I would have dropped my shorts there and then and blasted out a crater, but the place is packed and I'm running out of precious time. The beach is lined with palm trees that have huge, Arabic-style cushions beneath them, with rugs laid out on the sand where people laze about smoking hash and weed. With no other option left, I shuffle my way to the ocean the best I can. I'm bumping into trees, tables, people, proper all over the place, while scanning every overturned table for a cork. I'm so weak my rubber legs are giving way. I'm thinking I'm gonna have to crawl the last few yards to the sea. My target is in sight, I'm almost there. Flashes of the *Enola Gay* dropping its payload on Hiroshima fill my head, remixed with Chief Brody running along the beach shouting for every cunt to get out of the water. The pain in my gut is fuckin' unbearable. I have to reach back and cup my doughnut. People are pointing at me but still no fucker offers to help.

As I enter the sea, dark storm clouds mysteriously appear and completely block out the sun. Thunder, lightning, rain, biblical winds, it's all happening just as the water reaches my starfish. Starting at my forehead, I make the sign of the cross and unleash absolute Armageddon. I'm shitting myself inside out with an unnatural force. Over my shoulder the Grim Reaper surfs by in slow motion, pausing for a second to check his list of names. I kid you not when I say I end up fifteen yards away from where I started. My legs haven't moved at all; it's anal jet propulsion. Two hours later, I'm still in no rush to get out. As far as I'm concerned I'm in a happy place, plus the sun's back out now and it's a beautiful day. Not sure if my arse has changed the ecosystem in any way, but I'm safe, my quest is finally over.

Feeling ten kilos lighter, I finally leave the sea and make my way back to the oven hut from hell. I passed a complex of snazzy-looking, whitewashed huts along the way that had these huge palm leaves as roofing, plus a decent-sized hole cut in the side as a window, ideal for a much-needed breeze through. I asked the man how much and twenty-five pence was right up my street. I genuinely felt like I was moving up to the Ritz.

I get all my gear together and move double lively over to the new place, which turns out to be pretty sweet indeed. There's a double bed, even a cupboard inside, but most importantly fresh air blowing through. Things are definitely looking up, apart from my frayed arse that is in complete tatters. I lie face down on the bed with my backside in the air hoping for a mercy breeze to grace my rusty bullet hole. You know that sound you make when you blow across the top of a bottle? That's the sound I fall asleep to.

Chapter 11

"Hello Dubs, are you in there? Rise and shine fella, it's a glorious day for doing nothing."

"Dubs...? Pete...? Anybody?"

Hmm, interesting. Now where the fuck did they go? I've completely lost track of time. That episode with my possessed backside must have really drained me. That was one hell of a sleep I had, definitely feeling a lot better that's for sure. I've even got a little bounce in my step. Considering it's now 7.55 in the morning you'd expect the beach to be slowly filling up with people, but it's surprisingly sparse in every direction. Where the fuck are Dubs and Pete?

"Span, over here."

As I'm pretty much the only cunt about, I was easy to spot. Pete is with the girls over by a dive centre that looks nothing like a dive centre.

"Bruv, we're going diving. Where've you been, man? Me and Dubs were out all night looking for you."

"Are you trying to tell me you never heard any explosions? Or saw the mushroom cloud?"

"What are you going on about, Span man?"

"Mate, just read the front page of the *Egyptian Gazette*, it's bound to be in there, plus I don't really wanna talk about it."

"Fair enough, but you're here now so all's cool, innit."

"Where's Dubs?"

"He's over there with a load of kids learning to swim."

"Shit, yeah I forgot he can't swim. So what were you saying about the diving?"

"Check this out brother Span. You see that girl over there?"

"Which one?"

"The blonde one with the fit arse and green bikini."

"They've all got fit arses, and it's a turquoise bikini."

"OK, the one in the bluish-green bikini."

"Oh yeah, I see her."

"Bruv, you ain't gonna believe what went down last night."

"I fuckin' knew it! There's me bang in trouble with an arse like a furious Gatling gun while you and Dubs are in Caligula mode, bloody charming mate."

"Nothing like that Span, trust me. Anyway listen, she's got trips, man, microdots."

"OK and?"

"And last night while we were round their place smoking, she mentions to the other girls about scuba diving naked while tripping."

"Is that right?"

"Yes, bruv."

"And I take it Dubs is over there learning to swim so he can take part in the girl with the turquoise bikini's awesome idea?"

"Also yes, bruv."

Dubs is over in a crystal clear rock pool splashing about like a champion. A little dark-skinned boy of around eight with piercing green eyes is his coach, while nine other kids, perched on the surrounding rocks, cheer and clap for him.

"You move arm and leg," says the boy.

"I'm moving my arms and legs, dread, look."

"More fast, more fast," shouts the boy.

"Rasta, it don't make any difference, I keep sinking."

A tiny girl with golden, Shirley Temple hair hands Dubs her armbands which he puts on his wrists.

Then when he sees me approaching. "Blud, check me out, I'm swimming."

You know when a bird crashes into the water then tries to flap its waterlogged, heavy as fuck wings? That's Dubs right now, bless him.

"You've got your foot on the floor Dubs."

"What foot? There ain't no foot here, trust me."

"Mate, I can see it from here. Both feet need to be off the ground before you can say you're swimming."

"Nah man, I'm full-on swimming, blud, look again."

"Yeah, I'm looking Dubs, but all I can see are your arms doing their bit plus one leg kicking up behind ya, but that's definitely a foot bouncing along the ground I can see."

"What about now?"

"Nope, I can still see it."

"So this ain't swimming then?"

"Not really."

The little boy motions with his hands he's off for dinner and jets.

"Now what the fuck am I gonna do?"

"What do you mean?"

"He was teaching me how to swim. Have you spoken to Pete?"

"Yeah, just now."

"So you know why I need to be swimming, dread?"

"Yeah, but the dive guide will know you ain't ready for scuba, Dubs, that's just dangerous. Forget it, mate. Why not try a bit of snorkelling? You'll be in the shallows, there's a lot to see in the shallows, you know? You might even see a shark."

"A what?"

"A shark, there's untold here. I'm surprised you ain't seen one already."

"Blud, get me the hell out of here. Swimming is shit anyway."

Pete tells us the dive guide has said he's cool with the girls going nude, and why wouldn't he? Dubs has gone off to kick a few sandcastles, but I'm sure he'll calm down in no time. Other than that it's all super chilled here. Dahab is just one long beach in the middle of nowhere, fringed with palm trees and huts in all shapes and sizes. Nothing here matches, that's not important. What's important is that you relax and unwind, get into the pace of things leisurely and stop fuckin' rushing. Looking up and down the beach, I can see people slowly making their way to the water. Reminds me of turtles returning to the sea after laying eggs. So these must be what modern hippies are all about. There's no police here, or any kind of law, from what I can make out. Just people off the grid doing whatever the fuck they want without the hassle from any cunt in a suit. Most of them have slept under the trees all night on rugs, and fair play to them, I'd be up for that as well.

Dahab is super calm, without any violence or crime; still dangerous though because you could get far too comfortable and lose your way, and very easily. You can be stoned everyday for free if you fancy it. I mean, weed grows here naturally and everywhere. I passed a shitload growing wild on the way to the shower near my old hut. I'm sure you know what it's like when you've gotta get something done stoned, nine times out of ten you'll tell yourself you'll do it tomorrow then repeat when tomorrow comes. What I'm trying to say is you'd never leave the place if you got caught in that cycle.

The glow from thousands of candles dug into the sand the entire length of the beach is truly mesmerising. Now that's a beautiful thing. I should imagine at night it would be even more so. I like hippies, they just mind their own fuckin' business and wanna live the way they want, not how you want them to. I respect that because I'm the same. OK, if you're thinking I'm nothing like that, hear me out. If I can earn enough money my own way, regardless how I do it, then I'll be able to live how the fuck I want. So you see it's similar in a way, sort of, if you squint a little bit.

We make our way along the roasting beach to one of the dive boats. The girls already on board are laughing and joking about with the dive guide, who can't believe his luck. Pete passes me and Dubs a microdot that the American sort gave him that goes straight down the hatch, she's called Stacey by the way. Dubs is over the moon, because the Aussie has given him an inflatable flamingo to float about on while the rest of us are diving. We kit up and join the group of girls, wondering like a pair of perverts, when they're gonna peel off their clobber.

It takes us around forty-odd minutes to get to the dive site, as the acid starts kicking in, moments later the visuals arrive. As the dive guide goes through the usual safety procedures telling us what we can expect to see, I come to the conclusion that I'm extremely fucking messed up; have no clue what the guy is talking about or even what language. I'm more interested in looking at the kaleidoscopic rainbow of colours flowing from my mouth every time I breathe out. Floating all around me are living particles of multicoloured glitter that form into various different animals, vanish and reappear as a massive, neon whale in the sky plunging straight down into the depths of the ocean. Pete's lying belly down on the deck, one hand over his mouth transfixed at the tiny, silver dolphins on the Italian girl's ankle bracelet.

My vision is now in circus mirror mode, melting and warping the faces of all the people around me into an indescribable mess, like being inside a living Salvador Dalí painting crossed with a Picasso. The French girl curiously comes and sits next to me. She's a pretty little thing, I think. Tells me her name is Monique, but I can call her Moni, also I think; I'm really not too sure at this precise moment in time.

The ocean is a gigantic, blue silk sheet, rippling and breathing, dancing and tossing, looked alive, beautiful, menacing. My eyes make their way back to Monique but can see none of her beauty now, just a face in a constant state of change, morphing into a rather scary Medusa-type creature that I'd probably still bend over. She is talking to me but I'm in *The Twilight Zone*, trying my best to make out the words coming from her mouth. I can see them floating off into the air out of reach. I try my best to read them before they get too far away but it's no use. She puts her hand on my shoulder and gently shakes me back to earth. Actually, that's a lie, there is no earth, I'm in another dimension. I even try to style it out at one point that I'm not as mangled as I truly am. I'm standing here on the deck with more lean than a smooth criminal thinking I look completely normal.

So Monique says to me, "Hey, are you going to be OK? We are ready to go in the water now. Are you coming with us?"

I once again try my very best to process the words as they

float off into the sky, but end up tripping out on a tattoo of a butterfly that is fluttering all over the back of another girl. Every time I reach out to touch it, it flaps its wings. The girl turns to me laughing, knowing that I've dropped the acid already. She says something about them taking theirs twenty minutes ago, and they're waiting to come up before they go in the water. Then Stacey calmly takes off her bikini bottoms and swings them around above her head like a lasso, followed by a "Let's go, girls". All at once the others stand and take off their bikinis, strap on the scuba gear, and look fuckin' awesome.

Apparently, this little group get together every year to do similar stuff as this. Last year, for instance, was tripping naked while bungee jumping in New Zealand. Next year they're talking about naked skiing in Colorado. Have I mentioned I can ski?

A very happy-looking dive guide poses with the girls for some photos, then like synchronised swimmers they roll off the side of the boat into the water.

I'm kitted up, sat on the side ready to roll in. The yellow fins on my feet look huge; they appear to be breathing. I put the regulator into my mouth and hold on to my mask. Sitting with my back to the sea, I roll in and immediately start hallucinating on the tiny bubbles that rise to the surface, looking like little glass balls with screaming people trapped inside. As I release some air from my buoyancy device and begin my descent, I'm engulfed inside a huge shoal of transparent glass fish that flash with a mother-of-pearl shimmy; thousands of them everywhere darting in and out, up down, wrapping all around me. I feel like I have a connection with every single one of them; their little eyes observing me, always keeping an inch away from my outstretched hand. I can't see any blue of the ocean, just fish all around me. It's as though we are one complete organism moving in harmony. The feeling is pretty overwhelming, and I can't get enough of it. I'd be happy just to stay suspended where I am with those fish for the entire dive.

A hand slices through the shoal and grabs mine to pull me into the blue, where I'm greeted by Monique. Her eyes are smiling through her mask as she leads me down through a sun-drenched coral garden teaming with busy creatures of all sorts going about their daily business. To the left of me is Pete, desperately trying to get my attention so I can look at every single thing he points at, followed by an OK gesture as if he's Jacques Cousteau. A tiny, pulsating cuttlefish, no bigger than my thumb, hovers in front of my mask, either staring in at me or checking out its own reflection. An endearingly friendly little critter with curious eyes and fancy clothes that can change colour just like that, switching from transparent to a multicoloured, psychedelic light show in the blink of an eye. I know it's cruel to say, but if I had the chance that little bad boy would be my pet. I'd take him home, sort him out a tasty aquarium furnished with beautiful coral and he'd simply be fucking amazing.

Monique squeezes my hand to get my attention to a blacktip reef shark gracefully cruising by without a care in the world, leaving a slipstream of colourful holograms in its wake. I leave her by the coral garden and swim out into open water to a buoy with an enormous, rusty chain one foot across anchored to the ocean floor. Attached to the chain are hundreds of mussels clumped together, leading all the way to the surface, with manic red and white shrimp picking frantically at the algae covering the shells.

I'm holding onto the chain twenty metres down when from the corner of my eye in the distance I can make out a large, dark shape slowly coming towards me. My heart is thumping like crazy. Try as I might, I can't get the theme tune from *Jaws* out of my head. I have a go at squinting to see if that helps identify what is approaching, but all I can make out is a dark, shadowy figure looming towards me. I have a diving knife strapped to my calf that is soon in my hand. I can't make out if I'm just tripping or something is actually there. I focus, but all I can hear is my fuckin' heart beating. I look towards the coral garden for Moni but can only see blue. As I turn my head back round, the thing is upon me.

Fuck, does it make me jump, but I'm relieved to see it is just an old tuna fish plodding by. Big fella though, about six feet in length with cloudy, blind eyes just floating along waiting to die. Poor thing looks like it's a hundred years old, beaten up and scarred all over. I suppose it'll just keep on swimming in a straight line until it eventually grows weak from hunger and keels over, unless death comes sooner from a predator of some sort.

I swim back down to the coral garden to find Pete sitting on the seabed waving his hand in front of his face. I point up towards the surface at the five nude silhouettes looking very much like the beginning of a James Bond movie, then back at my air gauge; it's time for us to go. We stay for a while on the surface, bobbing up and down, watching the peaches glisten in the sunlight as each girl takes her turn climbing the boat's ladder.

"Hey, come on you guys," shouts Stacey to us, who's already on the boat taking off her gear.

Me and Pete are still busy looking at wet, naked girls climbing a ladder thank you very much.

"Yeah, I'm gonna need a bit more time until I can get out of the water," I shout back.

"Me too," says Pete.

"Me too," says the dive guide.

Back on the boat, spaghetti bolognese and refreshments are waiting for those that want it, followed by sunbathing and hashish smoking, which the girls naturally do naked, while me, Dubs and Pete sit opposite wearing our sunglasses, but definitely not looking at them.

"This is the life. What do you reckon Span?"

"About what?"

"About this being the life."

"Yeah, Pete, it's the life, mate."

"I mean, what more could you ask for? We're sitting opposite five completely naked honeys, blazin' some sweet ganja in the Egyptian sunshine. Look at the colour of the sea, man, fuckin' incredible. This is what it's all about, not what we got back home; Maggie Thatcher doing anything and everything possible to fuck up your enjoyment."

"Maggie Thatcher? Where the hell did that come from Pete?"

"I'm just saying, she's bollocks, man."

"I wonder if Reagan is slipping it to her."

"All day long, blud, he's definitely balls deep."

"I once had a nightmare about Thatcher. I was parked up on the Walworth Road getting me dick sucked. As I looked down at the back of this head bobbing up and down, it slowly turns to reveal her face. Woke me up with a shiver, mate."

"Bruv, look at the acid house situation. Never any violence, no pissed up wankers being pissed up wankers. Everything and everyone is cool, you know? People just wanna dance, so Maggie has to start throwing her weight around to stop all the happiness while pissheads cause grief in every pub on every front. It ain't fair, man, I swear we should do a rave just to fuck her off."

"Pete, it sounds like you're having a bit of a moment, mate. Are you alright?"

"Safe, Span, I ain't really buzzin' that much. That acid was kinda weak, bruv, to tell you the truth. How about you two? Are you still tripping?"

"A little bit, which is strange. I'm used to well over ten hours on a trip, and considering how strong it was a couple of hours ago I'm a bit disappointed. How about you Dubs?"

"I'm hungry, dread."

"Maybe it's got something to do with us diving that affects the acid, man."

"Fuck knows."

"So anyway, what do you reckon? Let's do a rave at my place. I'm serious, it's a bangin' idea and you know it Span."

"A rave?"

"Exactly, a rave, innit, and why not? My land is private, and you know we'll be selling our shit... I mean your shit. We'll make a fortune, bruv."

"I'm listening."

"Dubs can you get hold of any sound systems?"

"Of course Pete, but if you make me get it all together then let me down, I'll kill ya."

"Awesome. So there it is Span, on your lap, bruv. What are you saying?"

"I'm saying game on. If you're up for that let's do it."

And to think that fantastic idea came from Pete's deep-rooted hate for Margaret Thatcher. A rave, the perfect companion for my idea, burying filthy money made from selling Ecstasy tablets. Talk about perfection, talk about the right place at the right time.

"I can't wait, bruv, we're gonna smash it. Easy money,

man."

"Still needs planning, Pete. Getting the rave together is the easy bit, we can do that on the fields around the house like a massive garden party. The important thing is finding somewhere dense and well hidden away from the rave to hide the cash. It needs to be reasonably close though, like walking distance close."

"Why does it need to be so close to the rave?"

"So we can sneak off every now and then during the night to stash the money we make."

"Wicked, bruv. And we can signal each other with bird sounds when we're ready to sneak off, nobody will suss."

"What bird sounds? What the hell are you going on about?"

"Span man, check this out."

I ain't even gonna bother having a crack at trying to explain what fucking sound just came out of Pete.

"What the fuck do you call that?"

"That's a kestrel, innit."

"I dunno Pete, is it?"

"Yeah, man, but listen to this one. This is a crow, and then I'll do a kingfisher."

"Blinding, I can't wait."

OK, this is the only way I can explain it for your peace of mind, but don't have a go at me afterwards saying I've short-changed ya. Anyway, imagine somebody who in a million years will never evolve to have the delicate vocal ability to grace the universe with a song of any sort, and neither can he whistle. The kingfisher, by the way, sounded more like the noise a humpback whale would make as it watches its calf get slaughtered by a pod of orcas. The crow was a bit like my granddad clearing his throat after chain-smoking his sixth

Lambert & Butler.

"Mate, can we get back on track? For one, that racket sounds fuck all like any birds that have ever existed, and two, how the fuck would you hear it anyway over the music? And three, it'll be slightly easier to casually just stroll up and talk to me. Simple when you think about it. We'll just go the old-fashioned way and wander off when we're ready, but distance is important. The last thing we wanna be doing is jumping in your Land Rover every hour to stash our earnings. Plus, I know what you're like Pete, as soon as you drop an E and start buzzing you'll get us lost. We'd probably end up as two space cadets competing in the Camel Trophy, which we'd lose because you'd get us lost again. So it's definitely gotta be walking distance, mate."

Chapter 12

"Why don't you guys come and hang with us tonight? We're cooking it up later," says Stacey.

"Cooking what up?" asks a hungry Dubs.

"Pasta… with sausages."

"I'm there, blud."

That don't surprise me, Dubs loves his sausages, but I need to ask something important.

"Sausages? What sort of sausages Stace? And where would you get them?"

It's a fair couple of questions as there's no shops out here, plus I'm entitled to be slightly curious for the sake of my ring-piece which is still very tender.

"Just sausages, you know? Francesca brought them from Italy."

"Will they be alright though Stace? I mean it's fuckin' hot here. Ain't they supposed to be in a fridge so they don't go off?"

I'm only asking these questions because I don't fancy getting the shits again. Remember what happened to me? Because I certainly do. And I'll tell you something else, now it's been brought up, for the next two days after that incident my arsehole actually cried real tears. I'm fuckin' serious. I had odourless water seeping from my backside for two whole days and nights; extremely uncomfortable too when sand is added to the mix.

"No, they're dry sausages. No refrigeration needed, Spaniard. I'm sure you'll be fine."

She's talking about a chorizo sort of thing, so why not just say chorizo for fuck's sake?

"Nice. In that case put me down for some of that, and sorry for all the questions. I had quite an unpleasant episode when we first got here regarding my guts. Things got messy, and I believe I'll never be the same again."

"It's cool, Spaniard, no need for an explanation. So you guys be round for seven, yes?"

We agree and make our way back to ours for a freshen up. A quick glance at my watch tells me it's now three in the afternoon, and at this precise time Pete decides he's been silent for too long.

"A weekender, Span, that's it...! A fucking weekender, bruv!"

"What's he going on about now Dubs?"

"God knows, blud."

"I've been thinking, innit."

"I thought I could smell burning."

"Bruv, check this out."

"I'm checking."

"We make the rave a weekender, thus earning us double bubble for our trouble."

This could turn out to be something quite interesting, a weekender where all the drugs are supplied by me, and bloody good drugs too I must add.

"It'll be proper Radio Rental, bruv. Imagine... our weekender."

"Don't worry about that, Pete, I imagined it the second

you said it. That could be quite a fuckin' thing if we get it right."

Literally thirty seconds later.

"Get what right, bruv?"

"What do you mean get what right? Have you forgotten already what we were just talking about?"

"I dunno what you're going on about, man, this spliff has blasted me out. Kinda feels like it brought my trip back… What was you saying anyway, Span?"

"I wasn't saying fuck all, Pete. I was casually strolling along this beach with you and Dubs when all of a sudden you started talking about our rave."

"Oh, yeah man, the rave. I'm really looking forward to it, it's gonna be massive. What do you reckon Dubs?"

"Dread, can't you see I'm looking at titties on the beach? Fix up, man, and stop bouncing into me. Walk straight ya lightweight."

"Bruv, let's rest here for a bit, I can't feel my legs. We've been walking for hours."

Eight minutes to be precise, but I'm not gonna lie, my legs feel like elastic bands. We take a plot on the beach and motion to the fella selling drinks from a cooler to liven up in our direction. An ice-cold bottle of Fanta each and we're smiling.

"This tastes fuckin' incredible, dread."

"That is probably the best Fanta I've ever had, Dubs, absolutely amazing. I can really taste the oranges in it, and yet there's no oranges in it. Unbelievable."

"Yeah there is Span, there's five per cent real juice, trust me," says Pete the expert.

"Five per cent? Is that all? Tastes like an easy ninety per cent to me. What do you reckon Dubs?"

"Easy ninety per cent, Rasta."

"Is this normal Fanta Pete? Or am I that caned?"

"You're that caned."

"But it tastes so different."

That conversation went on for an hour, then we were back to the rave.

"Pete are you sure it's gonna be sweet with all those people stomping about on your land?"

"Super sweet, bruv, all day long. The more people the better, innit."

"That's what I like to hear, just making sure you wasn't getting cold feet, because that weekender idea of yours is fuckin' genius."

"I'm telling ya, Span, we're gonna get a reputation for running the sickest raves. We should do a membership thing too."

Another idea from Pete? This boy's on a roll.

"What do you mean?"

"You know? Like a membership thing."

"How is that an answer, Pete?"

"Well, after we've had a few raves and people know how amazing they are, we can charge for memberships, innit."

"And what benefits will the members get over any other cunt?"

"I haven't thought of that yet, but it's still a good idea."

"You know what, you might be on to something there, as it happens."

"I told ya, Span man."

"A membership could be a guaranteed entry to the rave, and we can hand pick who becomes a member."

It's moments like this I wish I had a long, thin moustache so I could roll one end with a finger and thumb whilst raising an eyebrow.

"Bruv, we could just let sorts be members, fit girls, you know? No moose allowed."

"That's a bit cuntish though, Pete. Money from a moose is as good as anybody's."

"But then I'll end up with a moose, innit?"

"How'd you work that out?"

"Come on, Span, you know I'll end up with one."

"Is that where your membership idea came from? You think by only letting pretty girls become members you're gonna end up pulling one?"

"Well it's a ratio thing, bruv."

"Who the fuck is Horatio, dread? Don't be bringing any weird, funky bods to the rave, Pete, man."

"That's not what I said Dubs. What I'm trying to say, Span, is if there's more pretty girls at the rave, then chances are I'll get lucky with one and not end up with a stegosaurus."

To be honest with ya, it wouldn't surprise me if the real reason Pete suggested having a rave on his land was just to meet a girl, that's how desperate the poor fucker is. I genuinely feel sorry for him. His luck is shocking when it comes to the ladies, and he deserves a decent girlfriend because he's got a heart of gold.

"Pete, forget about girls for a second. Let's concentrate on getting the rave running nice and smooth first, then you can worry about women."

"That's easy for you and Dubs to say."

"Why are you even bringing me into this, dread? I ain't said fuck all, have I? This is between you and Span, so shut up and have a look at the size of her tits over there in the yellow."

"Relax Pete. You'll be alright, mate. You've produced a cracking idea that ticks all the boxes. I mean Dubs can get the music side sorted."

"You know that, blud."

"And because of you the venue is sorted, not to mention the quality pills that are gonna be there that I can sort. It's gonna be awesome, Peter, and you never know, if you don't stand about looking as though your surname is Sutcliffe you might even meet the girl of your dreams after all."

We stay rooted to that spot on the beach chatting for what feels like an hour, but is actually six. Pasta and sausages... Sorry... Pasta and chorizo with the girls is obviously off as it's now close to ten, so we brush ourselves down and head off in search of some dinner.

Chapter 13

"Didn't I say those candles on the beach would look special at night?"

"Wow, bruv, that is sick as fuck, but it's sunset not night."

"Yeah man, wicked, Rasta."

"I told ya. How can you top that for a sight?"

We take a seat, bang centre of the candles, and look up to catch a shooting star trail off across a magnificent purple and orange, cloudless sky, boasting thousands of twinkling jewels.

"Now that's what I call a fuckin' sky."

"Hey, look who's here, dread?"

We look down to see Dub's little pal Shirley Temple, proudly pointing at her new sandals, rapidly whisked away by a smiling, apologetic mother.

"Cute kid."

"Yeah, blud, she gave me her armbands when I was learning to swim. I didn't even have to ask her and she knew, she's super smart."

"Look out, Dubs, here she comes again."

The toddler brings Dubs a seashell that melts his heart.

"You see how kids love me? Blud, I'd make a solid dad, you know that... Excuse me, madam, what's her name...? Lilu? Beautiful, and how old is she...? Nearly five... She has a special soul. Where are you from, if you don't mind me asking...? Sweden... Nice."

"Dubs you've probably already got untold kids running about somewhere that you don't know about, mate."

"That's true, Span, but maybe I'm ready to have kids that I know about, you know?"

"You better find yourself a nice, stable girlfriend then, and believe me they are few and far between. Spaniard's advice of the day, gentlemen, is to imagine a girl like an apple on a tree. Go for the one right at the top, the juiciest, ripest one that's worth your time and effort. The apples at the bottom of the tree are within easy reach of any cunt, so avoid them, they're all sloshers."

"And what if you can't even reach the bottom apples, bruv? Then what?"

"Anybody can reach the bottom apples Pete, but why would you want to?"

"Sometimes you ain't got a choice, man. I mean, take me for instance, I'm the perfect example, innit. I ain't had a bird in fuckin' ages man."

"That's because you don't leave the house. No bird's gonna come knocking on your door for a date, unless you pay them of course."

"It's true, Pete, you need to get the fuck out of that house more often. You know I've never seen you walk Wilson even once, dread."

"I don't need to walk him. I open the door, he goes and takes a shit and comes back when he's ready."

"You're missing the point, brother, Pete. This is about you leaving the house to go picking apples remember, not Wilson. Dubs is just underlining the fact you're a lazy cunt."

"Oh yeah, right. I see what you mean."

"When we get back home, try turning over a new leaf.

Use the thing we was talking about as a platform, remember? The rave?"

"Yeah, the rave. That's a good idea. There's bound to be plenty of fanny at the rave. Maybe you can set me up with one of Amber's friends if all fails."

"Here's a very important little tip for ya, mate. Don't go looking so eager, they can spot that a mile away, and you'll just come across as a clingy, creepy fucker."

"Yeah, and change the way you speak, dread, it don't suit ya."

"What don't suit me?"

"Your accent, what the fuck is that meant to be?"

"It's me, innit."

"Innit? And what the fuck is innit?"

"I think he means isn't it. Am I right Pete?"

"Anyway, you can talk Dubs. I hear you fuck-up a whole heap of times when you're chatting, bruv."

"Are you listening to him Span? Pete, you're a fuckin' grey man. You're a white boy trying to sound black, and it's not working out too well for ya."

"As long as people can understand me that's all that matters, innit."

"Pete, I personally can't understand what the hell you're going on about half the time, but I'm too polite to say, mate. Just thought now might be a good time to share that with ya."

"Cheers Span. Safe, bruv. Anyway Dubs you sound like a white bod."

"Shut up you mug."

"You see? How fuckin' white was that? And another thing, if somebody was chatting to you on the phone and they never knew you, they'd think you was white, trust me. You and Spaniard sound the same, and he's white. The only difference is you drop in a bit of Jamaican every now and then, but you're from Africa. How does that work?"

"I'm from Stockwell, not Africa, you plum."

"And actually, I'm more of a golden colour if you don't mind Peter. Also, I'm sure I've called you a bumbaclart more than once, mate."

"Yeah, but that's from the sun, innit, without it you're white, bruv."

"Not as white as you though. You actually look ill Pete. Have a look how white this cunt is Dubs. Plus, as a bonus, if you haven't noticed, being half Spanish I'm always gonna be slightly darker than you, my friend, it's got fuck all to do with the sun. Oh, and while we're chatting, how is it we've been here almost two weeks and you're still the whitest man in Egypt?"

"Protection man, fuck that shit, I burn easy. I bust out the high factor sun cream to keep me safe, that's why I always wear a T-shirt. My face is tanned though, innit?"

"Nope, in fact can you see what I'm doing Pete?"

"You're putting on your shades."

"And they'll be staying on while we're face to face. No offence, mate."

The night moves at a relaxed pace with much laughter and reminiscing. Lilu's mad, curly hair takes on a life of its own as it meets with the cool night's breeze while she sleeps draped over her mother's shoulder. Before long it's five in the morning and we've been chatting all night, and are pretty much the only people still about.

"Is that the girls over there…? Oi, girls, over here!" is my suave way.

"What happened to you guys? You missed an awesome meal," says Stacey directly to me, like it was all my fault they got blanked; unbelievable.

"Sorry about that, we kinda nutted out on the beach."

"Nutted out?"

"Fell asleep."

"Oh well, you probably needed it… So what have you been up to since?"

"Just sitting here talking, smoking, chillin'. How about you lot?"

"We're going swimming, skinny-dipping. Come join us. And why are you wearing sunglasses?"

"Pete's forehead. But you do know it's five in the morning, don't ya?"

"Yeah, the perfect time for going naked, nobody about. Come on, or are you wimps?"

"Blud, any second now and I'm gonna drop my man flesh on her chin."

"Behave Dubs, for fuck's sake."

"What? She called me a wimp."

Dub's unexpected comment has me and Pete holding our sides, and knowing Dubs he would indeed slap his cory on her chin if she wound him up too much.

"What's so funny, guys? What did he say, I couldn't hear?"

"It's nothing, Stace. He just said we're gonna swerve the swimming because we've not long eaten. We don't wanna get cramp, you know how it is."

"OK, but if you guys change your mind, you know where we are… See ya, wimps."

And with that parting shot that ricocheted around our table for a touch longer than we expected, the girls became naked and ran off laughing into the surf, deliberately jumping up and down so we could see their juggling chesticles.

"Fuck them prick-teasers, man. I swear, blud, if that Stacey bird's not careful, she's gonna get it."

"Yeah Dubs, man, bum her in the face!"

"Shut up Pete. That doesn't even make sense. I'm saying if I go all black Casanova on her, she'll fuckin' know about it. Tell him about the black Casanova, Span."

"Yeah, tell me about the black Casanova, Span?"

"Mate, if he goes black Casanova on her, then fuck knows, I don't even wanna think about the poor girl's heart."

"You hear that, Rasta?"

"Yeah, but I still don't know what it is, do I?"

"The black Casanova only comes out when prick-teasers are about, do you follow?"

"No."

"OK, look. Remember that time when Dubs was giving you tips on how to pull a bird?"

"No."

"Round your house that time?"

"When?"

"The time me and Dubs were chatting over the blower about the phone you was gonna sell him."

"Oh yeah, gotcha."

"Well, you're probably on the beginner level, Pete. No disrespect, mate. Now black Casanova, well that's on a completely different planet altogether."

"You know that, dread."

"You see Pete, what I'm trying to say here is that Dubs's black Casanova technique has been passed down through the generations. What are we talking here Dubs, four hundred years?"

"Six, blud."

"So you would need to pass beginner level stage three,

intermediate level, semi pro, all the way up to master of masters level super pro, and then it gets spiritual. We're talking another dimension here, Pete."

"Tell him again, dread."

"Another dimension, Pete. Don't go there, my friend, never go there."

"Have you been? I mean, do you know this black Casanova, Span? He must have shown you how to do it?"

"I've seen it, Pete, a few times... It's not pretty."

"I know Lucifer has a place for me at his side, blud. I've sinned so many times, Lord...! It's the black Casanova that makes me do these things."

"Scattered broken hearts everywhere, Pete. They don't stand a chance. It's wall-to-wall casualties."

"But I still don't know what it is, bruv."

"Let it go, Pete, just let it go... Plus, you're too white anyway."

"Fuck off, Span man."

"Come on, mate, you are one *Nosferatu*-looking fucker. Am I right Dubs?"

"All day long, blud. Pete's a haunting-looking bumbaclart."

And so the two weeks flew by. We pretty much just got stoned and relaxed the rest of the time. I'm kinda looking forward to getting back in the saddle, to tell the truth. I've relaxed, or maybe over-relaxed, if there's such a thing. No, I'm ready, time to get this rave moving, time to start earning.

On our last day, the fuckin' sun is insane. I'm talking cook an egg on the ground insane. So we're on our way back to the huts when we bump into little Lilu and her mum. Lilu is crying and the mother is pretty pissed off. The story is, Lilu runs across the scorching sand to a Somalian bloke selling ice creams. He drops a scoop onto a cone that he gives to Lilu that falls straight out of her tiny hand onto the sand. The fella has no intention of replacing the ice cream and just blanks her, while she tugs at his trouser leg. Even though we're running a bit late, Dubs stops to talk to the mother.

"So you're telling me that geezer over there sold little Lilu an ice cream that fell on the sand, and he won't replace it?"

Dubs drops down to Lilu's height.

"Stop crying, sweetheart. Uncle Dubs is gonna talk to the nasty man."

"Dubs mate."

"It's cool Span. You go on. I'll catch you up."

"Give me your hand Lilu, I think the man wants to give you some ice cream. Hey Mum, do you mind if I borrow Lilu for a second? Thanks. Come on, darling."

Lilu grips on to Dubs's index finger and smiles. Man he's gonna kill this guy, little Lilu is like one of the firm in his eyes. That thing with the armbands? That goes a long way with Dubs.

"Yeah, hello mate. Where are you from?"

"I'm from Somalia."

"Is that right? Well listen, first of all do you understand me OK?"

"Yes."

"You see that little girl there? I'm talking about this tiny, little thing here holding my finger with the cutest curly hair you've ever seen. Hold on a second, let me wipe her nose, she's been crying. You hear that, Rasta? She's been crying, you know? And do you know why she's been crying Mr Somalian? Because of an ice cream."

We leave Dubs to his diplomatic ways and head back to pack. Half hour later, he's at the door.

"Check this out, fellas, I've got lollies, Cornettos, some wafer things. All free, boys. Tuck in."

"Sweet, bruv! Where'd you get them?" asks Pete.

"That Somalian... Basically said he'd made a big mistake and he's very sorry, then gave me all this for free. Span you should've seen how happy Lilu was with her ice cream, it was as big as her. Chocolate and vanilla double scoops all the way, blud."

"What's that on your shirt, Dubs? Is that blood?"

"What are you going on about Pete?"

"There, on the side."

"What, you mean this here?"

"Yes."

"I swear to God you ain't gonna believe this, dread, but you know how hot it is out there? Well me and that Somalian fella were chatting away, when all of a sudden, out of the blue, he has a turn and collapses."

"Sounds like a case of heatstroke to me, Dubs."

"That's exactly what I thought, Span... So I'm trying to hold him up, but his head is bouncing off the wall. He drops onto the floor where he's now grazed to fuck, the poor cunt."

"Are you listening Pete? That powder soft sand is so deceiving, it's definitely gonna graze ya if you're not too careful. Still, you tried your best to help the bloke Dubs, that's all that matters, mate."

"Bullshit. You bashed him up Dubs. Am I right Span?"

"Who or what do you think Dubs is? He's no liar Peter."

"Yeah, what are you trying to say, Pete?"

"Forget it, there's no point... I'll have a strawberry Cornetto please."

"Coming right up. And for you Span?"

"I will go for one of these Arabian cherry lollies... So he

gave you his cooler too Dubs? What a fuckin' nice chap."

We only just make the coach, too busy eating ice creams and getting stoned. One last look at Dahab brings a smile as we slowly set off for home. I've had a good time, I think we all have. As I look out the window at all the places we've hung out and had great moments, I come to the conclusion we should do this more often. I feel like my batteries are nicely charged, and I'm ready to take on the world. Even Dubs's boat looks better, most of his stitches have gone; still looks like a cross between Frankenstein's monster and Clapham Junction, but I know he's had a good time. Pete, on the other hand, for some strange reason looks whiter now then when he first got here.

"STOP THE COACH!"

We all look round at Dubs. Well, when I say all, I mean me and Pete, nobody else is on board other than the driver.

"STOP THE FUCKIN' COACH!"

The startled driver, fearing for his life, puts on the anchors in a very lively manner.

"What's up Dubs? What have you forgotten?" I ask.

Dubs turns to me with the most ridiculous smile I think I've ever seen on a human. I say human because I once saw an Afghan hound with slightly a better one twenty minutes after eating a quarter of hash, he passed out soon after.

"Look, blud."

At the top of the sandy road by the first lot of huts we stayed in… Oh, by the way, when the other two saw my pukka Ritz hut they jumped ship and copied me; typical.

So anyway, at the top of the road stands a figure, holding onto a little figure, with really mad hair.

Of course we're gonna say goodbye to our little pal, who come to think of it, has never uttered a word all this time, just laughs, smiles and points at things. She's a happy little treasure, and I hope her big, blue, innocent eyes get to see all the beauty the world has in store for her. I hope she grows up into an awesome, unpolluted human being like she's meant to be, a bit like myself really... OK, I'm joking.

The second we jump off the coach, Lilu runs across the sand towards Dubs. He drops down to one knee with his outstretched arms to catch her. She seems to disappear into his huge chest for a second.

"How's little Lilu?" he asks.

Lilu smiles.

"You know we've got to go back home don't you, tiny one?"

Lilu looks up at Dubs's scarred and battered face. She places her tiny hand on stitches across his cheek and frowns.

"Yeah I know, sweetheart, I'm silly. Don't you go worrying about me though, this ugly face can take it."

With that, Lilu gives Dubs a super hug. Even when he stands up she's not letting go. Little Lilu has gripped his neck so tight she actually looks like a necklace. Her top lip has gone too, just a fat bottom lip, so you know she means it.

Dubs gently puts her down and fiddles with numerous chains around his neck.

"Here, little lady, a gift from your Uncle Dubs. You see this man? That's Haile Selassie. He'll look after you on your journey through life."

This chain, if you're wondering, is a gold belcher that comes down to Dubs's belly button, with a two-inch pendant of that fella he mentioned hanging off it. He literally has to wrap it five times around Lilu's neck, and it still comes down to her knees.

We wave and keep waving until all that's left are sand dunes and more sand dunes... Twelve hours' worth.

Chapter 14

Stepping through my front door, I spot a note lying on the carpet. 'Bell me' is all it says, plus a phone number. I make the call and find out it's the caretaker from the estate I live on, a punter who likes a bit of puff now and then. He tells me the Old Bill have been round the rent office asking permission to set up a surveillance team in an empty flat opposite mine. He told the police that people are moving into that flat so no can do. Whenever something suspect like this happens it's obviously very wise to lie low, but recently I've been lying lower than low. I've been out of the country, how much lower can I lie? I make a couple of calls and arrange for some trusted people to run my business from the other side of London while my temporary measures are put into place. Basically, I'm shutting down all trading my end until I know what's what. I know the police won't just leave it like that. They'll take their pick from a hundred other locations opposite my flat to be nosey. Any of the high-rise tower blocks from the surrounding estates will do the trick, no problem.

We decide to put the word out about our rave, making it crystal clear where people are meant to park, crap, dance and stick a tent. Obviously, the reason for a weekender is to sell as many drugs in as little time possible. If the weekender goes off the way it should, then those two days alone will earn us a nice bit of coin, and if I never do another it'll still be a life-changing touch.

I get a grim call from Dubs telling me that a couple of young girls have been found dead fairly local, dumped in an underground car park in Stockwell. Turns out they both died from a heroin overdose. All bets are on that they were Eastern European girls from Ratboy's thing. Sure enough, news travels fast underground, they were indeed two young girls from Latvia that Ratboy had lured over. When the girls arrive, he butters them up by staging out a little formal interview regarding their new job and accommodation. The Rat then sets up a mock party where the girls end up getting drunk, are taken off, locked up in a bedroom and jabbed with heroin until hooked. That's when they're pimped out, mainly to dodgy cab drivers that work around the clock so there's constant customers, after the Rat has first fucked and abused them himself of course. If one of the girls happens to die, she's simply dumped somewhere with a needle stuck in her arm for show, normally a squat. By the way, if you're curious, there's a hell of a lot of rancid squats to choose from in Stockwell if you're ever thinking of dumping a body. Go for one over near the bus garage, that's skaghead heaven. The addicts you'd find in there wouldn't even notice a corpse until it started chucking up. As far as they're aware it's another skaghead gouched out on the brown gear. Ratboy knows all the squats, that's partly how he got his name. When we were kids, you could put money on it you'd find him sitting in a dark, rancid squat somewhere in Stockwell. He'd be glue-sniffing or on mushrooms completely off his head, but in all honesty, we call him Ratboy because he looks like a mutated rodent. He's the colour of window putty, a skinny, veiny guy with bulging eyes, a tiny, lipless mouth, a huge fuckin' head, and teeth like a broken gearbox. In other words, a right ugly cunt. All the junkies, whether on crack or heroin, are in his pocket, so it'd be a piece of piss for him to have some crackhead dump a body in a squat looking like she's overdosed, and chances are it'll be an addict that finds the body and reports it.

I heard that, over the past seven months, four other girls have also been found in various squats scattered across Stockwell and the Vauxhall area; very sad business. Poor girls leave their country as normal, decent people hoping to change their stars in the UK, but end up abused beyond belief with their only salvation being death. Even when that happens, their body is abused further by being dumped in a shithole somewhere with a needle sticking out of them; a very decent way to go.

On top of that, there's a lunatic in the area going around murdering old ladies; such a wonderful environment I live in. Don't worry about the Rat though, I haven't forgotten what he done to me, I'll get him back. But that can wait for now.

While the police are busy finding another spot to sit and admire the outside of my flat, I'm gonna have me some fun. It's a little idea that came to me in Dahab. I wanna fuck-up Ratboy's trafficking business. It shouldn't need a lot of planning to work. Finding out where Ratboy keeps the girls should be easy just by sending a couple of bods into the pub he drinks and asking one of the local riff-raff if they know of any brasses in the area. If that don't work, I'm sure one of the dodgy cab firms around that vicinity will know something. Once I know for sure where the girls are kept, I'll have somebody very clued-up, posing as a punter, go in and check out the lie of the place. If all is cool, I'll pay for a little firm to go in and take all the girls out, leave them sitting in a rented minibus outside a police station with a note explaining that the girls have been rescued from hell and need taking care of, that they had been kidnapped, raped, imprisoned, pumped full of heroin by a right horrible cunt and are bang in trouble. That's all, signed Batman.

The police station has to be the best bet for the girls. There's no point in dropping them off at the hospital, as chances are they'll just start clucking for gear and walk straight back to hell. Plus, as far as I know, the girls are from all over Eastern Europe and don't speak much English. Dropping them off at their embassies would be grief, long and risky. At the police station they'd have a better chance because they're victims.

My only obstacle would be finding a firm that could at least speak some sort of Eastern European. Then it clicked, a few years ago I went to Poland to watch a fight and got chatting with a fella called Mirek. He's a blinder of a bloke, ex-army, that runs a security firm for music festivals and events across his homeland. When he came out of the army he couldn't get a job so ended up calling a few of his soldier pals together and started the business. If you're in Poland and want a reliable security team, with military precision, then Mirek is the man to speak to. He's already proven to me that he can handle himself in a situation, because on the night of the fight I saw him smash up two bods that were sitting along from us. They didn't seem to do anything wrong, and he never really explained why he battered them, but it was a beating and a half. Mirek had that marine look about him, well built with a shaved head, always stood upright with his shoulders back and chest out; a very regimental type of fella.

He was showing me these beautiful tattoos on his forearms of Japanese koi, and going on about how fascinated he was with the way of the samurai from ancient times, then out of nowhere he spots these two fellas, mumbles "kurwa" then calmly says "Excuse me for a second," in perfect English by the way, then slaps the souls out of these guys and comes back to finish our conversation like nothing had happened. Honestly, he was like the Polish Chuck Norris.

As we leave the venue, there are four other men waiting outside looking to do Mirek some damage for beating up the two guys inside. Mirek kicks off with the four men on his tod, like the Terminator, so at that point me and Dubs jumped in for a laugh, plus it would've been rude not to. After, we all went back to Mirek's place to try his wife's Polish cooking, which was fuckin' handsome, then get mangled up on vodka. Even though I'm not a drinker, on this occasion it would've been out of order, besides I had no puff with me and fancied getting caned with the others. As the saying goes, when in Rome, get off your fuckin' nut, mate.

I find out from Terry Taxi there are six girls being kept in a house in Streatham. He sent a bloke in for a spot of surveillance and was told the guy couldn't believe what he was seeing when he walked into the place. There wasn't any furniture, just white sheets pinned to the ceiling hanging down to form a row of private little cubicles the size of a single mattress. Inside each cubicle was a white paper, oriental globe illuminated by a red bulb. Each cotton cell contained a doped up, more or less unconscious girl wearing just her underwear. The only other people the bod could see were three men plotted on a sofa just inside the front door. They were doing lines of coke off a coffee table while impersonating Al Pacino from the movie *Scarface*.

According to Terry, his man was told to pick whatever girl was available. One of the men would walk along lifting the corner of each cubicle looking for a free girl, all the time thinking he was hilarious talking like Tony Montana. He'd lift the sheet and shout "Say hello to my little friend". Our contact says from what he could catch a peek at, inside the tiny makeshift cubicles, were of steaming fat, hairy arses humping away to the sound of crying.

I need to be sure the same men, or the same number of men, are there all the time. Two more visits later confirm they are, always three in total. With a bit of luck the job can be done at the same time as our rave, giving me an instant alibi. Mirek could come straight to the party after and unwind, plus I need to get him back for getting me so rotten on vodka that time. I puked my ring up half the night, woke up in the morning on the toilet floor with Sylvester the cat looking at me trying to work out what species I was. Mirek has never done an E before, that's not his cup of tea, so my revenge will be to get him totally off his rocker on one, or six.

I'm starting to get a little bit worried the weekender blows up and Dutch won't be able to cope with the amount of pills I'm hoping we're gonna need. I give him a bell and arrange for thirty thousand to be put aside with a promise he doesn't sell them.

"That's no problemo, Spaniard. If you pay now, I'll put two more lots of the same aside for you, that's ninety thousand, do you think that will be enough?"

"I fuckin' hope so, Dutch. Who knows? With a bit of luck we'll knock them out all weekend long. I've also put the word out to my regular parcel buyers to come along and grab some before they're all gone. Kinda told them that these tabs will be the last of that quality for a while, so guaranteed a few thousand will go straight to them. I'm telling ya, mate, everybody who serves up wants to be known to have pukka gear. I'll have to bell ya later about the money, gonna go count some pennies. How much are we talking here, anyway?"

There's a pause, then, "Five pounds each, because I'm generous, but only if you take the thirty thousand. From then on you'll always pay £5, whatever the order."

That's a very fair price, better than I was expecting. Problem is I don't have a hundred and fifty large lying around on the ready to spunk on a mega parcel of happy tabs. I drive over Battersea way for dinner with Amber; seems like ages since I last saw her.

I'm sitting at her place, totally in a world of my own, constantly racking my brains about the upcoming rave, the money for the pills, Mirek deciding on doing that little job, and for the life of me I can't get settled.

Amber leans against me and whispers, "What's the matter?"

I open up and tell her all about the rave and how it's a great opportunity to make a fortune, but my dealer will only give me the pills at a special price if I take a certain amount, which I can't really afford to pay up front. Knowing Amber has a few quid wrapped around her, I'm obviously using a very cunning technique to get her on board.

"So how much would you be guaranteed to earn on top of the 150k?" she asks, raising an eyebrow.

"Well, if we sell them all at £15 a pop we'll total £450,000, but to be honest, I'd rather sell them at £10 for people taking ten or more and £15 below that. That way you know you've got a guaranteed £300,000 plus for a weekend's work. There's also another sixty thousand tabs sitting there if needed, and you know that if this weekender goes smoothly, and everyone has a wicked time, the next rave will be even bigger, because word of mouth will spread about our thing and people will keep coming."

I explain all that to Amber as if I'm a veteran in the field, reeling her in like a kipper.

"I'm in," she says. "You need the money, I have it and can help you, but I want a partnership here; I'm trusting you, Spaniard, I'll give you the money. Shake on it, partner, what do you say?"

What does she think I'm gonna say? We shake on it.

Chapter 15

The more I think about what Ratboy is doing to those girls, the more I think a permanent solution is called for.

How many have already died?

How long has he been doing it?

How many more will die?

Why did he set me up for a bunch of murderous psychopaths to rob and try to kill me when we were always so cool with each other? Friends since childhood, I've got a lot of happy memories of us as kids fuckin' about on the estate getting into all sorts of mischief.

A classic example was one Guy Fawkes Night when Ratboy thought it'd be a stellar idea to find the biggest, softest, freshly laid, steaming dog turd in the area so he could stick bangers in it and watch as it exploded on a random passer-by. You probably already know where this is going, and yeah, the banger went out then exploded when Ratboy went back to check it *Road Runner and Wile E. Coyote*-style. The Rat even had his mouth open when the banger went off. Shit was all over his teeth, face and hair. He was running around in circles with his tongue out dripping with crap; golden moments that stay with ya forever.

I book a flight to Poland on the sly. Two days later I'm sitting on a plane watching a flight attendant vogue his way through the safety check procedure. Considering I only had an hour's kip on the flight, I'm feeling pretty good. Gdańsk Airport seems to be a refuge for every down and out wino in Poland. Everywhere you look there's pissed up tramps, resembling the undead, shuffling about begging for change. Don't help much neither that the airport is so tiny; dodging the zombies is becoming a challenge and a half. It's a bit like Michael Jackson's 'Thriller' video, with me moonwalking the fuck all over the place desperately looking for the exit.

Where the hell is Mirek? He was meant to meet me here. Said he was very interested to hear what I had to say, even more so because I couldn't tell him over the blower. Mind you, I'm half an hour early, so I'll grab a coffee somewhere to kill a bit of time. Not a lot going on in the airport foodwise, so I step outside to find a nice little pub. I take a seat and order a cup of coffee with a slice of 'szarlotka' which is pretty much apple pie. I could murder a joint now though; hope Mirek has sorted me out some green. I hear there's some nice weed being grown over here, plus most Poles I've met like a spliff, so for a face like Mirek it shouldn't be a problem.

Thirty minutes later, I'm standing back outside the airport waiting when a black G-wagon pulls up. True to form it's Mirek, bang on time.

"Siema, Spaniard. Welcome to Poland."

"Siema, Mirek. It's good to be here, mate."

We drive to a little place called Gizycko, which is a town situated in the lake district of Masuria, about a three hour drive from Warsaw; a pretty, green place full of forests, fresh air and boats. We pull up by a block of flats and make our way up four floors to Mirek's apartment. He tells me to be careful of his dog Hektor, a pit bull who's apparently disturbed in a

'I'll eat your bollocks while fucking this cushion' sort of way.

I've owned a pit bull, smartest dog in the world, in my opinion. If he didn't know a person that came to visit me, he'd sit in front of them watching, picking up vibes. If there was something about that person that bugged him, he'd growl every time they moved. The bod would pick up on it instantly, give an excuse and leave. Almost like they'd been busted for whatever little two-bob scam they were gonna try and drop on my toes. He was my radar, an extension of my senses that I took serious notice of, and I always felt the same way about a person he didn't like. I'd be sitting there chatting to some bloke that's been introduced to me by a friend of a friend and I'd be thinking, *You know what, mate? There's something about you I don't like, neither does me dog, and he's always right.*

I imagine walking into Mirek's place to find Hektor whistling while fucking a cactus. Luck's on my side, the dog checks me out and fucks off back to his beanbag wagging his tail. I go and give Hektor a well-deserved head scratching that Mirek and his missus find hard to believe.

"Ja pierdole, Spaniard. I have never seen Hektor like anybody else other than me and Karolina."

"He knows I'm a dog person, Mirek. What's up with his teeth? How come they're so worn down? He ain't that old is he?"

"No, he is still very young, three years old, but likes to chew bricks. If he sees one on the street, he will pick it up and carry it home."

Karolina comes back from the kitchen with a big fuck off pot of gulasz she's cooked up for us. Even Hektor the dog has some; finishes his in a flash then sits rooted under the table with his dribbling chops on my knee hoping to ponce seconds.

I dunk a fat piece of bread in my gravy and slip it to him under the table with a wink; Hektor and me are now best pals.

"So Spaniard, maybe we should talk on the balcony where you can smoke the ganja I have for you," were the words I'd been waiting to hear.

We pull up a couple of bamboo chairs and roll a spliff. I put the plan to Mirek, choosing my words carefully, making sure we understand each other.

"So, if you don't know any of the girls, why help them?" he rightly asks.

"Because the bloke running the thing is a right horrible cunt that nearly had me killed. So I wanna inconvenience him, for the time being, while I'm thinking about some good old-fashioned venganza to drop on him. He betrayed me big time, Mirek. I thought he was a good, trusted friend. Known him most of my life, but what he done is unforgivable. The longer I leave it the better. But if I personally deal with it head-on it could put my business at risk, as I'm sure to get comebacks from his old man's firm if I show my face. No, what I need to do is plan something where I'm nowhere near connected, and that takes a little bit more time. But time is on my side, brother, so I'll wait, and wait some more. Also, think about it, what he's doing to those girls is fucked up, mate. I'm not being funny, but you've got a young daughter, Mirek. Imagine her thinking she's off to the UK to better herself, but instead ends up meeting a monster of a human being who locks her up, forces her to become a heroin addict, then pimps her out to every scummy two-bob cab driver in London. Oh, and not forgetting that eventually she dies of an overdose and her body dumped in a nasty, little armpit of a squat somewhere in the arse end of South London."

I light the spliff and hold the smoke in my lungs.

"I'm also gonna give you ten grand for doing it, and that's just for picking up some wasted girls and putting them in a minibus to be left outside a police station. Ten grand for a couple of hours work ain't bad when you think about it. All your expenses will be paid too. There'll be a car parked up round the corner from the station waiting for ya, so you can come straight to the rave after and let your hair down, if you had some. I need you for the job because the girls probably don't speak much English, Mirek. You've got a better chance of understanding, also calming them down if need be. Chances are the girls will be more or less unconscious and you'll not hear a peep from any of them, but the main reason I could use you is because I know you won't fuck around, you'll be in and out faster than a fast thing."

"And who is this Two Bob you speak of?"

"Two Bob? No, that ain't a person, mate, it's just a thing we say when someone is a cheap, horrible cunt."

He gets it, because he half smiled.

"Ten thousand pounds is a lot of money for two hours' work, Spaniard. I know you mean it, because you are here."

He rings a number and talks to someone that makes him laugh while Karolina brings out coffee and biscuits. I can see she's a touch curious to know what we are chatting about. For a second I think she's having a go at Mirek about the idea; hands waving in the air, stomping up and down, shouting at him, full-on animated. All looks a tad aggressive from where I'm sitting. Mirek spills the good news to me, she wasn't shouting at all, just a bit excited when she realised she could help out.

As it happens, Karolina has a friend called Marika who works at a tourist office in London that speaks most Eastern European languages. She goes on to say it'd be better to have a friendly female there on the night to calm the girls if they're freaking out. I agree, if she's up for it. I ask Mirek to explain to his missus it'll be a grim sight walking into that hellhole. Would this Marika bird have the stomach for it? Karolina bursts out laughing; no need for me to worry. Marika is a tough, clued-up sort who grew up on the streets of Warsaw. If she'll do it, that'll be a result, and I'll gladly see her sweet for her troubles. Karolina goes off to call her pal while me and Mirek decide to get caned. Twenty minutes later, she comes back smiling saying all's sorted; Marika is looking forward to it.

Good news all round then. Mirek wants me to meet a good friend of his, an old army pal. I gather it's the person he spoke to on the phone. We grab our coats and make for the G-wagon. Fifteen minutes later, we pull up outside a bar to meet Hugo the Bear King.

"How exactly did he get that name, Mirek?" I need to ask, expecting to hear stories about a Goliath of a man snapping grizzly bears in half then scalping them. Legend has it a bit differently to my imagination, but it's still epic in anyone's eyes. Many moons ago, Hugo was sitting in the front row at a circus pissed out of his tree. When the bear act came on, the biggest one, for some reason, had the hump and flipped out, broke free, and rushed into the crowd causing mayhem and panic all over the shop. There was a fair bit of screaming going on, people trying to climb over each other to get away, plus a touch more screaming; full-on pandemonium, I should imagine, with a ridiculous amount of screaming thrown in. Hugo was the only person left sitting, because he's fast asleep snoring away. The snarling monster of a bear roared and growled, rolled back its lips, flashing its huge teeth, as it slowly approached Hugo. The bear got within biting range, reared up on its hind legs fucking huge. This cunt was nine-foot tall. If it was my story it would've been close to fifteen, but anyway. The beast was towering over Hugo while he slept, its massive shadow had already consumed him completely.

Now this part of the story, or legend, might be made-up just a little bit.

The place was deadly silent; everybody held their breath as the ferocious animal looked down on the sleeping Hugo, unaware of his fate. The bear stretched out its monstrous claws and opened its mouth wide for a killer bite. Then from out of nowhere, Hugo still snoring, leaned to the left, lifted half his arse and let out a thunderously loud fart that totally confused the bear. Hugo, meanwhile, who's slept through all the racket up to this point, woke up from the sound of his own trouser cough. He saw the huge silhouette standing in front of him, that he probably thought was a geezer squaring up, and threw an almighty punch into the bear's chest, knocking the animal on its backside. As the bear is sat there wondering what the fuck just happened, Hugo sat back down to finish his kip, probably totally unaware it was a bear he'd just punched. The confrontation between Hugo and the bear gave the crowd time to filter out and the handlers time to get their shit together and restrain the loopy beast, thus making Hugo a hero, and a legend was born.

Meeting the man is a brief, quiet experience. The only words I hear him say over the hour are Polish cuss words that seem to tickle Mirek no end. Hugo is all ready to set off night fishing on a nearby lake, so we say our goodbyes and part company. The Bear King wants to come along on the job so he doesn't miss any fun, Mirek tells me. That and because he wants to visit London to see the Changing of the Guard at Buckingham Palace. I'm leaving it all down to Mirek to recruit his team for the mission. He mentions bringing three men on the night plus Marika. Hugo's one, the other is a Polish Sparks who lives in London, and some Russian bloke.

He wants the Sparks there to cut the power when they storm the place; he's keeping it military-style because that's how these boys roll. The Russian fella is also based in London; he's the bloke supplying the team with whatever tools they need for the job. Mirek's plan is to go in with pistols and night-vision goggles, but assures me nobody will be shot. The guns are just for show in case the coke-heads really do fancy themselves as characters from *Scarface* waving shooters around. One look at the Bear King alone should be enough to change somebody's mind about being a hero.

Hugo stands around six foot six with no neck. The legend says he's eight-foot tall, but trust me on this one, I've just met the man. He's in his forties with a shaved head that looks like it's made from marble. He's got these piercing, grey eyes that give away a sign they've witnessed or created a death or two. You come across that look all the time where I come from. It's like a cross between an empty and ultra-focused stare.

I've enjoyed my little stay in Poland, but need to start making tracks back to Blighty. I hand Mirek £3,000 plus flight money with the understanding he'll get the rest when I next see him. I'm driven to the airport where Mirek tells me he'll be in touch over the next few days. I salute the man and I'm off.

Chapter 16

It's about time I gave Pete a bell for an update. The last time I spoke to him he said all was sweet, an ideal place was found and he'd already started digging holes for our cashola. Pete's a night owl, so he'll be out until the crack of dawn getting his hands dirty in total secrecy.

"Any luck with those holes, Pete? I ain't heard from ya since last week, mate. Kinda getting a bit worried, as you've been so quiet."

"I'm here, bruv, and well fucked. I've been digging like a cunt for two days solid. My back is proper missing."

"You see what I mean about you, Pete? I'm proud of ya, my friend. I don't believe what they say about you."

"What do they say about me?"

"The holes are finished then?"

"Done, man, and I put two of them green wheelie bins in the holes too for weather protection... So who's talking about me then, bruv?"

"Nice fuckin' move, I like your thinking. Read the papers, it's all in there about you."

"Fuck off, Span, but yeah, all we need to do is put the money in bin bags and drop them straight in. When the bins are full we just flip the lids over and fill in the holes, safe."

"Blinding. I hope you ain't told anybody about those

precious holes, Pete. Not being funny, mate, but I don't trust anyone these days."

"I ain't said fuck all, Span man, trust me. I'm being proper careful. I see this as my light at the end of the tunnel. The dough my old pops left me has more or less dried up. I'm serious. Between me and you, I'm down to my last twenty grand."

"Oh, is that all? You cunt."

"What? But then I'm potless, innit. I ain't got any cash coming in, and you know I can't sell the house. When I think back to the money I spunked on crap; not gonna happen again, trust me. You wait until you see where I've dug them holes. Couldn't have found a better place if I tried."

"Well I hope you tried."

"I have put blood, sweat, tears and a shitload of love into them holes, Span. I'm stung to fuck all over, because the location is in nettle city. I've got lumps on lumps to prove it."

Pete sure sounds like he's been on a mission sent from God. I leave it with him that I'll be over to see the holes tomorrow and hit the gym. As I walk in I'm greeted by one of me old training pals Mikey, who I ain't seen in ages. He goes on to tell me that he sees Ratboy every couple of weeks up at a pet shop in Kent buying rabbits to feed his caiman; must be the same place Terry Taxi told me about.

"Can you believe he was boasting about feeding it live kittens too!" grunts Mikey.

"Yeah I heard, mate, it's grim stuff. Just out of curiosity, have you seen Terry about?"

"Terry who? Taxi?"

"Yeah."

"Last time I saw him was a few weeks back, when he took me to the pet centre we were just talking about."

So, it is the same place Terry was going on about. I fantasise for a little while about Ratboy being ripped to pieces by a huge, fuck off crocodile. That genuinely makes me smile. I picture it just like you see on those animal documentaries, where they show hundreds of migrating wildebeest crossing a river. One by one, they get taken down by an armada of super hungry crocs that haven't eaten in a year. Man, if only that was possible to pull off. Imagine... that would be the perfect way to end Ratboy, eaten and shat out by the thing he worships; fucking brilliant. It could easily look like a stupid, pissed up tourist decided to take a dip in the wrong river; accidents happen.

The perfect murder, thinking about it, and now I can't stop thinking about it. Can't even concentrate on my workout, just keep turning that ridiculous thought over and over... Is it doable? I call Dubs to bounce the idea off him.

"Blud, you're insane. I love it, man. Of course it's doable, I just don't know how. Give the Fox a bell. He's always going to Kenya fishing, remember? That big-arse fish he's got on the wall in his pub was caught in Africa. The one you put your sunglasses on that time over the fireplace. The Fox has gotta know somebody who can deal with that sort of business."

The Fox-Meister, or as we like to call him 'The Fox', is a fella we know who runs a pub over in Tooting that also doubles up as a shady poker house, running all the way through the early hours of the morning, ending when every cunt is skint, except the crafty Fox of course. Mad about his fishing, the Fox has won many a trophy. He shoots over to Kenya eight weeks a year just to sit on a boat looking for marlin while topping up his perma-tan.

The interesting thing that's got me raising an eyebrow,

is that the Fox has a few quid wrapped around him and is well respected by the locals because of the amount of cash he puts their way, what with chartering boats and getting everybody hammered in Hemingways' bar every night and day whenever he's on a visit. I've seen it myself. I popped over to Kenya once to meet up with the Fox regarding an idea we had about importing wooden carvings to the UK. We met up in Hemingways on Watamu Beach to discuss business. The locals had the utmost respect for the man. I'd go as far as saying they treated him like a king, always making sure he was happy and comfortable. As I was in his company, I also got the same treatment.

So I'm here now thinking that the Fox must surely know someone out there, who knows someone's brother's mate's cousin's uncle, who knows a river where crocs hang out. At this point, I'm not even thinking about how the fuck would we get Ratboy out there, I just wanna know if there's a place tucked away it could happen.

We make our way to Tooting where the Fox greets us as we pull up outside his pub. He's got his signature, year-round suntan and is wearing the brightest yellow shirt you've ever seen.

"Hello boys, what brings you to sunny Tooting then?" asks the Fox.

"Crocodiles," says Dubs.

"Crocodiles? What do you mean 'crocodiles'?" The Fox looks a touch confused.

"You know, those big fuckin' dinosaur-looking things that live in African rivers that eat anything with a pulse," I put to him.

He tells me he knows what a crocodile is, but knows fuck all about them as he doesn't allow them in the pub anymore, apparently they always fuckin' wreck the place. Did I mention the Fox was a funny cunt? And too much sun has made his face looks like a cowboy's saddlebag? He reckons he looks like a young Dean Martin, but somehow I can't see it. I ask him about the likelihood of him knowing anybody in Africa who could help out with a little fantasy project of mine regarding a river full of very large, murderous reptiles. The Fox has no clue where to even start but has a South African fishing pal living in Kenya who might know something.

"This guy drives tourists around all day in a jeep showing them the 'big five', like a mini, one-day safari type of thing."

"What's the 'big five'?" I ask.

"The rhino, lion, buffalo, leopard and the elephant are the big five. I'm out there fishing in three weeks' time. If it helps, fellas, I can bell ya when I've had a chat with the South African geezer."

"Mate, that would actually be a big help, but keep it under your hat though, Foxy."

"Don't I always?"

We shake hands and leave.

"Mate, this is so far-fetched. I mean, how the fuck would we get Ratboy to Africa?" I ask Dubs.

"Dunno, blud, your idea. I was gonna ask you the same thing."

Driving back home we sit in silence, in deep thought, racking our brains with insane ideas on how to get the Rat to Africa... And I finally, come up with a brainwave that could have legs, which Dubs agrees with. If I can persuade, with a shitload of cocaine, a South African prostitute I know from back in the day called Pippa to get involved, then the wheels will most definitely be in motion. She's a full-on freak that I'm sure would do anything for a large parcel of lemon, so it's fair play to give it a try.

Pip came banging on my door at five in the morning once totally off her face. She was on her way back home from an acid house rave twitching, begging for a free gram of charlie as she had no money. Now even though I personally can't stand coke, and hate everything about it, I still knock a bit out every now and then for the sake of a pound note. So anyway, first thing she asks me, as I opened the door, was why I'd never made a move on her in all the time we'd known each other. Using all my intelligence, I came to the conclusion she was saying I could fuck her for some coke, and you know very well that when a pretty damsel is in a state of extreme mash up, it would be very easy to take full advantage of the situation. Somehow with Pip though, maybe because she's a brass, I've always swerved her when it comes to a spot of passion. Not that I've got anything against prostitutes. It's just the thought of slinging it up one, knowing that eight other cocks have probably already gone through it for the day, just doesn't really do it for me. Pip's a party girl, quite a looker too. OK, excessive use of cocaine hasn't done her appearance that many favours, but the times I've seen her out clubbing she's always looked decent enough, so she scrubs up well. Maybe she could be persuaded to start drinking in the same pub as Ratboy to chat him up. Pip could easily pass as a South African student over here in the UK doing English studies or something. Maybe say her brother's business just so happens to be in Kenya driving people around on a big five safari, that's where the Fox's man could come into it. Pippa could make out she's the person who takes care of all the bookings for the tours whenever she's over there.

Anyway, so what I'm thinking is, somewhere down the line, after Ratboy and Pippa have become good friends, he's bound to proudly tell her all about his pet caiman and his passion for crocodiles. Then maybe, at some point, her brother could invite them both over.

I know the word maybe has been dropped a few times back there, but I figure she'd be fucking him at that point, so it's plausible, they'd be a couple. When they get to croc central, a romantic table for two with candles would be laid out by the riverbank, with someone tossing steaks on a barbecue for good effect. During the evening, Ratboy is sure to wanna go take a piss at some point, leaving an opportunity for Pippa to drop a sneaky sleeper into his drink. The minute Ratboy is snoring all would leave, except me and Dubs who would've been hiding close by watching everything unfold. All the way through, leading up to this point, everyone would've been kept completely in the dark about our intentions with the Rat. Myself and Dubs would then get to work making the crime scene look believable. A small campfire burning away with a backpack leaning against a tree, empty cans of beer scattered about as the icing on the cake, or a cherry on top if ya fancy. Then we'd roll the sleeping Rat to the river's edge, maybe sling a dead chicken on top to lure the crocs in, bon appetite; job done.

Chapter 17

"Hello Pete, can you hear me?"

"Yeah, but your signal's bollocks Span."

"What about now?"

"Still bollocks, but I can hear ya. What's up, bruv?"

"That night when me and Dubs were at yours overdosing on *Star Trek*, did I see a shitload of nature vids in that box?"

"National Geographic, yeah man. Why?"

"Mate, I fancy watching something about crocodiles, because you know why."

I slip back over to Pete's to hopefully gain some knowledge on the behaviour of crocodiles, plus it's hot dog day and Dubs is already there.

"Can you believe I'm driving around these days hiding my face? I'm thinking every bod coming my way is Old Bill in an unmarked car looking for me. I'm fuckin' well paranoid."

"You should always hide your face Span, Wilson's been getting nightmares, bruv."

"That's pretty quick for you Pete. Well done, mate. But if you must know, I'm hiding my face because I don't want the police thinking Paul Newman has nicked my motor, am I right Dubs?"

"You know that, blud."

"Paul Newman? Span you don't look anything like Paul

Newman, trust me."

"Hang about, Pete, you're not looking properly, mate. Have a look now that I'm gazing into the distance."

"Still no."

"Hold up, ya cunt, I ain't done the look yet."

"Well go on then."

"OK. Are you ready?"

"Yeah, I'm ready. Show me Paul Newman."

"Bam...! Now what are you saying?"

"No fucking way, innit, that's what I'm saying, bruv."

"Well then you're blind Pete, because as it happens, the other day in Sainsbury's some fella walked up to me and said: 'Paul Newman! Fancy seeing you here. I thought you was fucking brilliant in *Cool Hand Luke*. Can I have your autograph?'"

"Whatever."

Pete's still not convinced I look anything like Paul Newman, and the weird thing is, everybody else I know, other than Dubs, thinks the same. Must be my accent. Yeah, I'm sure that's what it is.

"Here we go, bruv, crocodiles and alligators."

"Nice one Pedro, stick it in the Ferguson. Also, where are the hot dogs, ya tight cunt?"

So the video is ready to play, the hot dogs are coming and spliffs are circulating.

"Pete, fast forward, these are alligators; no good to us."

"Why not?"

"Because he just said alligators are from America, completely different country."

"They look the same though, so they must act the same, innit."

"No mate, crocs look evil. These here look fat and placid,

plus crocs have got more teeth. Have a look at the railings on those alligators and compare them to a croc. Pete, fast forward, for fuck's sake."

A fast forward later.

"I see what you mean Span, definitely more teeth, and check it out. They look like they're smiling."

"Yeah, but the thing I wanna know is will they go for something that ain't moving? All these poor fuckers crossing the river getting munched are moving, and probably giving off a vibe that's full-on panic mode too. I mean, take that zebra there for example, where the fuck is he going?"

"Blud, he's swimming out to deep water. It's all over for him, trust me."

"And here come the crocs right after him. Hold up Dubs, have a look how fast that zebra's shifting now, and he's doing the butterfly. Did any of you see him slip on a pair of Speedos before he went in? Look at him going for gold. And he's made it to the other side; impressive. Not so good for his pal though. Have a look at that dozy fucker. Swims out to the middle, then decides he's got half a stitch and turns back. Now what are you gonna do? And he's gone... Survival of the fittest right there, gentlemen."

"He got proper fucked up, blud, but we still need to see about them snatching something from the edge of the river, unless Ratboy decides to go swimming; that would be a nice, easy day for us, you get me?"

"And that's the problem Dubs, even those animals standing still that are being grabbed are drinking, so they're kinda moving, plus standing up, that's a big difference on its own."

So really, I'm still none the wiser. OK, I know a little bit more about crocodiles, but I ain't seen them take a sleeping man at the river's edge yet. Pete insists that before we have any more hot dogs and videos, we need to check out the holes he dug last night. So we kinda check them out but at a distance. Imagine stinging nettles for as far as you can see, then sling in some tall holly bushes and various other nasty-looking plants that snag your clothes. Now fill every possible open space with trees, that's it pretty much, and my shins don't need to get any closer to the nettles thanks. Come to think of it, what's that gonna be like at night pilled up off your nut? Imagine tripping over and rolling about in it, fuck that. We head back to the house for a conference.

"Pete about those holes, mate."

"What holes?"

"Where have we just been, ya clown?"

"Oh, right. Is that a safe spot or what, man?"

"Well, let's just talk about that word 'safe' for a second if you don't mind, Peter."

"Now what?"

"You know, I appreciate the graft you put into those holes, and I'm not having a pop at ya, but didn't you put yourself in a scenario of what it'd be like on the night having to navigate through all those nettles pilled up?"

"Not a problem, Span. You see how you have no faith in me? I think of these things, innit. I know exactly where to place my feet without getting stung. Besides, I'm gonna leave wellingtons close by for full-on protection."

"What size are they, just out of curiosity?"

"Seven and a half. Why?"

"Gutted, mate, I'm an eight. I'll have to walk with you up to where the nettles start and wait for you to plug the dough up. I'll be keeping dog, thank fuck."

"You can follow me through, Span man, it'll be easy."

"The Normandy landings were easier, Pete. I ain't getting stung to fuck on rave night, no way. I said find a sweet place, meaning well hidden and easy for us to sneak off to. Not find a place where it would be very fuckin' easy to ruin our night with a good old-fashioned stumble. Look at me, I'm already scratching, for Christ's sake."

"Fine, I'll stash the cash then. I don't have a problem with that. Leave it to me, as usual. Leave it to Super Pete to save the day."

"Blinding, well that's settled then, but promise me you ain't gonna call yourself Super Pete from now on."

I'm not being a cunt for letting Pete deal with plugging the cash on rave night all on his tod. In a perfect world, I would have opted for picking another spot and help dig the fuckin' holes, but we're short on time now, so we're gonna have to see how it turns out. Besides, I'm still gonna be there just not in the stinging nettles.

An invitation for dinner has me reaching for my car keys. Amber reckons she's made my favourite munch, paella. Don't worry though, I only had a couple of hot dogs at Pete's, there's always room for paella.

As I climb the gleaming marble stairs to Amber's apartment, I stop to catch my reflection on the last step, and for a second I think it's Paul Newman.

"Come in Spaniard. Would you like some wine?"

"You know I don't drink."

"Oh yes of course, silly me. Juice then?"

"Sounds good. What have you got?"

"Elderflower."

"Behave."

"Too dainty for you?"

"Yeah, I'm far too macho for that. Ain't you got anything

else?"

"There's Coca-Cola."

"Coca-Cola? You mean Coke?"

"That's what I said, Coca-Cola."

"Don't you just call it Coke?"

"But it's Coca-Cola."

"Yeah, I know that. It's just nobody calls it Coca-Cola, it's always Coke."

"I'm going to hit you in a minute."

"What with? A bottle of Coca-Cola?"

"Dinner will be ready in about forty minutes. I'll be back in a second. Put some music on, sweetie."

I roll a joint to the sound of Jim Morrison belting out 'Riders on the Storm'. The weather outside is a perfect match as a crack of thunder rumbles the windows.

"Wow, was that thunder I just heard?" asks Amber as she begins to lay the table.

"Sure was, it's pissing down. Looks like I made it here just in time."

"I think you should stay the night, if you want to that is."

Well that's a bit sudden. Could mean she's after some tummy banana.

"Sounds good to me. Do you want a hand with anything?"

"No, I've got it thanks, but you can sit at the table. I'm ready to bring it in."

Now things are getting fucking strange. Amber brings in what looks like the perfect paella. She told me, a while back, she wasn't that great at cooking, which I agree with. Some of the stuff she's put in front of me tasted and looked pretty fuckin' indescribable. There's no way on earth you can knock up a paella like this if your cooking skills are shit, and I'm an expert when it comes to what a paella should look and taste like. I slip my way to the kitchen, suspicious that some other bod is hiding in there that cooked it, but no, Amber definitely made it. I like her even more now.

"This is fuckin' handsome. I can't believe you made it. Did you see me just go into the kitchen? I was checking to see if you had a proper chef hidden in there."

"You flatter me, kind sir. I thank you."

So the meal is amazing, and the rest of the night is going that way too, sort of. I mean, we're lying on the sofa, all comfy, watching a movie, when she starts going on about my Ecstasy supplier Dutch. She thinks it would be a good idea if she met him. I don't think so and tell her so.

With that she gets up and says, "But it's OK to use my money? Fine."

Don't get me wrong, I'm grateful for her help, but not enough to start introducing her to all my business contacts.

"I'm sorry, Spaniard, I didn't mean to be pushy."

"No worries. You're just stoned, that's all."

"What's he like though, this Dutch character?"

"He's good as gold; looks like Sting."

"From The Police?"

"Yeah."

"So he's good-looking then?"

"You can't ask me a question like that. I'm a straight man."

"You are funny Spaniard, really."

"Well he ain't an ugly cunt, if that's what you wanna know."

"You don't have to use that word, sweetie."

"Sorry, he isn't an ugly cunt, if that's what you wanna know."

Amber going on about meeting Dutch goes on far too

long for my liking, especially when I'm caned. Am I being over sensitive? Maybe. Is she trying to make me jealous? Maybe, but that won't work, I can take it or leave it, easy come, easy go. Well, that's how I used to be anyway... before I met Amber. Then the interest switches back to me.

"So tell me, Spaniard, how did you get into the whole dealing thing in the first place, if you don't mind me asking?"

"Not at all. Simple really. Me and a couple of pals got fed up with buying shit weed to smoke ourselves, so we shot over to Holland to see how they grew it. Got all the knowledge necessary then came back, and the rest is history. I don't grow it anymore, just get it off my pals at a great price."

"And what about the tablets?"

"What about them?"

"How did they come about? Sorry, but I find your world fascinating."

"Nothing fascinating there, Amber, I just met a bloke at a rave once that sold me an E. I liked it and arranged to buy a small parcel from him that slowly grew. Now I've met Dutch, that's pretty much it really."

"So Dutch is the Mr Big then? How exciting."

"I don't know about him being Mr Big, but he's certainly a godsend in my eyes, that's for sure."

I sleep like a baby all night, nearly nine hours straight. The smell of coffee and freshly cooked toast is all I need to get me up. Amber shouts from the kitchen something about it being a beautiful day, and I should sit out on the balcony. She's right, that storm last night has made way for a nice spot of sunshine. The spread in front of me ain't bad either. I've got a pot of fancy coffee, toast and jam, freshly squeezed orange juice and my very own pain au chocolat, all laid out on a red and white, checked tablecloth. She's even got me a newspaper;

it's like staying at the Hotel Amber. I could seriously get used to this, and I've not heard a police siren since I got here which is incredible.

A cute, little robin flutters down onto the table and sings me a beautiful morning song. Now that deserves a corner of toast, so I break a piece and place it on the newspaper and slide it close to him. He happily hops over to inspect it, cocking his head from side to side to get a better look. I reckon that piece might be a touch too big for the little fella, so I break it into crumbs, but he's still not having it. What else can I give him? Then it all makes sense, I should have known. A slight breeze blows the toast crumbs across the table, as we make eye contact. The robin's eyes narrow as he realises he's been rumbled. We stare at each other like gunslingers, waiting for just the right moment. The rippling sound of the tablecloth blowing in the wind is all that can be heard. I roll a toothpick from one corner of my mouth to the other, never taking my eyes off him even for a second. Something is about to go down and get pretty messy. This robin is out for my pain au chocolat, and I'm not feeling that. Slowly, and I mean very slowly, I take the newspaper under the table and begin to roll it so tight that my knuckles crack. The bird pauses, keeping one eye on me and the other on my pain au chocolat. I'm ready for him, and I think he knows. If he tries it, I'm batting him across the Thames.

"Come on, you little cunt, try it, I fuckin' dare ya."

"Who are you talking to, sweetie?"

He's lucky he flies away when Amber turns up. I was about to hit him for six, which is over Battersea Power Station.

Chapter 18

Really need to get my shit together, I'm blazing way too much these days. The second I wake up I'm reaching for the skins. It's wake and bake seven days a week for me. There's a load of that mad cheese going about that gives you mental red-eye from just a couple of tokes, and that makes you look like a hot cookie the minute you step outside. Normally, if I'm out and about with a severe case of red-eye and bump into someone that doesn't need to know I smoke weed, I tell them I'm flued up, even in the summer. I've perfected the fake cough followed by a sniffle that's worthy of an Oscar nomination. My mum thinks I've had the flu for the past fifteen years, bless her, but I'm getting so absent-minded in my everyday life. Forgetting to call people back from missed calls is such a bad thing for business, because it makes you an instant messer. People get pissed off quick time, and rightly so, I do when it's done to me. Gotta focus on the next few days leading up to the rave, or I could miss a little detail that'll fuck something up big time. Mirek is meant to get here within the next couple of days. He said all he needs is the address of the place and he'll take care of it. That's what I like about the Poles, they're like the Germans, very clinical in their operations; you can rely on them.

The set-up for the rave is turning out to be a blinder. Dubs has put a quality sound system together that I can hear crystal clear all the way from where I'm standing over in the chill-out field, which is a fair way away. The acoustics sound crisp with a heavy bass that made me look up to the sky thinking it was the rumble of thunder. Huge, fuck off speakers the size of telephone booths stacked high dominate the main field. It's all surprisingly, very professionally done and laid out, which I've gotta say is a relief. Pete and Dubs have done a cracking job getting all this together on time. I've been so manic the past few days, getting the last little details together for Mirek that time has flown by in a blink. I've passed him the bits of info he needs to know so it's now out of my hands, and that most certainly is another relief. Looking down into the bottom field where the rave will be held, I can't help but feel proud of the boys tinkering about making sure the last little details are how they should be. Of course, it's always possible to overdo things.

"You've done really well Pete. See, you can get your arse into gear when you try, ya lazy fucker."

"Cheers, but I'm not quite done yet. You wait until you see the smoke machine, it's gonna look sick, bruv."

"Smoke machine?"

"Yeah Span, you know? A smoke machine. You gotta have a smoke machine at a rave. It ain't a proper rave without a smoke machine."

"Pete, are you fuckin' winding me up?"

"Nah, man, I've got the biggest smoke machine you've ever seen. Had it delivered this morning from a place up north that hires them out; got a great price for the whole weekend."

"Pete, I'm not being funny, but we're not a club in Ibiza. Yeah, we want people to have a good time, but a fuckin' smoke machine ain't the way to go, especially outside, mate."

"Well I kinda figured that the smoke would blow across the fields and into the woods where we'll be stashing the cash, thus hiding our tracks, innit."

"Thus hiding our tracks? Pete I'll be pilled up off my fucking face, lose my bearings and end up somewhere on the M25 looking like Animal from *The Muppet Show*. I've got the worst sense of direction in the world, and that's when I can see where the fuck I'm going. We can't have smoke, Peter, because even though it's your private land and we've been plugging the rave through underground methods, you're still gonna get undercover bacon trying to slip in. If they find a reason to raid the place and shut us down they'll do it. Seeing a few hundred people walking about with a jaw like a cashier's till will definitely twig them off, people will get nicked. Having smoke at the rave makes us as easy as you like to find, you could see us from the fuckin' moon. I'm liking the green lasers though, Pete, they look pukka, plus can be controlled. Smoke does whatever the fuck it wants to do and that's always go up, like a big smoke signal in the sky for every copper in the land to see. Believe me when I tell ya, they'd be coming out the fuckin' trees, my friend."

"OK, Span, you got a point. It's this crazy skunk, bruv, frazzling my brain."

I know what he means by that, but I've held it down today. Gotta say it's sharpened me up a touch too. It's been just over five hours since I last had a spliff and I feel nicely awake; a pleasant change. I swear to God that fuckin' smoke machine is going back tomorrow morning first thing though.

My mind switches over to Mirek, what day will he do the job? I told him I'm gonna be at the rave from Saturday to Sunday, that's when he's gotta do it. Last time I spoke to him, he told me Marika was gonna meet him en route where they were gonna go straight to pick the girls up, then drop them off outside the nick in one quick swoop, blitzkrieg-style. So any time from now then. For fuck's sake, I hope it goes well for them. I make a quick call.

"Dutch, mate, all set for tomorrow?"

"Of course Spaniard, it's all ready for you, amigo."

"Nice. I've got a mate posing as a courier who's gonna pay you a visit as my stock gets low. He's on a motorbike, so business should be speedy."

"No problem, my friend. I hope to maybe join you later at the party when business dies down. I will even bring my dancing shoes to have some fun with English girls."

"Sounds like a plan. You get in there, my son. I've got another call coming through from Pete. I'll speak to ya later, Dutch. Pete what's up?"

"Bruv, I've just sold three thousand little fellas for £10 each to Chinese George, he's bringing half of Soho to the rave."

"Result! And for tenners? Make sure you get the money first though, Pete. You know how slippery he can be."

"I told him already, he knows the score."

"Might be worth me getting some more dropped off then, I've got a geezer who'll be picking up for us as we need them. He's old-school, as reliable as a Rolex. My friend Tina is putting the word out about the rave through her pirate radio contacts, so all four corners of London should know about it by now. This could be a rather busy weekend, brother, Pete."

"Man, we are gonna smash this, trust me... Who's Tina?"

"I fuckin' knew you wouldn't let that slide. The second I mention a girl's name I knew you'd be on it."

"But is she single though?"

"How the fuck do I know?"

"Well she's your friend, innit."

"She ain't a close friend, Pete, more of a contact."

"That's even better then... Hook me up, bruv... What's she like?"

"So you want me to set you up with her before you even know what she's like?"

"I know she's gonna be fit, man."

"How's that then?"

"Her name, innit, and the whole pirate radio thing. She's gonna be cool, Span, you know that."

"No, I don't know that, but what I do know is I'm not calling her. What's the matter with you Pete?"

"Bruv, it's alright for you, you know you've got Amber to buzz with on rave night. Dubs will pretty much have whoever he likes, but what about me? I wanna buzz with someone too, you know? Like when everyone's gone home and it's just me and her getting messed up in private. Those times are wicked, Span."

I'm completely with him on that, there's nothing like holding back some pills for after a rave to get wasted with that special person. A lot of the time it turns out better than the rave itself.

"You'll meet somebody at the rave, Pete. I can't call a bird I don't know that well and just come out of the blue about you wanting to meet her. She'll think I'm a fuckin' crank. I'll tell ya what I will do though."

"What's that?"

"I'll give you some advice, mate, that's absolutely priceless, so listen up."

"I'm listening."

"You clearly are one frustrated cunt, Pete, am I right?"

"I'm always frustrated, bruv, it's because…"

"Hang on, let me finish. The problem with you, my friend, is you've got what the Romans used to call 'Sakisfullus'."

"Eh?"

"Your sack is full, mate. You need to tug one off… but not this very second. It'll calm ya down, for Christ's sake. There's a thin line between how a rapist looks at a woman, and how lately you've been looking at women."

"I'm not a rapist, Span."

"I know that, Pete, I'm not calling you a rapist. I'm just saying you're ogling birds and it probably fuckin' scares them."

"What the hell is ogling, bruv?"

"It's what you do, I've seen ya. You'll look at a sort as if you're undressing her, and you never turn away. That makes them really uncomfortable. You need to hold that down, or they'll always run for the hills. Do yourself a favour, throw it over your thumb. Don't walk about with a loaded pistol. The second you've unloaded, you won't be thinking about girls every second."

"I'm unloading three times a day already, bruv, like a champion, innit."

"It's at this point, Peter, that I no longer wish to continue with this conversation."

But he done well knocking them bits out to Chinese George like that. I'd much prefer to shift as many pills as possible before people actually get to the venue. I'm uneasy serving up out on the floor to bods I've never met before. I'm getting a bit old for that method, plus it puts a lot of heat on ya. You can quite easily sell to undercover Old Bill and before you know it your feet don't touch the ground.

"I've got this awesome idea how to shift pills on the floor," says Pete.

"Go on," I reply.

"Well you know Mandy from Clapham? She's got one of those mobile fruit juice stands you find in shopping centres. The ones where you pick your fruits and they whip you up a smoothie. Anyway, when I saw her last week pitched up on Clapham Common, she had somebody walking around dressed up as a giant orange; fuckin' sick costume, bruv. We could get that stand set up at the site for people that have had enough buzz and wanna turn in. You know what they say? Vitamin C kills the E. We get somebody in that orange costume to punt out pills, sweet as a bug in a rug. Think about the shape of the costume, Span. Now imagine how many tabs could be stashed inside. Also, he'd be part of the fruit juice stand looking like he's got a reason to be there, he won't draw attention to himself."

"Draw attention to himself? Pete, he's a giant fuckin' orange. Please stop smoking drugs, mate. We ain't having any giant oranges walking around the party loaded with my narcotics. You may as well have somebody dressed as a giant pill. For fuck's sake, Pete, behave, mate."

"Just a thought, bruv. Only trying to help."

"Really?"

Pete does have his moments; ya gotta love him for it. He's been hitting the White Widow all day and night the past few weeks, the brain cells that used to knock about in his head are on vacation somewhere, not expected back anytime soon. I'm genuinely getting a bit concerned about him. He used to be as sharp as they come, but since his dad died he's lost a bit of spark, and as time goes by he's getting dimmer. Can't really blame the fella though, he was pretty close to his old pops. His dad looked after him maybe a bit too much in most people's eyes. Pete never had to struggle for money or anything else, come to think of it. When he wanted a car he just had to ask the old man, the same thing if he fancied a holiday. Now that his dad has gone and left him alone to fend for himself, he just sits about at home getting stoned and watching videos.

"Pete, seriously mate, I've slowed right down with the puffing. I think you should too. We all need to be totally on the ball with this thing. Let's just get it out the way then we can do what we want, treat this thing of ours like a proper business. We need our marbles in place. Do you understand what I'm saying?"

"Yeah, I know, Span, live at the end of the day not on the day. Just a bit stressed, bruv, that's all. I'll be fine, besides, Prague is calling. You should come out there after the rave to kick back, man."

"I might do later Pete. I've decided I'm gonna chill in Amsterdam for a while first, just until the buzz dies down a bit. A lot of people know it's our do, so you're gonna get all sorts of lost friends coming out of the woodwork reminding you how much they always considered you one of their best pals. I'm blanking any number that comes up on my phone I don't recognise."

"Good idea. I think I'll be doing the same, bruv. I fancy a bit of the 'Dam myself, to be honest, been fuckin' ages since I was there. I might have to pop over for a couple of weeks. Where do you normally smoke when you're over there?"

"Anywhere really, I seem to find a new, favourite coffeeshop every time I visit. As long as there's a nice selection of weed plus a cracking hot chocolate I'm happy. Come out there, Pete, put your feet up for a while, and think about what you're gonna do with all your money. Speaking of money, I think we should take our time before we go digging about, it ain't going nowhere. What do you reckon?"

"I reckon you're right. What shall I do with the cash from Chinese George?"

"We'll use that to pay all the people helping us out with the rave. I've put some money aside, which I need to pay Mirek when he's done that thing, but come Saturday we start plugging it straight in the bins."

"I'm looking forward to this, Span man. It's about time my fuckin' boat came in."

Chapter 19

"Hey Spaniard, sweetie, what are you up to later? Fancy dinner and a lazy night in?"

"Nothing much, and yeah, that sounds like a great plan. No need to go crazy with the cooking though Amber, I'll order us pizza if you're up for it. Come to my place and take it slow for once."

"Wonderful, pizza it is then. Wow, that was easy. What time shall I be at yours for?"

"Make it eight and we've got a deal, plus bring some popcorn because *The Great Escape* is on the box."

Strange how things turn out, they say opposites attract, Amber being so upper crust and what have ya, and me the polar opposite. We've been sort of seeing each other for a few months now. Things are going pretty sweet. I've put off meeting her parents a few times, as I fuckin' hate that sort of thing. Kinda feel like the old man would have a field day grilling me about my past and future plans with his princess. Amber knows the score too, that's why she's not done my head in over it, where most girls would have by now.

I sink down to eye level and imagine the bubble bath foam drifting across as icebergs. With my ears beneath the water, I'm in the most peaceful place on earth. The rain crashing against the window tells me things are not so peaceful outside for Amber. She's not a fan of rain and hates driving in it more so. Personally, I love it. The harder the downpour the better, throw in some thunder and I'm happier than a happy thing living in Happyville; the perfect weather for not getting random police stops. How often have you seen Old Bill pull someone over in the pissing rain? Not often. My reflection in the bathroom mirror suggests I need some rest, I'm looking tired; feel it too. My staggered sleep pattern isn't helping much; two hours here, four hours there, doesn't seem to be doing the trick.

A buzz on the intercom tells me it's eight, Amber's arrived. I open the door and she's standing there in a Burberry mac and heels, dripping wet. Without taking a step forward, she undoes the buttons and shakes the coat to the floor revealing a very naked Amber. She drops to her knees, pulls my strides to the floor and sucks my cock right there on the landing.

"I've been looking forward to this all day," she says between mouthfuls.

"Well no need to be shy about it. I'm always looking forward to it, so crack on anytime," is my romantic reply.

Eighteen minutes later, I'm on the phone ordering a large, thin crust meat feast and chicken wings.

"I want some more of what just happened at the front door," says Amber.

Sensing more romantic chat is in order, I tell her that we should maybe hang on for a while as my spunk bunkers are empty. Or at least wait until after the Steve McQueen motorcycle jump scene which is coming up pretty soon. Five minutes of silence goes by, then Amber turns to me and says the most normal thing you could possibly say whilst eating pizza and watching *The Great Escape*.

"I want to take you to Amsterdam so I can choose a

prostitute to suck your cock while I watch. Would you be up for it? It's something I've had on my mind for a while, and the thought of it drives me insanely horny, to a point I can't even concentrate at work."

"Blimey, I thought you was gonna ask me to pass you the garlic bread. Where the fuck did that come from?"

"I have no idea, but it really turns me on. I feel like a bit of a freak. Am I a weirdo?"

"Yeah, you're a full-on weirdo, but that's one of the things I like about ya. Listen, whatever floats your boat Amber is OK with me. You've just got a little kink going on, that's all. Everybody has a kink. I'm as kinky as you like, as long as you don't try and stick something up my arse, that's where I draw the line."

"No, I wouldn't dream of it, although I heard a man likes a finger up his bum just before he's about to climax during the missionary position."

"If you ever try that on me we're gonna fall out big time. Stay away from my ring-piece, or we're gonna have a serious problem. And you can stop laughing, it ain't funny."

"It is a little. Why are you so protective of it?"

"I'm not. My bottle is out of bounds, that's all... Pass the chicken wings, please."

"OK, I think I've got it. So you don't like your anus played with."

"Call it what you like, but if you go near it I'm setting my dog on ya."

"You don't have a dog."

"So I'll buy a dog just to set on ya."

"OK then Mr Man of the World, what really turns you on? There must be something you haven't done that we can do together? Think of something kinky you want me to do, and I'll do it. We could do both of our kinks, one after the other, in Amsterdam."

I don't have a problem with her little fetish, if you can call it that. Thinking of something for me is turning out to be harder than I thought though. The thing about kinky sex is, if you're getting it that way all the time, it's harder to get turned on when you go back to normal sex. It's as though the bar has been raised to a point that if you split from that girl and find yourself in a new relationship with a normal sex life, boredom will come knocking pretty sharpish. It's not all doom and gloom though, it just takes more time to adjust, to get back to normal, so to speak. I don't want that to happen with us, and I can't give Amber an answer to her question just yet.

"OK. I'll think of something and let you know."

"Awesome! So you'll do my thing then?"

"Yeah. So let me get this straight, you want me to do nothing while a woman of your choice blows my trumpet while you sit there and watch?"

"Exactly."

"Ain't you gonna at least strum one out while you're watching? Just seems a bit weird otherwise."

"What do you mean?"

"Well wouldn't you wanna polish the pearl?"

"Pearl?"

"Yeah, you know? Circle the wagon...? Rough up the suspect?"

"Sweetie, you're talking another language."

"Play with yourself, for Christ's sake."

"No... I just want to watch... I'll touch myself when I'm alone, thank you very much."

"Fair enough. It doesn't matter to me whether you do or

don't; just thinking it was the normal thing to do. Anyway, sweet, I'll do your thing. Just don't go picking an ugly, cockeyed bird to blow me, or we might have a performance issue."

"Great...! And I promise she'll be beautiful."

"She better be."

"I'm so happy you said yes, sweetie."

"Yeah, I can see that. You really are a freak."

"But I really want to do something special for your thing. Please think about it, Spaniard."

"Don't worry Amber, I will do just that and report back when I have a suitably filthy idea."

I'm surprised to not hear from Mirek yet; had the whole thing running around my head all night right up to when Amber left this morning, and I feel a bit unsettled. Mind you, it's just gone midday, so maybe I'm stressing a touch. Hundred press ups and a shower later has me reset and feeling a lot better. Checking my phone, there's a missed call from a foreign number; could be Mirek. I ring it back and chat to a member of staff from Hemingways who expected the call. I'm passed over to the Fox who's sitting at the bar, and judging by the racket in the background, seems to be missing out on the conga.

"Mr Fox, I take it you're not in Streatham then?"

"Hello, mate. No, I'm in Africa. Remember I said I was coming out here fishing when you was round me pub?"

"Yeah, yeah, I remember. Mate, that was fuckin' weeks ago. How's things?"

"Things are good, but do you remember what we spoke about?"

"Of course, crocodiles and the Rat, if I'm not mistaken."

"Spot on, son, I'm impressed you remember what with

the amount of that weed stuff you smoke."

"It's better than being a pisshead, mate, believe me. One day we'll have a blaze, and you'll see. I'll make you a believer yet, Foxy."

"No thanks, you can keep that shit. I'll stick with what I know. Booze is my business, happy cabbage is yours. Anyway, that thing you was asking about could have legs after all."

"In what way?"

"In a way that one of my fishing pals over here has been importing parrots on the sly from some poacher-type character, who's prepared to meet and show you the perfect place where you'll find a shitload of handbags with teeth, if you know what I mean?"

"Really? Fucking hell, Foxy, tell me more."

"Not a lot more to say really, mate. The fella thinks you wanna poach yourself some croc skins, which he's organised before for some Yanks. He reckons it's a case of showing you a spot where no cunt goes and that's pretty much it."

"And I take it he's totally in the dark about the reason?"

"Yeah, he thinks you're a spender. He said he can supply you anything you want while you're over here; women, drugs, diamonds, he's the man to ask."

"Is that right? Maybe not all at once though."

"Whatever you like, according to him. Only thing is, being a poacher, he's a right slippery fucker. I know he's gonna be about for the next couple of days, but after that God knows when he'll show up again."

"Fox, mate, if it ain't any grief, and you know I'll see you sweet, can you get him to show you where we need to go? I can't get out there just yet, because things are happening this end. Ask him how much and I'll sort it?"

"I could ask him, Span, but he won't show me fuck all

until he's paid up front. That's how they trade over here."

"Can't you pay him? Fuckin' hell, Foxy you should be ashamed of yourself. I could have the money back with your missus in Streatham before you open your wallet, ya tight cunt."

"I'm only joking. I know you're good for it. Let me get back to ya when I know a bit more."

I must admit, I'm getting a bit excited now. Time for another call.

"Dubs, mate, remember our little visit to the Fox's that time?"

"Yeah, blud, is it on? I'm game if it is, you know that."

"Could be, according to the Fox. He reckons some poacher bod over there has got all the answers we need. From what I gather, if we can get Ratboy out there, it should be a piece of piss."

"How do we do that, by the way, Span?"

"Planning I suppose, mate. I've gotta first find sloshpot Pippa though. I can't plan fuck all until I know what my options are. If she's still on the game and up for a well-paid acting job with no questions asked, we could be in business. I think that idea I mentioned about her luring him over and putting him to sleep by the river is the way to go, Dubs. What do you reckon?"

"Yeah, that's pretty cool, blud, but it's a pity he won't suffer. He should really suffer, you know? Like them girls suffer."

"I think if he wakes up surrounded by crocodiles we might get some suffering."

"Dread, we should wake that cunt up just as the crocs come in for the kill."

"That ain't a bad idea, thinking about it. I wonder if he'd

wake up from the sleeping pill if I was to kick him in the balls?"

"Probably, man."

"I'm thinking maybe a classic toe punt would do the trick. Have you still got them old football boots with the steel studs? Might be worth bringing them along."

"Of course, dread, but they'll be better for stomping on his balls I think."

"Maybe you're right. Stomping's good though."

"Stomping is very good."

"I just thought of something funny, Dubs."

"What's that?"

"Do you remember me telling you about that time me and Amber bumped into Tommy the Cannon in a restaurant?"

"Yeah, when he told you about the shit on his chest thing."

"Yeah, that's the one. Anyway, do you remember the size of that cunt's feet? He's a size fourteen, mate, I kid you not. We all used to take the piss out of him up at the gym. How funny would it be to nick his right, steel toecap Dr Martens just to kick the Rat in the balls with it?"

"Blud, that would be hilarious. And what size are you again?"

"I'm an eight."

"And he's a fourteen, you say?"

"Yep, and I'll put on that Sasquatch boot, take a run up and kick Ratboy's balls through his eye sockets."

"That would slay me if I saw it, blud, but if you slip up on that wet mud by the river, you'll be like one of them deer things in Pete's crocodile video being tossed about while your arms and legs are twisted off."

And that was the end of my big boot kicking a sleeping man's bollocks fantasy.

Chapter 20

"Spaniard, it's Mirek. Can you hear me?"

"Hello, Mirek? I can just about hear you. Where are ya?"

"Hello, hello."

"Must be your phone, Mirek. I've got full signal."

"Hello."

And gone. Always the way when it's important. Four times I've tried to call him back, but no joy, not even a ringtone. Each unsuccessful attempt stresses me out, so I roll a comfort zoot, slump on the sofa, and get thoroughly baked. It's normal for me, at this point, just when I get myself beyond chilled, to have some cunt call me.

"Hey sweetie, I've been thinking about you all day with a silly smile that doesn't seem to want to go away."

I'm not saying she's a cunt for calling me... I just mean... Well, you know what I mean.

"You're only human Amber."

"Cheeky thing. There's a reason I've called you. Can you deliver some goodies to a very good friend of mine?"

"What and when?"

"Half an ounce of charles please to Knightsbridge. Sorry about the short notice, but I only got the call five minutes ago. One of my girlfriends is having a party. She said we're more than welcome to go, if you like."

"I've got too much going on today, to be honest, Amber, but I could meet her in Victoria an hour from now for the other thing. Buzz her back and let me know if she still wants it, also what she'll be driving."

I hate hanging around for a call when time is tight. I never know what to do with myself while I'm waiting. Pacing up and down works for a minute or two, then I start to get bored, then angry because I can't plan fuck all until I know the apple.

"Yeah, she's cool with meeting you in Victoria. Nicola will be driving a yellow Beetle. I told her to look out for a white Triumph Stag. Where exactly in Victoria shall I tell her to be?"

"Tell her to park up by the McDonald's on Victoria Street in an hour. When I see her, I'll give her a toot or flash my lights, so she can follow me round the corner; job done."

How is it that whenever I've got some kind of deadline, other shit mounts on top to slow things down? As soon as I open my car door to set off, Pete pulls up in a black taxi.

"Span man, any chance I can take the Stag for a couple of hours?"

"Nope, sorry mate, can't do it. Got a little job to do. What do you need it for anyway? And since we're chatting, you do know you're sitting in a taxi, don't ya?"

"Bruv, we need backup amps for the rave. Dubs is on site as we speak tweaking the equipment, and we only now just realised we'd be fucked if the amp blew without a backup. Look what happened at my last house party, shortest party in the world, man."

"Yeah, but you're still sitting in a taxi, ya cunt."

"Yeah, I know, but I might have to go all over London until I find the right gear. A Sherbet will fuckin' cane me, bruv. Terry Taxi ain't answering his phone; I would've been sorted otherwise."

"And what about that old Land Rover of yours?"

"Flat battery, innit."

"Fuckin' hell, Pete… OK, ask that cabbie if he'll be sweet taking me to Victoria. Tell him I'm going to look at a yellow beetle I might be buying."

"You're buying a yellow beetle?"

"Of course not. Just ask him will ya?"

I give Pete the keys to the Stag and jump into the taxi. Parked on Victoria Street, I keep one eye on the meter and the other for any passing yellow Beetles. Amber's phone isn't responding, or it's switched off, which definitely ain't doing my stress levels any good. In other words, this Nicola sort I'm meant to meet has no idea of the slight change of plan, plus I have no way of contacting her. I waste forty-five minutes of my life sitting in a cab talking to a stranger about things that don't interest me then call it a day and head back home. No joy getting through to Pete either, his phone is off for some reason, so fuck knows if he's managed to get the stuff we need for the rave.

Gotta say it feels amazing being back on my sofa. The half-smoked joint resting in the ashtray is teasing to be blazed. It's also a pretty rare thing; when was the last time you was round someone's place who puffs and saw a half-smoked joint sitting in the ashtray?

There's a buzz on the intercom, and a breathless Pete is on his way up to see me.

"Bruv, listen to this! You know when I left you earlier? I got a tug from the Old Bill as I was pulling out of the estate. They were all over your car like chimps at a safari park, man. Proper thorough going over, like they were on some kind of mission."

"For fuck's sake, I had half a wizard of lemon on me when I jumped in that taxi. That was the little job I was telling you I had to do. Did they search ya?"

"Bruv, I dropped my strides and underpants on the spot. One horrible cunt wanted to nick me for getting my dick out in public, but I turned on some drama screaming harassment that drew a nice little crowd that took the dairy off it. They found nish on me, or in the car, so they fucked off, just like that."

Being caught with half ounce of cocaine would have done me no favours at all just before the weekender kicks off, which reminds me it's tomorrow. We head off to the site for some last-minute checks then check again. All is sweet other than a shitload of missed calls on my outstanding communication device which decided to switch itself off. Twelve missed calls, three of those were from Dubs, a couple from Amber and one from Mirek; the others don't matter.

"Dubs, me fuckin' phone went all silent on me, it's got a mind of its own. What's up?"

"Have you not heard? Blud, you should phone Mirek lively and call that thing off. There's been a mad fire at that place. It's wall-to-wall with Old Bill."

"What, the place where Ratboy has got those girls?"

"More like the place where Ratboy used to have those girls. Now it's a smouldering shell, dread. Fuck all left of it."

"Anybody dead? How'd it happen?"

"I ain't gotta clue, blud. You can't get near the place at the moment. The road's blocked off. Probably started by one of them idiots washing up some coke or piping rocks. They're all fuckin' crackheads up there, I'm telling ya."

I try Mirek again, but still no joy. Checking what time the missed call was tells me six hours ago. He's probably on his way over, switched his phone off and is sitting on a plane about to have his time well and truly wasted. I'll see him sweet for his troubles though, plus it'll be good to have him and his crew at our little rave enjoying themselves. With a bit of luck, they'll party hard enough to feel like they haven't had a wasted journey after all.

Driving over to Amber's place, I can't stop thinking whether those girls died in that fire. I make a few calls and nobody knows a thing. Then, as I pull up outside Amber's place, I get the call from Mirek.

"Hello Spaniard, my friend, it's Mirek."

"Mirek. Fucking hell, brother, where are ya?"

"I'm in Poland."

"Thank fuck for that. Stay there, it's all gone tits up over here, mate. That target has been burnt down. There's police everywhere you look."

"Yes, sorry about that. Bloody Russians always want the fun."

"Russians? You've lost me there, Mirek."

"One of the girls in the house was Russian, she is eighteen years old. My friend Vlad is also Russian, and took it very personally that a Russian was being held. He went back to the house, after we took the girls, to make sure the people understand not to fuck with any Russians again, or next time they will be in the house tied to chairs as the building burns."

"Fuckin' nicely done. There's me stressing away thinking you was on your way over to do the job, and you've already done it. That's quite epic, even for you Mirek. When the fuck did you do it, anyway?"

"Some hours ago, my friend, but I had to wait to come back to Poland to call you. Even though I know your phone is secure, I just feel better speaking from a phone I know for sure is secure. No offence, you understand."

"No, that's cool, Mirek. So where's your pal Vlad now then?"

"He's in France."

"France? What's he doing in France?"

"He loves escargots."

"Fair enough. And the girls?"

"The girls were left with Marika in the minibus. Not your minibus, we took another one. Marika followed the plan we spoke about; the girls are safe, Spaniard. There were six in total."

"You took your own minibus?"

"Yes, from the airport car park."

"You stole some poor cunt's minibus? So where's the other one?"

"We left the girls in the stolen bus, and Marika took the car you arranged back to her house. No time to call for a taxi."

"Mate, I'm sweet with her taking the car, don't worry about that, it was a rental anyway. They'll pick it up from wherever she leaves it. I'm just still taking it all in, and I'm rather impressed."

"It was a fun time."

"I can believe it. And nobody got hurt?"

"There was no resistance, no noise. We entered very quietly. I put a pistol to the man's head, and told him I was taking the girls. Vlad said to me after, in the bus, he will be back in a minute. That is when the fire happened."

"So he sets the place ablaze, then fancies some snails and fucks off to France?"

"Yes. He said 'I go to France for escargots' and goodbye."

"Is he a bit unhinged, Mirek?"

"Very much so."

"Superb. So how come you went back home? I thought you was coming to the rave tomorrow."

"Another time, amigo. I have things to do in Poland."

"You're such a sly old dog, Mirek. See what I mean about you?"

"What do you mean?"

"You knew I was planning to get you back for the vodka that time. That's why you're dodging the rave. Come on, admit it."

"You're funny, Spaniard, but maybe another time. Karolina and Hektor say hello to you. Oh, before I go, can you give the rest of the cash to Marika? She will bring it to me here in Poland next month."

"No problem. I'll get Terry Taxi to drop it round to her tomorrow. What's Marika's number? I'll bell her to arrange it."

Chapter 21

I hear the sound of music, and I don't mean Julie Andrews. What the fuck is going on? Sounds like a carnival on my doorstep. There's a huge convoy of cars gathering below, each trying to out-stereo the other. Imagine twenty or thirty cars all with different music blasting at the same time. Surely they can't all be waiting to follow me to party land? That's a dead cert for getting a tug from Old Bill. Gonna have to be sly and swerve all these hot cookies. None of them are people I really know, so slipping out the back way unnoticed should be easy.

Feeling a bit like a ninja, and with *The Pink Panther* tune in my head, I'm all set to jet. I leave my block the back way and quickly look for shadows to blend into all the way to my car. I've not been spotted, so I'm feeling rather clever, as I slip behind the wheel and head off to the rave. A short trip to Kent later, I park up in Pete's garage and make my way on foot across the lower field up into the main one where it's all happening. From the three hours since the music started, it's already filling up nicely with sweaty, happy faces everywhere I look. I'll be dropping a pill or two later on no doubt, but first I wanna feel comfortable with my surroundings. I'm using Tommy the Cannon as my security that so far has proved to be money well spent. He's got eight other giants together to form a menacing sight just in case of trouble, and has even agreed to loan me his size fourteen Dr Martens if I really want it, and you know what that's for.

People are nicely parking where they're meant to park and going where they're meant to go. It all looks and more importantly, feels like a proper rave, so I'm smiling. My little posse of friends are plotted up by the DJ area which has been roped off making a nice mini haven. Pete tells me he's already been putting cash in the sunken bins and that maybe I should give Dutch a bell to keep it going, which was a good call.

The arrival of my courier puts our stock back up ready for second helpings. Through the crowd, I notice Amber waving at me, with a jaw that looks like it got here a few hours before she did.

"Wow, these pills are amazing, sweetie. Are they from Dutch? Have you done one yet? We should go and make love," is the mangled response I get from a simple: "Hello Amber, fancy meeting you here."

"You should try and find out who Dutch gets them from. Cut out the middleman. I'll go in on anything, partner, as long as the pills are the same as these."

"Slow down Amber. Dutch is a good man. No need to be greedy. We'll do fine doing things this way. Think about the story of the hare and the tortoise."

"Sorry, I've been told before I'm too ambitious. Have you thought about something kinky yet? God, I feel so horny. We could go to Pete's house for a quickie. Nobody would know, and we'd be back in no time. Come on, let's go."

"Amber I've just got here, sweetheart, I need to be on my toes. We've got all night and tomorrow to go, so let's just enjoy the rave and talk about bumping hips later shall we?"

"That's easy for you to say, you haven't taken one of these pills yet. I've never had them this good before."

"Well you have, they're the same pills as what we done at your place."

"I feel so amazing. Look at all my friends hugging. They're so loved-up, totally blown away by the quality. You need to try these, Spaniard."

"I tried them at yours, don't you remember? I already know they're blinding."

"Take one, sweetie, please. Come join us."

"Later Amber, honestly. I'll come look for ya, I promise."

I leave Amber to get back to her group and find Dubs chatting to the DJ.

"Dread, have I got news for you. Guess who I bumped into clucking in Brixton Market?"

"Go on."

"Trappy."

"Trappy?"

"Yes blud, slosher Trappy, Pippa's mate. She told me Pippa's locked down proper, gone clean. She met some geezer who turned her around big time. She's been hitting the gym too, apparently. Looks really well."

"Really? What a cunt. I'm happy for her, mate, but my selfish side is reminding me she was the key to getting Ratboy out to Africa. Talk about throw a spanner in the works."

"So what's plan B, dread?"

"Ain't got one."

"C?"

"Nope."

"Why don't you just go old-school and pay some cunt to shoot him?"

"Too risky, Dubs. I could always do what he had done to me and have him tied up and stabbed in the fuckin' head a couple of times and left to bleed out."

"Sounds reasonable."

"Yeah, but he needs to go in an untraceable, epic way. The crocodile thing would definitely be epic however you look at it; plus no trace of a body which is always gonna be a bonus. Do you believe Trappy though, Dubs? You know she talks a lot of shit, mate."

"God knows, she was all over the place when I saw her. I got her number, if that's any good. Maybe she can lead you to Pippa."

As far as first-time raves go, we've done really well up to this point. Better than I thought, and still another day and night to go. The DJs have access to free Es over the weekend to keep them on top of their game, pulling them through to Sunday. They've been dropping them like Smarties and playing on top form so far; let's all hope that continues and doesn't end up a disaster. The first DJ up has breezed through a three-hour set and looks like he could go another three. Pete tells me it's because he's on a pill every hour, it's how he likes to pace himself; no problems there then.

"Excuse me, do you know there's goats running about loose?" says a mashed up girl, with pupils the size of saucers.

"Goats?" I ask.

"Oh, fuck man, my goats have got out." You know that has to be Pete that said that, and I need to know more, so I ask the girl.

"Where did you see the goats?"

"Where everybody's dancing; over there in the field."

"Cheers love. We'll sort it out."

Then with impeccable timing, as me, Dubs and Pete are about to set off goat hunting on the dance floor, three chickens run past us and off into the heaving mass of gyrating sweat monsters.

"Pete, did I just see three chickens run past us and into that crowd of people? Please tell me there's a KFC around the corner, and they're not your chickens, mate. Tell me they're escapees that were on death row from the Colonel Sanders State Penitentiary, because I ain't quite got me head around the raving goats on the dance floor thing yet."

"I know what's happened, bruv, it's all my fault." As if it's anybody else's. "I fed them earlier and got a bit stoned, innit. Forgot to lock up their enclosure... Fuck man."

"Pete, I've gotta ask ya, but what the fuck have you got chickens and goats for anyway?"

"The goats eat the grass around the house so I don't have to cut it."

"OK, yeah I can see that, that's not a bad move. And the chickens?"

"For eggs obviously, but they're also my pets. You two think chickens are only for eating, you don't know chickens like I do, bruv. Trust me, they're smart."

"Well if you want my opinion, I'd say those Chanteclers that ran past us look a bit fat, Pete. Should be well easy to catch. Lucky they weren't Lakenvelder chickens, those fuckers can shift, dread."

It doesn't matter how long I've known Dubs, he never ceases to amaze me. As for Pete, I'm beginning to think I really know nothing about him at all. I mean, a good friend of yours keeps things like goats and chickens and you don't know about it? Surely you'd know if your pal had these things, wouldn't ya? Talk about a dark horse. Don't tell me, I bet he's got one of those as well.

"So, what other animals you got that you ain't told us about then, Pete?"

"That's it, Span... Oh, there should be a couple of cows

down in the other field, but I ain't seen them for ages. Other than that no more animals."

"What are you talking about? Are you telling me you've got a couple of cows that you don't know whether they are dead or not? How's that even possible, mate?"

"Span man, I know it sounds cruel, but trust me, them cows have it sweet."

"Had it sweet you mean."

"The fields they're in has the best grass in Kent, plus they have their own private stream. What more could they want?"

"Maybe someone to check if they're still breathing comes to mind. When was the last time you saw them?"

"About eight months ago man, relax. An old fella comes and milks them every now and then. If there was anything wrong with the cows he would have told me by now, innit."

"An old fella?"

"Yeah, he's in his nineties, bruv."

"You are joking?"

"No. Why?"

Do you know what's turned out to be so funny about the goats and chicken thing? People are so loved-up and happy buzzing away, that they honestly want us to leave them alone to mingle. There's a couple hugging and talking to one of the goats like long-lost friends reunited. Another girl is sitting against a tree, cross-legged, cuddling a chicken against her cheek. The animals seem cool and relaxed with the attention, so Pete decides to leave them to rave on. Something I never expected is the amount of people plotted in the surrounding woods. Some are chillin', most are dancing, but all are having a brilliant time. There's a slight mist in the air, perfect for our lasers as they swoop in time to the music, over a sea of bouncing heads.

I keep getting a reminder flash up in my mind regarding Pippa. I need to find out for sure the score with her. Trappy is called Trappy because she has a problem with constant flapping of the gums; never fuckin' stops talking. Most of what she says is total bollocks purely because she's a crackhead. She's the kind of person that'll make something up if she has nothing genuine to talk about. I'm strongly thinking Trappy was more than likely convinced Dubs needed Pippa for some work, so told him a load of bullshit to sway him into choosing her instead. I decide to drop a pill and enjoy the rest of the night, I mean morning, as it's now 2 a.m.

"Span have you seen Sid?" asks Pete.

"Who, Slippery Sid?"

"Yeah, he's looking for ya. Asking if you can still get rid of jewellery. He said he's got some pukka, antique stuff for you to look at."

"Where is he?"

"Over by the khazi last time I saw him. He looked full-on mangled, bruv, proper gruesome."

Sid is gruesome from any angle, that's easy for any cunt to see, but he sells some decent stuff on the cheap. I rarely turn down any antique tomfoolery, regardless where it came from, as it's always gonna be worth a fair bit of coin. Sid comes from a family of alcoholics. His dad fucked off when he was a baby, leaving him with a drunken slut of a mother that would dump him off to anybody willing enough to babysit for a couple of cans of Tennent's Super, while she went in search of stray cock. He ain't the sort of bod I normally like to do business with, purely because he's one creepy fucker that freaks me the hell out. There's a story behind it all though. He was trapped in a nasty fire a few years ago that nearly killed him. In actual fact he died on the operating table twice, but they managed to jump-start him. He's seventy per cent crispy all over, three quarters of his face is one big, shiny red mottled scar, framing a tiny, melted, all white eye. Or should I say was an eye. The other eye is sweet as, but either way you look at it, he's a mad-looking character that speaks with an even madder lisp. If a snake could speak I'd imagine it would sound like Sid. Never ever seen him without his trademark, black, full-length leather coat and black hoodie up whatever the weather. He'll walk around like that in the summer, hot as fuck and still have the hood up. He appears now and again out of the blue with a pretty sweet bargain then vanishes like a phantom in the night. I find him loitering by the Portaloos.

"Hello Sid, long time no see. How ya doing, fella?"

"Spaniard, nice rave, man. Nice... Nice... Nice."

When Sid talks to you, you can only guess where he's looking, as he always finds a shadow to stand in. He's a permanent silhouette, and it always feels like he's staring into your soul. Sid goes on to dig out one piece of jewellery after another from his bottomless pocket to show me. Problem is, I'm now starting to come up on that pill and really don't wanna be standing here talking to Sid while I can see Amber and all her pretty friends at the end of the rainbow, dancing about all sexy in a mass of happy colours.

"Sid, mate, I'm not being funny, but I'm just starting to come up on a pill I dropped twenty minutes ago. Can we do this later?"

"Dunno, man, I might be gone soon. Things to do, you know? There's always things to do, Spaniard."

"As it happens, rewind what I just said. That ain't a bad-looking ring there."

"Which one?"

"That one... Show us it a second."

"That's a real diamond, Spaniard."

"Is it bollocks... Have a look at that sparkle... Do you see that? A diamond don't sparkle like that Sid, mate. That's a zirconia all day long, but anyway I'm not interested in the stone, I'd sling that and mount a ruby in it for me girlfriend."

Of course it's a diamond, and a fat one too; I'd say at least a carat. But Sid can only see out of one eye, plus it's dark and he's on drugs; I'd be a fool not to take advantage and so would you. He'll only end up getting double wasted here and lose it somewhere. One thing you need to know about Sid, is when he gets messed up he becomes one of those dribbling casualties that stumbles around bumping into every cunt in his path. Not aggressive by any stretch, just a fuckin' nuisance that quickly outstays his welcome.

"Looks like a diamond to me, Spaniard."

"You're havin' a laugh, Sid. Just taste that... It's glass, mate."

Yeah, I really did just dab my tongue on it, and now Sid thinks I'm on another level of expertise.

"If that was a diamond, Sid, it would feel warm on your tongue. A diamond adjusts to the temperature of the person wearing it. Do you follow?"

I've got no idea where that came from, but Sid looks confused.

"But I wasn't wearing it."

"But it was on your person Sid, mate. You had it in your sky, which is pretty much wearing it."

I actually fucking amaze myself sometimes. All that shit I just said; completely on the fly. One thing I forgot to mention to ya is how much this geezer stinks. He's chucking up a strong fusion of BO and piss that's burning my nostrils and making my eyes water.

"So what are you saying, Spaniard? You wanna give me silly money for it? Is that what you're saying?"

"Mate, I don't take the piss, everybody knows that, including you. I've given you top dollar in the past for your goods, am I right?"

"Still looks like a diamond to me though."

"Pop the stone out then ya cunt. Honestly, it's the mount I want. Give it here Sid, I'll pop it out with me car key and you can keep the Jekyll stone."

"So you just want the gold?"

"Exactly... Now what do you wanna do, Sid? I'm rushing off me nut here, geezer."

"Give me seventy quid and you can take it as it is?"

"Sid, I swear on my life this is all I've got on me, forty quid and three pills. These go for £15 each, so you've had a touch."

"Are they any good?"

"Any good? Look at the state of me; I'm bang in trouble, mate. They're fuckin' blinding."

Shit, I shouldn't have said that last bit, the poor soul's blind in one eye.

"OK, £40 and three pills."

"You know you've had a result Sid, you crafty fucker, and trust me you're gonna love them bits, but I need to fuck off over there lively, me bird's waiting for me. Nice doing business with ya."

The ten second walk to Amber and her group is like moving from winter to spring. I can feel Sid's stare burning into the back of my head all the way as I join her, probably thinking I was a cunt not to invite him over. I'm gonna keep the ring under me hat until the right time, and that includes not telling Dubs or Pete. Maybe I can give it to Amber in the Dam? But is it too serious a gift to give her at this point? I dunno, I've never given a girl a ring before, let alone one with a fuck off diamond lodged in it. What's she gonna think? I don't want her getting the idea I've gone all super serious on her. I just wanna give her something nice to let her know that I think about her once in a while.

"Gosh, sweetie, that man you was talking to looks like he's melting. Where do you know him from? He's staring at us. How creepy."

"Don't worry about Sid, he's harmless. The bod was in a fire and got badly charred. I'm proper buzzing now though, so forget about him. What was that you was saying earlier on about popping into Pete's house?"

Chapter 22

"Blud, the DJ is asking if you want any requests."

"Yeah mate, 'Everything starts with an E' and 'Break 4 Love' if he's got it."

"Cool, and you Pete?"

"'Pacific State' by 808 State, bruv... and also 'Tears'."

"Frankie Knuckles?"

"Yeah man."

"How are you feeling Pete?" I ask.

"Non-stop rushing, bruv. I don't even know how many bits I've dropped... How about you?"

"Same as, feeling nicely mashed though. I just wanna plot here and listen to the music."

"Me too... This DJ is alright, bruv. Maybe he'll let me spin some tunes later."

"Behave Pete."

"What...? I know my music, Span, and I can mix. I've been thinking of making some music for a while now. I reckon I could proper smash it."

"Is that before or after your medicinal cannabis oil business?"

"Oh, I forgot all about that... But fuck it; I'll do both, innit. I'm a musician for real, you know?"

"So am I, Pete."

"Really? I don't believe ya. So what instrument can you play?"

"The mighty recorder, my friend, and my version of 'Greensleeves' will blow your fuckin' eyebrows off it's that strong."

"Man, you're talking about way back in school days. That ain't a proper instrument anyway, bruv."

"That's bollocks, Pete, of course it is. If you can make music with it, it's a fuckin' instrument, and so what if it was at primary school, it still counts. Anyway, what can you play then?"

"I can play any instrument, innit."

"Yeah alright, mate. I bet you can't play the recorder."

"Bruv, I can even play the spoons, my old man showed me how to do it."

"Not a lot of call for that on the rave scene is there, Pete?"

Dubs comes back to find Pete missing.

"Where's Pete, dread?"

"Mate, you are not gonna believe this. He's gone back to the house to get a couple of spoons."

"Spoons?"

"He's lost the plot, Dubs. I can't even remember what we were talking about... Instruments I think. The next thing he says, 'I'll show ya how sick I can play the spoons' and fucks off to get them. Pete's gonna be rattling them cunts up and down his legs until tomorrow if we don't dodge him. It's gotta be done, Dubs, I'm hiding in the bushes."

"Good idea, blud, I'm with ya. Take one of those torches under your seat. I've got mine here already. Signal if you see him."

"Two flashes means he's back spoons in hand, one means he's gone to probably look for us... Sweet Dubs?"

185

"Sweet."

I've got one leg inside the bush when Amber turns up, potentially ballsing up my escape from Pete and the musical spoons from hell. My first thought is to chin her, but then I'm not like that, so I spin her around, place my hand over her mouth and drag her backwards into the bushes. Then through the darkness came Pete, spoons in hand, smiling like the crazed lunatic he is. I hold Amber close, still holding her mouth tightly. The hot breath from her nose warms my chilled hand, as I quietly explain the apple. I gently release her like a trapped butterfly and she instantly understands, slowly nodding her head in agreement while slinking further back into the shadows. There's two quick flashes from the bushes opposite that are quickly answered with two from me. This is tense stuff. Pete's not sure if he caught a glimpse of light from Dubs's bush. He stands there motionless, stainless steel cucharas chinking in the moonlight. There's a small log to his right that makes me nervous. If he spots it, and us, there's a strong possibility he'll put a foot up and really go to town with them spoons, and there'll be no stopping him if that happens. A snap from a twig Amber just stepped on means certain capture if it wasn't for Silver Bullet and 'Bring forth the Guillotine' played at volume setting eleven. Pete heads back off towards the house kinda dancing, but completely out of step with the beat. A single flash of light is fired from the opposite bush confirming the coast is clear; we made it, all of us. Pete comes back empty-handed. Why he bothered to walk all the way back to the house just to leave the spoons is beyond me, but that's Pete for ya. He finds me, Amber and Dubs sitting back by the DJ area.

"Oh, there you are. Let me just go back and get the spoons, bruv, wait there."

Pete turns to go back to the house.

"Pete, Amber's gonna try and set you up with one of her friends... Aren't you Amber?"

Well what else could I do? Get back in the bushes? I'm buzzing off me nut.

"Really, bruv? Really, Amber?"

And that's why I said it, the spoons are instantly forgotten.

"Er... Er... Yes Peter, I'll try."

"Told ya, mate. Take a seat and skin up, I'm sure it's your turn anyway."

White lies are passable, especially in this case, because they're little, soft fibs designed to not hurt people's feelings. When the time was right, I told Pete that he was bang out of order for making us hide in the bushes because of the spoon thing, which he found hilarious. A bit too hilarious for my liking, and slightly annoying really as I've got a strong feeling Pete ain't done with wanting to show me he can play those bloody spoons.

I can't say for sure how many tabs I've dropped so far, but the number six is familiar, or is it nine?

"What day is it, blud?"

"Sunday night, Dubs."

"What happened to Saturday?"

"Yeah, I know it's gone quick, mate. What do you think of those bits?"

"Dread, I'm proper missing. I'm having trouble keeping my eyelids open."

"What about you Amber...? Oi, Amber, are you asleep?"

"Sorry... What? No, I was just resting my eyes."

"Bruv, it's Monday morning not Sunday night."

"What's he going on about Dubs?"

"I've got no idea, blud."

"You said to Dubs it was Sunday night. It's Monday morning, innit."

"What's that up there Pete?"

"Where are you pointing?"

"Where does it look like?"

"The sky?"

"Exactly, and it's dark, so it's Sunday night."

"What time is it?"

"Fuck knows. I can't focus on me watch. Why?"

"It's just dawned on me... I forgot to let Wilson out. Man, it's gonna be shit city when we get back."

"Oh, for fuck's sake Pete, sort it out. We can't all pile back to yours in this state if there's gonna be shit everywhere."

"Yeah, Pete, fix up, man. What's wrong with you?"

"Shall I go and have a look, bruv?"

"Yes, have a fuckin' look, mate, please."

"What's happened, sweetie?"

"Nothing Amber, you go back to sleep."

"Span man, I'm too fucked to be picking up shit, man."

"You don't even know if he's done any yet, and if he has whose fault is it?"

"OK, OK, I'm going, but this is bollocks."

Ten minutes later.

"Sweet as, Wilson was fast asleep, innit. What a touch."

"I hope you let him out though Pete."

"Fuck, I forgot. I'll do it later, man."

"Mate, don't start all that bollocks. Let the poor cunt out to lay a cable, then you ain't gotta worry anymore about it. Am I right Dubs?"

"Absolutely, blud. Pete you're on shit duty, Rasta... Sort it out, ya bumbaclart."

Shit duty out of the way, we stand proud of our achievement. Hundreds of people having a great time makes it all worthwhile, and I'm not talking about the money we've made. Pete's right about what he said back in Dahab, about Thatcher doing her best to suppress your enjoyment. Not here though. I know I'm pilled up and might sound like I'm talking bollocks, but this is a beautiful thing right here; nobody miserable and everyone smiling. The DJ is on another level, not sure how he's mixing, as his hands seem permanently in the air. The surrounding forest looks manic through strobe lights, freeze-framing nature and madness in perfect harmony. People are skinning up everywhere, just how it should be. How can you call a plant illegal? So are you telling me God's creation is wrong? Fuck off.

As Monday morning got brighter, we all got dimmer, and coming down off these pills ain't so bad at all. I just feel kinda tired and dirty, but really sweaty. Nothing a nice shower and kip can't handle. Quite a few people have already left. Hardcore nine to fivers probably, and fair play to them. The last pasty, dark-eyed faces of over-raved ravers with their trembling jaws shuffle their way to wherever they're going until completely gone, and that includes us, crawling into Pete's house and each claiming one of his eight sofas to crash on. Amber has no idea what's in store for her, and I'm not sure if I should tell her, but out of all the Chesterfields she could choose from, Amber's on Wilson's. Now this should be interesting.

Chapter 23

We've not been anywhere near our hidden earnings just yet. Police decided to turn up at Pete's place Tuesday morning looking for Ecstasy tablets, which they never found because we ate them all over the weekend. It wouldn't surprise me if some dozy, mashed up raver got pulled over on the way home and told the police exactly what they wanted to hear; the pills came from our rave. None of us have a clue how many we sold, but according to Dutch, we done pretty good that's for sure. He reckons for the whole weekend we've made roughly around 300k profit, which ain't bad for two days' graft.

One thing we never thought about would be a clean-up team. I can't even begin to explain the fuckin' mess all over Pete's land. It's now Wednesday, and the cleaners we hired are still there. According to Tommy 'Shit Chest' the Cannon on security, the only bit of trouble over the two days was from Crispy Sid feeling up some bird lying on the grass who was out of it on Ecstasy. Sid sat next to her, making out he was skinning up, then decided it was a great idea to help himself to one of her tits, which didn't go down too well once she took a peek at his boat.

The constant police presence buzzing around the area is making things far too risky for me to do any sort of business these days, so for the meantime, I'm thinking of shooting over to Amsterdam for a bit until it cools down. Pete's jetting off to some place in Prague to get out the way, while Dubs is happy to stay round the manor, because he doesn't give a fuck. I spoke to Dutch earlier on, and he said something about joining Pete in Prague at some point to get full-on wasted, as he's a bit gutted for missing our rave.

Amber is still doing my nut in about that kinky thing she wants to do, and for the life of me, I still can't think of anything really filthy enough that I haven't already done. I've got this cracking opportunity to be absolutely fucking disgusting, and my mind is as blank as can be. I know what I'm into, I like spontaneous sex. It's the things I don't expect that do it for me, and the timing is crucial. As an example, a little while ago I went to view a flat in Kennington Lane I was thinking of buying. Rebecca the estate agent appeared in a navy blue, pencil skirt and crisp, white shirt buttoned all the way to the top looking very classy indeed. She's got her hair tied up and a pair of silver-framed, rectangular glasses perched halfway on her nose, that for some reason, came across as quite sexy. She'd peep over the top with these beautiful green, smokey eyes and a filthy smile that really got your attention, also in your pants. Fifteen minutes into showing me around, we're laughing and joking about like a pair of kids. Anyway, we're now sitting bang opposite each other in the front room. She crossed her legs and dangled a shoe while we chatted about the flat. Whenever I began to speak, she put the tip of a pen in her mouth and gently sucked it whilst looking straight into my eyes, which to be fair, was gonna raise more than an eyebrow. Rebecca then went on about the kitchen surface being genuine granite while taking me by the hand to show me.

As I ran my fingers across the surface of the stone, she put her hand on mine, as it came to a stop, and said, "Feel how cool this is compared to how hot my hand is. This is all real granite, nothing fake here."

She was standing a foot away from me, so that's well inside my bubble, plus she'd come to me not the other way around. I looked straight into her eyes, gently lifted her onto the shiny, granite surface, pulled her undercrackers to the side and plated her like a Walnut Whip. Other potential buyers were at the door a few minutes later to spoil the fun, but it was still fuckin' sweet all the same.

I've got a missed call from a foreign number I recognise, so I bell it.

"What's the score Mr Fox?"

"Hello, me old son. Listen mate, I've paid that fella to show me where you need to go. So now I know the spot, there's no rush your end."

"And what's the spot look like?"

"Secluded and full of crocodiles, just what you was after. You've also gotta watch your back for lions though."

"Sorry Fox, for a second I thought I heard you say lions, mate."

"Yeah, there could be lions. You're gonna be in lion country, it's not a tourist park, Span. You'll be just off the track but well hidden by greenery."

"Nice... but not exactly hidden from lions though. You see that's a slight problem, my friend. No cunt told me there'd be lions strolling about."

"Common sense really. You're gonna be in Africa, that's where lions like to knock about."

"For fuck's sake, we're gonna need shooters then."

"Don't worry about that, I've already sorted it. There'll be a sawn-off waiting for ya when you get here."

"What the fuck am I meant to do with a sawn-off? You are joking? You might as well just leave me a catapult, ya cunt."

"It's all I could get at short notice, Span. You'll just have to learn to reload double quick on the run."

"Reload double quick on the run? Are you listening to yourself? There won't be any reloading double quick on the run, Mr Fox, because I'll be lion food. Think about it for a second. Look at the range of a sawn-off, and now imagine a charging, fucking mental lion that's rather keen on eating your face and bollocks. I'll have two shots then I'm fucked. Oh, and not forgetting lions always hang about firm-handed so then what?"

"You could always use it as a club."

"I'm gonna club you when I next see ya, you tanned cunt. Who do you think I am? Conan the Barbarian? And don't think I can't hear ya laughing, Foxy, this ain't a laughing matter."

"I ain't laughing, mate, you're overthinking the situation. Listen, if you need something else I'm sure you'll find it when you get out here."

"I'm not even slightly overthinking the situation. You clearly have under-thought it though. You couldn't even get me a pistol? What sort of villain are you?"

"I'm not a villain, I'm the landlord of a pub."

"Don't change the subject."

"How is that changing the..."

"Do you know what, Foxy? Forget it, mate. I'll make a gun when I get there. What do you think of that?"

"You're gonna make..."

"A gun."

"And how are you gonna do that?"

"I dunno… Leaves and twigs probably."

"Leaves and twigs?"

"Leaves and twigs."

"And what are you gonna use for bullets?"

"Meerkats, you cunt."

"Span, mate, honestly if there's anything else I can get ya while I'm out here just say so."

"Well, as it happens, I'd like 200 kilo of catnip please."

As it turns out, the Fox, being a bit of an old prankster, was winding me up after all, and assured me the poacher said there's definitely no lions in that area because they'd all been shot. I've also been given a number to a clueless bod who can supply me with transport while I'm out there, plus a number to a clued-up bod in case it all goes boss-eyed. So far so good then, just need to find Pippa and hope she's got a South African pal who'll be up for the challenge.

I find Trappy where she always is, Brixton Market. I'm told Pippa is very sick, gonna die and the complete opposite of what she told Dubs. After a hell of a lot of bullshit on my part, I managed to get Pippa's number and arrange to meet up for a well overdue chat.

"Spaniard, long time, eh? How are you?"

"Always good Pip, or at least I try to be."

"That's good to hear. They must be so proud of you at your church."

"They sure are. I'm top boy in the choir."

"I can believe that. So what do I owe the pleasure, Mr Spaniard?"

"Well, it's pretty delicate Pip. I know I haven't seen ya

about for ages, but I'm gonna come straight out with it. I need a level-headed, South African girl for a bit of work. She needs to be cool with conning some guy, over a period of time, into thinking she's romantically interested in him, eventually becoming an item; temporarily of course. The whole point of the job is to lure some fella out to Africa where we then take over. It's easy money, Pip, for a working girl."

"Why does she need to be South African?"

"For the accent, it makes the whole thing more believable."

"Why do you need to get this guy to Africa?"

"That would be part of the job, Pip, no questions asked."

"How much does the job pay?"

"Five grand, plus a bonus if the girl gets him out there sooner."

"Sounds interesting. And a free holiday?"

"Not exactly a holiday, Pip. As soon as she gets him where we want him, she's gotta leave."

"Well that sounds easy… and I'm sure you knew I'd say yes, but for seven and no questions asked. As soon as I get him to Africa I'm gone."

"Well, you need to get him there and send him to sleep first, then you're gone."

"Send him to sleep?"

"Yeah, but don't worry, I'm not talking about singing him a lullaby. There'll be a table for two set up by a beautiful river, looking all cosy in the sunset, with candles and flowers. It's gonna look as though your brother has set it up for you two as a surprise, romantic dinner in the wild type of thing. There'll be a little campfire burning with a couple of steaks sizzling. All you need to do is slip him a sleeper when he goes for a piss. The second he's snoring is your cue to fuck off. That's also been taken care of, by the way, somebody will be standing by to take you back to the airport."

"And you can promise me I won't get any comebacks from this guy? I mean, what happens if I bump into him one day in London? He's going to flip out on me big time."

"That won't be happening, Pip. Look at it just as a job, once it's done it's done. It'll be a forgotten chapter in your life, but if you're not up for it I understand. Dubs bumped into Trappy and was told that you're out of the game, if you know what I mean?"

"I do Spaniard, and no, I'm still in the game, or even on the game, but let's just say I now make the rules and get to choose my clients, so it's my game, if that makes any difference."

"Well you're looking good, so it must be making a difference."

"No, that's from hard work, man. I stopped all that shit I was on before. No more class As for me, thank you, just smoke a little weed at the end of the day to relax. You may laugh, but I also go to the gym three times a week and watch what I eat. Who'd have thought, eh?"

"Fuckin' hell, that's a bit of a turn around."

"Had to do it, man, look how Trappy turned out. I was going the same way. No, I had to break away from those girls quick time."

"Fair play to ya. So about that job we were talking about. I'll give you six not seven. Trust me, Pip, I'll find someone else to do it for a grand."

Having Pippa now onside is a massive fuckin' touch. For a start, she looks on point and not like a brass anymore, which is handy. I'm not sure about the Cleopatra-style eyeliner, but her hair looks good in a black bob instead of the blonde, greasy mess that used to be tied back all the time. Snaring the Rat will be a piece of piss now. If I remember correctly,

Ratboy likes the old mod scene. Sling a Quadrophenia T-shirt on Pippa and it'll be game over. Her looks are way out of his league, as he's such an ugly cunt. Next thing that needs doing is to find out what day the Rat visits the pet shop, so Pippa can be there to get noticed. I've met girls in shops before so it does happen.

Ever since Pete got that tug from the Old Bill, my car has become a magnet for it. I got pulled twice the other day on my way to and from the dry-cleaner's. It's time to change motors. I need something that easily blends in with every other car on the road. Common sense directs me to the low-key, invisible cars that you never notice. On my way through the showroom to buy a Ford Escort, I spot a silver Jensen Interceptor having her body waxed, and that was the end of my common sense.

Chapter 24

It's been over a month now, and the police are still watching Pete's house. Not harassing or stomping all over his land, just quietly parked up in an unmarked car looking very obvious. Terry Taxi has been doing what he does best and that's gather juicy information. A trip to the pie mash shop later and I'm told by the man himself that Ratboy buys a kitten to treat his caiman every other Saturday. Pippa is let loose on the right day, but the Rat's too high to notice. The same thing happens the following time.

"Fuck this man! I'm gonna bump right into him next time. He'll notice me, or he's straight up fucking gay."

"Sounds like a good plan Pip. We'll be here all year otherwise. Do the eyelash thing on him, that's bound to work."

"What eyelash thing?"

"The thing where you girls make your eyelashes flutter like the wings of a butterfly."

"Spaniard, you little romantic softy, I never thought you of all people would be into poetry?"

"Don't fuck about, Pip, be serious for a minute."

"How can I be serious when somebody who looks like you mentions fluttering eyelashes and butterflies in the same sentence?"

"Furry muff."

"What?"

"Fair enough."

On the following Saturday, Pippa's eyelashes hit a home run. She made the move and got noticed. The way it happened was pretty slick. She first blazed a joint in the car and got nicely stoned, then went into the pet shop carrying a tiny, open bag of skunk. Pip then, stinking of weed, bumped into the Rat. The Rat, instantly smelling the skunk, burst out laughing, as he was also stoned. He told Pippa she reeked of weed, and they both ended up having quite a giggle in the shop about it. No contact details were exchanged, but the ice had been broken.

Pete tells me he's been checking on our buried cash every few days and reckons badgers or foxes have started taking an interest in the area, judging by the odd bit of digging and paw prints about, plus they've shit all over the place. Not bad going considering the cash has been buried for over a month now. God only knows how much we made in total, but I'm thinking it's a lot more than what Dutch says.

The police parked up can only really see the side of Pete's house, none of the land is really visible unless they're on foot. All the way around the house are massive pine trees plus a wall. They already came knocking once with the proper paperwork, didn't find what they were tipped off to find so fucked off, so now what do they want? Pete's remarkably relaxed about the whole thing. He said it's because they'll never find our money in a million years. I fuckin' love Pete's rare flashes of confidence sometimes. I make my way over to his place for a smoke sesh. Dubs is already there and both are seriously baked.

"What are you boys smoking? Fuckin' hell, look at the

state of your eyes."

"Blud, I got some of this murderous Jamaican sinsemilla. Look at Pete, the lightweight, he's finished already, dread."

"I'm sweet Dubs, just hush and pass me the joint, man, I'll show you the proper way to blaze," says a very pale Pete, who then has a moment that only Pete could have. "I've been thinking about you two in Africa."

"Oh yeah, what about us in Africa?" I ask.

"Well, you was saying that poacher fella says there's no lions around, but what if the crocs come onto the land after ya? Have you thought about that?"

"What are you going on about Pete?"

"Crocodiles on land are fuckin' quick, bruv, you can't underestimate them, trust me."

"If it's on land, I'll kick it up the bollocks and run. How's that?"

"You can't do that though, Span, that's one of the reasons the crocodile is an apex predator, innit. It's designed a way that nothing can get to its balls when it's kicking off. That's one of the reasons they're so low to the ground, I'm telling ya."

"Crocodiles don't have balls on the outside Pete, or there'd be wallets made out of their sacks, mate. And even though I'm dead against the killing of animals, unless you're gonna eat them, I for one would have to have one of those bad boys just so I could tell people my wallet is made out of a croc's nut sack."

All three of us give that one a nod of approval. Pete swears that back in the day, while he was at school, he read a book where Charles Darwin said crocodiles do have bollocks but can't remember the name of the book.

"I've just had a brilliant idea, bruv."

"Here we go. About what Pete?"

"The Ratboy thing, man. You could wait under the water like a camouflaged frogman, innit. You know it'd be sick Span, think about it. Remember the video? Crocs only attack things on the surface or at the water's edge. You'd be safe underwater breathing through a snorkel. When Ratboy is asleep, Dubs rolls him onto a blow-up lilo at the edge of the river, then you drag him out to the middle with string already attached. High five...! Don't leave me hanging, Span."

"Put your hand down Pete."

"Dubs?"

"Shut up."

"Just out of curiosity, did that same Charles Darwin book you was going on about earlier happen to mention anything about crocs never attacking underwater? What's with the shrugging? I thought you were an expert. You see what I mean Dubs? The things he says when he's caned. How would I get passed the feeding frenzy going off all around me then Pete? Because that's what's gonna happen the second I pull that string of yours and Ratboy enters the water. It'll be absolute carnage, and I ain't Johnny fuckin' Weissmuller, mate, there's no way I'm outswimming those cunts."

"Do a Bond, bruv, run across their backs, innit." He really did say that.

"I told ya Dubs, now you see what I've been saying about him. He's not all there."

"Pete slow down with that herb, man, you're talking shit again."

"Yeah, you say that Dubs, but what about when the hyenas come for you and Spaniard? Oh, you never thought about them did ya?"

"Hyenas hang about where lions hang about, Peter. If

there's no lions, there's gonna be no hyenas."

"OK, what about cheetahs then? Don't tell me there ain't no cheetahs, Span man."

"Cheetahs are wankers, it's a well-known fact. David Attenborough even said so on his programme, *Life on Earth*."

Dubs follows up with, "Yeah, I saw that episode, that's exactly what he said. It's a scientific fact."

"What, that cheetahs are wankers?"

"Yep... no claws, small teeth, can't have a row, wankers mate. Every other animal with a pair of bollocks about them will mug a cheetah from its kill. That's why they have to eat so lively. Not to be confused with a leopard though, that is a different beast altogether and will kick your arse," I say, feeling pretty damn smart with myself.

"OK, so what if there's leopards about then?"

"Fuckin' hell Pete, are we going through Noah's ark here or what?"

We laugh and joke until the early hours, then I make tracks for home. I glance into the rear-view mirror, and it seems I'm being followed. As I stop at the traffic lights, the car is right behind me, almost on my bumper. I give the mirror another sly look at the driver, who's looking right into my eyes. I don't recognise him. The passenger is ducking down, so all I can see is the top of a head. I have a feeling they don't wanna to do me any damage, as we're the only cars on the road, and they've had some superb moments to do so witness-free. The rain starts to fall making the car behind look like a stain on my mirror. I can make out it's a blue Volkswagen Golf, that's easy. My mind races through a list of friends that own one. At least two come to mind, and they're both girls. The good thing about roads in the leafy parts of Kent at 4.30 in the morning is the absolute lack of any other drivers. The road ahead of me appears to go off into oblivion. The lights are still red, as I gently slip the Interceptor into drive, keeping my foot on the brake, taking very good care not to relax it. As they change to green I slowly waft away, gaining a steady speed, then slam my right foot down. The VW no longer has a place in my mirror, so I continue my munchie-induced journey over to a burger van in Battersea, where I indulge in a burger that tastes like the Virgin Mary made it herself. The hot dog was also quite special, as were the chicken and chips.

The morning sun slices its way through my curtains to wake me with blinding beams of light. I'm feeling good, I'm feeling happy. I flick on the radio and do an amazing little shuffle to Kenny Lynch's 'Half the Day's Gone and We Haven't Earned a Penny'. Shower, dress, coffee and good to go. Pete just told me over the blower that the police ain't parked outside his house today. Thank fuck for that then, it's about time. He also thinks he might be just a little bit paranoid because a helicopter keeps hovering high over his land, but also admits he just watched *Goodfellas* the night before so that might have something to do with it.

Amber calls me to say she wants to suck my cock, and I'm already there.

The Fox calls me to say he's back in the UK and gives me the name and number of some African fella who's an expert at shooting crocs; he's another poacher with a name that sounds like a burp going backwards. If I need any tips on poaching crocs he's the man to speak to. When the moment is right, the Fox will be over there waiting to show us the spot. At this moment though, all he wants is his money, which he gets plus a bonus for keeping schtum about the whole thing.

As time goes by, Pippa and the Rat are getting closer. She told me they now have a puff in his car when they see each other at the pet store. I say pet store loosely, it's one of those huge garden centres that also doubles up as a pet store. They sell parrots, dogs, cats, fish, anything furry plus reptiles. In fact, I fancy popping down there and having a look around, as I've never actually been inside the place. Also... truth is... I want a little goldfish for my kitchen. I've already got a bowl, had it years, but never got round to getting a fish for it. Today is the day, I wanna change all that.

I hit the shop and head for the fish section, smiling like the happiest man on the planet.

"Can I help you, sir?"

"Yes love, where's the goldfish please?"

"Straight down on the right, past the aquatic plants."

"Cheers."

Seven minutes later.

"Excuse me, mate, where's the goldfish?"

"See where it says marine fish?"

"Yeah."

"Go past there and turn left, the freshwater section is downstairs."

"Gotcha."

Five minutes later.

"Can I help you?"

"Yeah, I'm looking for a goldfish, love."

"They're just over here."

I don't remember goldfish looking anything like these monstrosities; fuckin' *Elephant Man* fish.

"What the hell is that?"

"These beauties are called Oranda goldfish, and those there are Ryukin."

"Nope."

"You don't like them? I think they're amazing fish. We sell

a lot of them."

"Ain't you got any normal goldfish? The sort you win at the fair? I only want a little one."

"That's the common goldfish. We're all out of those, I'm afraid. Next Thursday we should be getting more in."

"Next Thursday? I'll try and pop back then."

"What about a Lionchu goldfish? There, behind you."

"What, that?"

"Yes."

"Fuck off, love."

I'm gutted. I set my heart on getting the easiest pet in the world, instead got nothing. I stop by the exotic section to check out the unusual stuff like stick insects and wacky, multicoloured, trippy frogs to cheer myself up, when all of a sudden I hear screaming and laughing, in that order, and really loud. Being a bit of a nosey cunt, I feel the need to investigate. A quick left later and I'm there, watching this absolute cock rocket, idiot member of staff, largin' it with the biggest spider I've ever set eyes on. I ain't even seen anything on TV as big as this fuckin' thing. I think I heard the bod call it a Goliath bird-eating spider. Whatever it is, it's as big as a dinner plate. There's a couple of young girls he's trying to impress by chasing them around the shop with it. Don't get me wrong, by the look of things, they were having quite a fun time. I've seen enough though, it's boring, so decide to leave, but not quite. That fella skids around the corner of the aisle to where I'm standing and bumps straight into me, causing that monstrous, eight-eyed, hairy bastard to scamper from him to me and take a plot right on my shoulder. I've said it before, plenty of times, spiders in your home are a good buzz, I leave them alone to do their thing, because they get rid of the bugs that annoy the hell out of me, but this is different. This you could put a fuckin' saddle on and ride into battle.

"Listen, mate, you wanna take this off me lively?"

"I'm trying to, sir, but she's a little skittish; they don't really like fast movements. It'll calm down in a minute. It's just a bit freaked out, that's all."

"So why were you running around with it then? You fuckin' sigh."

"Excuse me?"

"You heard. Listen, if you don't take this cunt off my shoulder sharpish, I'm gonna very calmly go out to my motor, get a car jack, and end this thing's life, and it'll be your fault."

I'm not being a party pooper, it's just when that spider's walking on me I can feel its footsteps, it's got weight behind it. Then it fancies marching further up my shoulder to screw me out with all eight eyes. I can see my own reflection eight fuckin' times, can you believe that? It's enough to give ya the horrors. When I move my head this thing lifts up its two front legs, that tells me it's got the hump and I'm close to getting a bite, right on me Gregory. If it wasn't for the fact I have on my best chinos I would've done a piledriver on the beast. I'm standing pretty close to the rabbits at this point so have access to handfuls of sawdust ready to throw in the spider's face if it comes back at me swinging punches. Dirty tactics, I know, but I don't play by the rules.

Chapter 25

Does this fuckin' alley ever end? Feels like I've been walking for ages with no end in sight. Then again, I can't see much further than ten yards in front of me what with the fog, and that's kinda different to the fog I know; white and wispy, almost like the clouds have dropped down. To my left is a wall that goes up and up, so far up it disappears into the mist. To my right is another wall that's the height of my shoulder. If I stretch my arms out to the sides I can almost touch both walls, so we're talking really narrow. I'll tell ya something else that's a little bit strange, considering there's no sun about all seems to be unusually bright, but grey. The only sounds I can hear are my own footsteps echoing back at me through the fog. I'm sure I've passed that old Coke can by the drain before, and more than once; this is fuckin' weird. As I continue forward through the white mist a voice up on my right takes me by surprise.

"Well, well, well, look who's here. If it isn't Spaniard himself."

"Who the fuck said that...? Where are ya?"

Up on the wall, strolling towards me is a cat, a tabby cat.

"Behold Spaniard, it is I, your conscience."

"Did you just say something to me?"

"Yes... I said I'm your conscience."

"No disrespect, and I'm not being funny, but why would a cat be my conscience when I'm a dog person? Doesn't make sense."

"You say that, and yet here I am."

"Which makes me think you're talking bollocks, mate."

"Mate is it? Well at least you see me as a friend then."

"Not really, I'm just being polite. I called you mate because I don't know your name."

"I have no name, but I've been toying with the idea of Zoltan the Great."

"I'm not calling you Zoltan the Great."

"Oh, go on."

"No."

"Why not?"

"Because I'm not calling you Zoltan the Great."

"But I'm your conscience. I should have a strong name, and you gotta admit Zoltan the Great is pretty fuckin' strong, Spaniard."

"If you're my conscience, then as far as I'm concerned you're Conscience the Cat."

"Conscience the Cat? Hmm, interesting, that does have a certain ring to it."

"And I'm still a dog person, so why are you following me?"

"Because I'm your co..."

"Yeah, you told me already, you're my conscience. Can we move on?"

"You really don't like cats do ya?"

"No, they fuckin' scratch and bite me whenever I've tried to be kind to the cunts. I don't trust them."

"That's a bit racist... Look Span, do you mind if I call you Span? The problem with you and cats is you're too heavy-handed with us; you touch cats the same way as you touch dogs. We don't like to be manhandled that way, do ya get me? We're sophisticated. We like to take care of our appearance. Have a guess at what I was doing before you showed up?"

"I have no idea."

"Cleaning myself. All us cats do it, all the time. That's why our fur is so much softer than a dog's."

"Well that's debatable."

"Oh fuck off, you are joking? Come and feel this bit of fur on my belly."

"Are you serious, cat?"

"Yeah, I'm fuckin' serious. Come on, right in the centre. Don't go too low or I'll bite ya, and don't go too high because I still might bite ya."

"Jump down here then."

"That's a bit of a problem. I can't get down off this wall. You'll have to reach up."

"What do you mean, you can't get down?"

"Don't ask me, that's how it's always been. I've tried to jump down a couple of times, but my feet don't let me. It's as though they have a mind of their own, or like they've had orders from up above to make sure I never get down off this wall. It's a mysterious thing, Spaniard, and even more reason to call me Zoltan the Great."

"That's not happening."

"Just give me one reason why not? And I won't ask you again."

"For fuck's sake. I'll pluck one reason from the air and that's it."

"Hit me with it, Span."

"You're too small... Zoltan the Great would suit a lion, or a tiger. Something big and powerful... Can you stop puffing up your chest? It's not making any difference, you're still small."

"Anyway, Span, moving along, and as I was saying, reach up here for that bit of fur I was telling you about. Put your hand up, I'll lie on my side; should be easier to reach now."

"What there?"

"Left a bit."

"There?"

"That's it. What do you reckon?"

"Fuckin' hell, as it happens that is super soft."

"I told ya didn't I? So what I'm trying to say is, yeah, have your rough and tumble with dogs, but be a bit gentle with us cats, and we'll get along as sweet as a nut."

"You might have a point there. Now, when I think about it, I do play a bit rough with cats. I thought you liked it though?"

"Yeah, we do when we're a fuckin' kitten, that's part of growing up, Span, but take it from me, when we're adults and fancy a wrestle, we'll come to you. Don't come to us when you fancy a wrestle, that just won't work."

"Fair enough, and quite well put, as it goes, cat. I'll take that on board."

"Cheers... So I suppose you wanna know where you are?"

"It would help."

"You, my friend, are somewhere in the back of your own head. When I said I was your conscience, I wasn't joking. You see that wall on your left?"

"Yeah."

"Well that runs all the way around your skull, through your mind and keeps going, there's no end to it. Doesn't make any sense at all, but then neither does your mind most of the time."

"And you're seriously my conscience?"

"Absolutely, although I do a bit of instinct work for you as well."

"Really?"

"Oh yeah... Remember that time when you was eleven and that weird cunt tried to drag you in that dark alley to do God knows what to ya?"

"Yeah."

"That voice in your head that told you to 'FUCKIN' RUN!' was me. That was my first true test, my first true job at instinct. Imagine if he would have got you in that alley, Spaniard. You was so small, so young, we both were, but as your conscience I had to get it right. When you looked down at the pavement and saw that shadow creeping up behind you, I was going fucking mental here on this wall praying that you picked up my vibes, and you did. You see all this mist here? It went the colour red, it's only ever happened twice. Like a red alert for a seriously deadly situation you're in. The other time was quite a few years later. I think you was about seventeen... No, hang about, you was eighteen."

"And where was I this time?"

"Clapham Junction, remember? The tower block?"

"Fuckin' hell, the fire."

"Yeah... You got the little boy out, and his mum, but got trapped inside didn't ya?"

"I thought I was gonna die that day."

"I know you did... Do you remember how all the windows exploded at the same time, and the fuckin' ceiling collapsing?"

"Of course I do, like it was yesterday. I can still smell it."

"When you was standing in front of that burning door, while the whole place was crumbling around you, it was me that made you take that chance and go for the handle."

"Thanks, cat... seriously."

"You're very welcome, Span. I'll always do the best job I can for ya, believe me. I know you don't trust cats, but have I steered you right so far?"

"You have indeed, and you know what?"

"What?"

"Hang about, cat, there'll be an old, rusty coat hanger coming up in a second, should be lying right next to a squashed Coke can. What's with the constant déjà vu by the way? I keep passing the same things."

"Fuck knows."

"Here it is. Give me a second, let me just bend this about a bit."

"What are you doing?"

"Trust me, you're gonna love this. Now I know you can't get down, but I'm gonna need you to turn and face me, with your head bowed."

"What the...? That's a sword shape...? You've made a sword...? I'm gonna be knighted...? I'M GONNA BE FUCKIN' KNIGHTED!"

"Calm down will ya...? Where are you going now?"

"I can't fuckin' calm down. I need to go for a run. If only I had some curtains, I'd go mental."

The cat, feeling slightly excited with his news, takes off full speed along the wall and into the mist, and now he's back again, puffing and panting.

"OK, how'd ya want me...? Like this...? Or with my shoulders down more...? Maybe I should tilt my head slightly this way?"

"Cat, just bow your fuckin' head."

"OK, OK."

"Are you ready?"

"I'm ready."

"Cat, wilt thou, upon this day, pledge thy fealty to myself, and stand as a knight of my crown?"

"Absofuckinlutely!"

"Do it properly or I ain't doing it."

"I'm sorry, just a bit excited... Yes, Your Spaniardness."

"I, Spaniard, do hereby dub thee Zoltan the Great, may your courage and devotion become a shining example of how to make a dog person like cats... Why are you saluting? You don't need to salute."

"I'm sorry, are we all done?"

"Yeah, why?"

"Gotta run again, I'm buzzing, man. Wait there."

"Zoltan!"

Zoltan comes to a screeching halt.

"Did you just call me by any chance?"

"Yes."

"Say it again. Go on, please."

"Zoltan."

"Man, that sounds fuckin' awesome. You know what we gotta do now though, don't ya?"

"What's that?"

"Smoke a celebratory joint. I know you've got some Orange Bud on ya. Should be in your inside pocket. I can't skin up though, as I don't have opposable thumbs."

"So how will you hold the joint?"

"With my front paws. Like this."

"You look like you're praying."

"I am praying, for a joint, so skin up."

Me and Zoltan smoke and speak about the times he'd done me proud, always telling me to listen to my inner self. I do anyway.

"So how's Pete?"

"He's fine."

"Good, good."

"What?"

"Nothing. Just asking."

"Come on, what?"

"Well… You already know for sure I'm your conscience, yes?"

"Yes Zoltan."

"And I'd do anything for ya?"

"OK."

"I can't alter the future, or even see into it, but sometimes you just need to observe closer to home. You're doing too much at the same time to notice the little details, my friend."

"What do you mean?"

"You've got some good people around ya, Span, that genuinely care about your well-being. Dubs would kill for ya, or should I say, is gonna hopefully kill someone with ya. How is the planning for the Africa thing going, by the way?"

"Pretty good, pretty good."

"That's what I like to hear."

"So as my conscience, you're fine with what I wanna do to Ratboy then?"

"All day long."

"Well that's good to hear."

"Anyway, the thing is, Span, sometimes it's better to observe the bigger picture, to sit down and really have a go at fitting all the pieces together. Am I making any sense?"

"Not really, but go on."

"Use your ears, your nose, your eyes, amigo. They'll never let you down, and I'll never let you down. That's a fuckin' combination right there, am I right?"

"Yeah Zoltan… I guess you're right, mate."

"Because when you wake up, you're back on your own, and you probably won't remember any of this, but the only thing I can really get away with telling you is to think about when your problems first started; trace it back, Span. Search for the root and things will become clear."

"Hang on a second, did you say wake up?"

"Yeah, you obviously know you're dreaming right?"

"How the fuck am I gonna know if I'm dreaming, I'll be asleep."

A sudden shift in the mist has Zoltan frantically looking in every direction, then back at me.

"Oh shit...! Time's running out, Span. Quick, listen to me."

"What...? What's going on?"

"Always listen to your feelings, make sure your heart is aware of fake intentions. Sometimes deliberate short-sightedness will reveal people to show themselves as not who or what you think they are."

"What do you mean by that...? Zoltan...! Zoltan come back!"

"I'll always be here, Spaniard. Maybe we'll see each other again sometime... Good luck and Godspeed, my friend... Godspeed."

And with those parting words echoing around me, Zoltan the Great is gone, vanished into the mist, as it slowly begins to turn lighter and lighter; too bright now. It's dropping down all around me, now I can't see anything. I'm still in the alley. What's that noise? Sounds like metal scraping on the floor, coming from straight ahead of me. OK, I'm no detective, but I could swear I've heard a very similar sound when I've picked up a kitchen knife I've just dropped while cooking. Now what the fuck is that? The sound of a woman's shoes slowly clicking and clacking behind me, getting faster with every second step, louder and louder. The echo is deafening. She's now running at full speed towards me, but I can't see a thing through the mist...

Man, it looks like another glorious day. Do you know what? I've got a super king-size bed that's so fuckin' comfy it's bordering on ridiculous.

Chapter 26

I'm sure I had a dream last night, something about an alley. I can remember mist, thick white mist, but that's about it, or was there a lion? I hate it when you know you've had a dream but can't remember fuck all about it.

I'm off to Amsterdam with Amber next week, only for a few days. She said she'd like to sample all the different strains of weed the coffeeshops have to offer, but I'm not stupid, I know the real reason is she wants to see a brass munch on me gristle. I told her I'm still thinking of something naughty for her to do, and it'll probably come to me while we're over there. It's nuts how Amber is so proper, so posh, yet has this other saucy side. I'm actually feeling a bit excited about giving her that ring I got off Sid, but also genuinely worried she might think it's an engagement hint. Maybe a diamond ain't the way to go, a touch too soon and slightly over the top, but at the right moment it could work. I mean, it's only a gold band with a wicked diamond in it. Of course she won't think I'm looking at marriage, would she?

I order double pie, mash and liquor, and sit down opposite Terry Taxi.

"Hello Tel, how's you today?"

"I'm always fabulous, Span. How's life treating you? Beautiful car, by the way... Juicy?"

"Yeah, too juicy, mate. I get about 12 mpg if I'm lucky."

"I bet the ladies love it though."

"Wouldn't know, Tel, I'm locked down in that department."

"So I take it you're still with that posh bird then? The solicitor."

"Who Amber? Yeah, still seeing her. She's an estate agent in Mayfair. I see what you mean though; she does look a lot like a solicitor. We just have a laugh every now and then, nothing too heavy."

And yet I wanna give her diamond ring... What am I like?

"Did Pete tell you I'd be here?"

"He mentioned you might be here, and if you were, you may have something interesting to put to me. Pass the chilli vinegar please Tel. Pete says you're taking him to the airport when he shoots off to Prague."

"Yeah, I said I'd take him. You're not going then?"

"Nah, Terry mate, Amsterdam for me every time when it's cold. Sitting in a cosy, warm coffeeshop smoking a pukka bit of weed while it snows outside appeals to me somehow, plus Amber's never been, so it'll be her first time."

"It's Amber I wanted to chat to you about, to be honest, Span."

"What about her?"

"Well, I could be wrong, and I hope I am for your sake, but a few days ago I had a job taking some Arab bloke to Savile Row for a suit fitting. He was gonna be a while, so I parked up by West End Central Police Station to have a sandwich while I'm hanging about. I'm bang facing the nick and had a pretty good view of the people going in and out. Amber, or her doppelgänger, comes strolling out of the station carrying some folders, which she hands over to coppers in a marked car, has a laugh, then goes back in the nick. Ten minutes later, she comes back out and fucks off in the back of an unmarked car."

"Tel, that can't be Amber, mate."

"What makes you say that?"

"Well she takes too many drugs for a start. You should've seen her at our rave; shocking. Also, one of the reasons we're off to the Dam is for some diabolical deeds, and I'm talking double diabolical here, mate; all her idea not mine, Tel."

"That doesn't prove much really though, Span. If she's Old Bill and on to you, she'll do whatever she thinks necessary to win that prize. Have you ever picked up any weird vibes from her that made ya suspect foul play?"

"Not even slightly, Tel."

"Just be careful, mate, I'm seeing a lot of Old Bill around the manor these days. Pete was telling me he got a tug in your old Stag not too long ago, as he was pulling out of the estate. Imagine if it would've been you, and you was holding."

It was at this precise moment, I knew I'd fucked up.

"I don't believe it... Fuckin' hell, what a cunt I am."

"I won't argue with that."

"Talk about a piece of the puzzle falling into place."

"You alright, Span? You've gone a bit pale, mate."

"I can actually feel the blood draining away. Me mouth is as dry as a nun's crutch. I can't even swallow, I've got no spit."

"So are you gonna tell me, or what?"

"Let's have a sip of your tea, Tel."

"Help yourself."

"Cheers."

"I didn't mean all of it."

"That day when Pete got pulled, coming out of the estate,

that was meant for me."

"Go on."

"Amber asked me to do a little job for her, literally a couple of hours before, which only me and her knew about. I switched transport with Pete at the very last minute, he then gets a tug. How suspect is that?"

"Well there you go. You're gonna have to think very carefully about your next few moves here, Span me old son, could make a difference between sinking and swimming. Are you any good at chess?"

"No... But I can find a black, rubber brick at the bottom of a swimming pool dressed in me pyjamas."

"Let's just hope those skills come in handy for ya then."

"Why didn't you say something sooner, Tel? About seeing her outside the nick?"

"Because I didn't wanna worry ya, Span, plus I half thought she was an actual solicitor; she certainly looks the part. I couldn't remember for sure if somewhere down the line you told me she was one, but I saw her again yesterday coming out of the same nick and alarm bells started ringing."

I say my thanks to Terry and arrange a little conference with Dubs and Pete at his house.

"So gentlemen, the main things I've got rattling around my canister are: Amber constantly asking me to find out who Dutch gets his Ecstasy from; Amber also telling me more than once she's really ambitious; Pete getting a tug that day in my motor; and the Old Bill snooping about Pete's place, plus not forgetting what the caretaker said about the police wanting to get into that flat to do surveillance on me. I'm starting to think the money Amber gave me for the pills wasn't hers but the Old Bill's. Maybe they know the money is somewhere on

Pete's land but are standing by waiting for Amber to blow the whistle."

"Blud, you can't let her know you're on to her. You've gotta play this smooth, man. We seen her take them drugs, Span. She could be one of them renegade cops that'll do all sorts to get to the top," says a wise Dubs.

"Maybe you was the original target, bruv, then when Dutch came along she saw a bigger fish, innit. How much does she know, Span?"

"She knows we get pills from a bloke called Dutch, also that the money we got from selling them is buried somewhere. On the upside, she knows fuck all about the Ratboy project, so that's a bonus."

At this moment, Pete actually has a valid point.

"Or what if she's just a bent copper who's thinking about retiring early? Amber could be using Span to make that financially happen off the record, do ya get me?"

"Or she could just be waiting to get me banged up for a ten stretch, Pete. Listen, I think I may have the start of a plan brewing that could potentially solve our little problem, but first on the agenda is a phone call to Posh Mark. Surely he must know the score about Amber? It was him that gave me her number in the first place."

After three unsuccessful attempts at belling him, a match has well and truly been thrown into my gasoline pit of paranoia... Cheers Mark.

The plan I'm talking about is quite simple, but very dastardly; it has to be to work. Whoever Amber is, I need to get something on her that'll make her think twice about her intentions, whatever they may be. Now Amber, at this moment in time, has no idea she's been rumbled, and if I can keep it that way until we get to Amsterdam it'll be all over for her.

221

You see, what she's doing is unknowingly giving me a blank canvas to create my beautiful exit. I'll take full advantage of the kinky thing she wants me to choose for her to do. A photo of Amber doing the unspeakable could do me a rather big favour. If she is a copper, or even a bent copper, then the right picture at the right time could work wonders in a way that she'll be the one looking to find the exit for me. She's probably at home now, all smug and chilled, sipping a gin and tonic, thinking it's just a matter of time before I slip up.

She's got no fuckin' idea. As the saying goes, I'm street, look both ways before you cross me.

"So what are you gonna get her to do, blud?"

"I'm still thinking Dubs. It's been giving me a fuckin' headache, to be honest."

"Bruv, I've got it…! Do a Ratboy on her."

"Clarify please Pete, because I'm exhausted, mate."

"What are those sleepers called? The ones you're giving Pippa to slip Ratboy in Africa?"

"Temazepam."

"Why don't you bring Amber round here and slip her one of those?"

"What's the point of that?"

"Naked photos, innit."

"I dunno Pete, that's on your doorstep, mate. Plus, it ain't rude enough."

"I'd be happy to bang her while you take photos."

"I'm sure you would, ya cunt, but that somehow seems like rape."

"I've got it, bruv."

"What again? Didn't you only just have it?"

"Wilson."

"What?"

"Wilson. He's perfect, innit... Bring Amber round here, slip her a tomatopan. We strip her naked, bend her over, and let Wilson smash the granny out of it."

"God give me strength."

"Imagine the photos, bruv. Plus you'd be doing Wilson a big favour; he's never had a bunk-up in his life. Look at the size of his balls, man, they're huge."

"Yeah I know, Pete, I've been up close to them, remember? Stop all that thinking, for Christ's sake, it's disturbing. I just need to think of something really kinky, and she said she'll do it no problem, so that's what I need to do."

I take a seat on a sofa that's far away from Pete and his maniac ideas. Next to me is a pile of his educational mags he always leaves lying around: *Astronomer Monthly, Horse & Hound, Practical Fishkeeping, SAS Survival Skills Volume One*, and *Bondage Dykes from Venus*. That's when I had my Eureka moment. I grab my car keys and make a dash for Amber's apartment with my hopes soaring.

"Hi sweetie, what an unexpected surprise. I was about to make dinner. Anything in particular you fancy?"

"Yeah, I fancy seeing you hog-tied, getting fucked by a woman of my choice wearing a strap-on."

"What, right this minute? Can't it wait until we've had our pudding?"

"You asked me to think of a kink, and I've given you one."

"Oh wow, you're actually serious. Spaniard, I can't do that."

"Why not?"

"Because."

"Because what?"

"Because… Well… Just because that's all."

"That's cool then, no problem. Don't worry about it. But please stop doing my head in about choosing something really kinky for you to do. It's taken me fuckin' ages to come up with that, and you just brushed it aside."

"Why on earth would you even want me to do something like that?"

"Listen, you told me you wanna see a woman of your choice give me a blow job while you watch. It's your fantasy you said, remember? You then asked, no correction, stressed me in picking a saucy thing I haven't done or seen before. I came up with that idea because it's something I've never seen, and as an added bonus, it happens to give me half a thick'un when I think about it."

"Really? It turns you on?"

"Yes."

"Me with another woman?"

"Yes."

"And she's wearing what again?"

"A rubber cock."

"Like a dildo you mean?"

"Exactly, only it'll be strapped to her. You wouldn't even see the woman; you'd be facing the other way."

"Come again?"

"Hopefully."

"Spaniard."

"Well, you'd be tied on all fours with her behind you, so no eye contact to make you feel weird. Even if you and the woman decide to have a marathon staring contest after, you're still never gonna see her again, so no worries."

"And where will you be?"

"Sitting there, smoking a spliff, enjoying my private show."

"I know I won't enjoy it, even in the name of fun."

"But it's not for you though, is it?"

"Bloody hell, Spaniard. OK look, never say never. We'll see how I feel when we get to Holland, OK?"

"In other words you'll do it?"

"I'm going to cook us dinner. I'll leave you with that smug look, and please try to get rid of it by the time I come back. It makes me want to throw something at you."

She leaves me with my smug look and heads for the kitchen. I take a little chance, because I'm pretty fuckin' daring like that, and slip onto the balcony out of earshot to give Dutch a bell.

"Dutch mate, gotta be quick, I'm being super sneaky."

"Hello my friend."

"Dutch, please tell me you know people involved in the red-light district?"

"In what way? You want a girl? Sure, no problem."

"I need a girl who's cool with me taking a photo of her while she's doing something to another girl, if that makes any sense."

"You want to take pictures? Of course, I know girls. What kind of a Dutchman would I be if I didn't, eh Spaniard?"

"She's gotta be a prostitute, Dutch. I need her to wear a strap-on and fuck a woman who'll be with me, who also needs to be hog-tied."

"Tying people up for fun is not new, my friend. Don't worry, your secret will always be safe with Dutch."

"It's not like that Dutch, mate. Well it is and it ain't, but anyway, I know those girls don't like to have their picture taken, and I can't afford to cause a scene."

"Like I say, amigo, it's not a problem. There's a lot you don't know about me, Spaniard. Let's just say that if you're ever in Holland and would rather a girl come to you at your hotel discreetly, Dutch can arrange this for you."

"Sweet, but it needs to be done at a proper place, Dutch, in the red-light district. I think it'll need the full backdrop to work. The tying up bit is really important too, mate."

"I know a girl who is a specialist, it's her job, she's very skilled. The ropes never cross, they touch but never cross. It's an art to her."

"That was a bit deep, Dutch. I was thinking maybe a granny knot will do."

"Granny knot?"

"It's not important, but if she could make a work of art out of it I'd be quite chuffed. It would be even better if the woman wearing the strap-on was mature. Maybe dressed like a school headmistress or something, kind of important but sexy-looking."

"Give me something difficult, Spaniard, a challenge, my friend. This is too easy for Dutch. Call me whenever, wherever, and it will not be a problem, trust me."

Chapter 27

So this is nearly it, ladies and gentlemen. Amsterdam and the moment of truth are just around the corner, and I'd be lying if I told ya I wasn't looking forward to it. Got myself the smallest, sneakiest camera I could find. Even found the need to laugh out loud in a Dick Dastardly-style, as I handed the cashier at Jessops the money for it. My brother says he'll do me a favour and develop the money shot for me, as he reckons Boots the Chemist on the high street might not be such a good idea. Dutch and Pete are now in Prague as we speak, and I've also clued Dutch up on our suspicions with Amber, which he took surprisingly well, but even so, Prague is a safe haven for him while we get to the bottom of things. The constant feeling of a major raid has us all on edge, so what was originally meant to be a week out there has turned into an open ticket. Before he left, Pete dusted down his ninja suit, and over the course of a week, in total secrecy, has moved the buried cash to another part of his land, which he described as the deepest part of the Congo, placed in the middle of the Amazon jungle; a part of his land that's never been stepped on since he was a kid. In other words, stinging nettle city knowing Pete. He said he had to move the money, because when he last checked the site, one of the buried bins was slightly exposed due to more digging from bored animals. He told me that news yesterday, when he touched down in Prague; knew I had a lot on my plate so didn't wanna bother me with it. He was keen to tell me down the phone where the new site was, but I had to tell him to hold back because you never knew who's listening.

I've gone and shut down all my usual little ventures for the time being, and have been staying at a local hotel over on the Embankment that Amber has no clue about. We're off to Amsterdam tomorrow, so she'll never find out anyway. Could be the last time I ever see her now I think about it; sad really. For the first time in my life I actually thought I'd found the one, and maybe I have; the one that's gonna take me down. I fabricated a little story to her that Dutch no longer deals, that he's fed up with the drug game and is moving on. Amber got unusually angry about that. I wonder why? He hasn't, of course, but leading up to this trip she's been mentioning Dutch's name a bit too frequent for my liking. It's always the same topic, me finding out who his contact is so we can get the merchandise at a better price, sweetie.

I've also slipped in a crafty side lie that I have a number for someone in Amsterdam who can help us regarding that situation. I kinda styled it out like it could be the Mr Big she thinks Dutch deals with; a tiny fib that cheered her up immensely. The reason for that little porky was to stall her ambition, to see if she slips up while we're in the Dam, but the main reason was simply to shut her the hell up because she was doing my head in. If Amber really is a copper, she's fuckin' good at what she does though. I mean, none of us had a clue, even Terry Taxi thought she was a solicitor, you heard him yourself. You know what makes matters worse, or better depending on how you look at it? Dubs sat with Terry in his cab on two occasions in one week, and both times Amber was seen strolling into the nick at midday in broad fuckin' daylight. If Dubs tells me it's definitely her, I believe him.

I'd be lying if I said the whole thing hasn't made me super paranoid, but come on, don't I deserve to be? It's keeping me on my toes after all. Last night didn't do my paranoia any favours either. I ain't had time to tell anybody about it yet, but check this out for a freaky moment. While I was relaxing in my quaint, little hotel room, I fancied a spliff around two in the morning. On any other day, I'd happily pop down and smoke it in me motor, but as it was pissing down outside I thought I'd blaze it by the window. I put a towel along the bottom of the door, switched off the light, pulled the battery from the fire alarm, and got myself all nice and comfy perched by the window.

As I sparked the spliff, my eyes were drawn to a figure down below across the road from me. The rain coming down was unreal, not a soul about, yet standing underneath a lamp post, completely still, was a bod holding a bag staring up at me, just like the poster from the movie *The Exorcist*.

What the fuck does this cunt want at 2 a.m. in the pouring rain? He stayed looking straight up at me as I smoked, or in my direction; it was hard to tell with all the rain. Was it Ratboy? A hitman? Or could it be someone Amber sent to watch me? I curved a complimentary digestive biscuit at the figure that hit the lamp post; no reaction. Even when I carpet-bombed the cunt with six chocolate bourbons he didn't flinch. Nobody knows where I am, that's what's troubling me.

I made a cup of coffee, and by the time I came back he wasn't there; rather spooky if you ask me. I've been extra careful not to be seen when I come to this hotel of an evening. I'm in super secret agent mode; even wearing black polo necks for fuck's sake. Every night, until I get to the safety of my room, I'm James Coburn as Flint.

Pete's called again, from Prague, itching to tell me where he's moved our cash. He says he'd feel better knowing that I know, but told him to hold it down until I next see him; I'm still far too bloody para at the moment. I might even make a rapid exit from the Dam straight to Prague as soon as I've got my million-dollar photo. It'd be an easy enough trip to do. Besides the buried cash, I've got a fair bit plugged away that'll last me ages. I could even rent myself a little flat out there, nicely tucked out the way so nobody would ever find me. The Pippa and the Rat situation also seems to be moving along nicely. According to a very quick phone call, she says they're pretty much dating, as they see each other every day.

Knowing what I know, I feel surprisingly relaxed walking with Amber through Gatwick Airport. I'm in a pretty good mood and so is she. We've spoken briefly about the woman I'm gonna choose to bang her come kinky day, but Amber keeps changing the subject back to Dutch and the main man, or the made-up contact I was telling her about.

We get to Amsterdam in the afternoon and hit the Bulldog coffeeshop like a couple of first-time tourists. I must admit it's great though, we get proper fucked up. The snow is falling, and it's absolutely freezing outside. To prove it, the canal has frozen over solid like it does every December. I'm happy sitting here in the warm, all cosy, sipping on my hot chocolate, openly puffing away. Amber thinks it's magical that we can smoke without a care, she's in absolute amazement, or she's acting like it. There's not a lot that could make me wanna leave this moment, I feel like I'm home, in my element, safe. I know that sounds strange, what with her sitting right next to me, but as the saying goes, better the devil you know. Amber leans in for a delicate whisper.

"Can we go to a sex shop so I can see what a strap-on

looks like?"

"Let's go."

Some of these toys are just plain mental. I'm looking at a rubber forearm with a clenched fist. There's everything you can think of here, and everything you can't for sure. A magazine in the shop window has a woman on the front cover with a horse's cock in her mouth, and not a soul passing by bats an eyelid. The next window we look in has got a very tasteful magazine on display with a dog spunking all over a girl's face; her mum must be beyond proud of her achievements. I'm enjoying the stroll around this porn shop with an embarrassed Amber, who looks incredible, by the way; surprised and innocent, like a lost angel that took a wrong turn and ended up in Sinsville. When I see this side to her it really does confuse me. Surely Amber can't be that good an actress, can she? She honestly seems blown away by it all.

"Here you go Amber, that's a strap-on."

"Oh my... I see... Gosh that's big."

"Yeah, it is a bit, but don't worry, they come in other sizes too."

"That's reassuring to hear."

"I like the look of this thing though."

"What on earth is that?"

"Says here it's a paddle for spanking."

"Looks more like a cricket bat with knobbly bits."

"I reckon we should get it."

"Why?"

"So I can smack your arse with it while you're getting sorted."

"No, thank you."

"Well that's a bit boring."

"We didn't agree on any extras, Spaniard."

"Fair enough, but surely I'll be allowed to put my cory in your mouth?"

I managed to sneak Dutch a call while we were in the Bulldog, letting him know I was in Holland, also to give me the contact's number regarding what we spoke about. I said there was no rush, as we'd only just arrived; a minute later, I knew everything I needed to know.

The contact's name is Tess. She's expecting me to call anytime from now. Dutch has given her the heads-up, in their own language, in case of any confusion, which suits me fine. Last thing I need is to be tied up with some bird knee-deep in my arsehole by mistake, and trust me, I'm not even gonna mention the horse or spunking dog pictures we saw earlier, just in case we get severely lost in translation and I end up somewhere down the line in the middle of a dispute between a shire horse and a Siberian husky on which end they should be when I'm spit-roasted.

We get to a steakhouse and fill our empty bellies. It's here, at this very place, that I see something that gets my attention. Amber never leaves her handbag alone for a second. Even when she's eating her meal the bag is on her lap. In the two hours or so we are at the restaurant, she dashes to the toilet three times in total, with her bag tucked so tightly under her arm that she looks like a wide receiver from the San Francisco 49ers. I picked up on it way earlier on, though. I first got suspicious at the airport; at the steakhouse it's simply underlined.

Man, is she gonna get it. That woman's arse, who'll be wearing the strap-on, is gonna be going like the clappers, like a woodpecker's beak. When Amber is all nice and tied up, that's when I'm gonna take the photo. I'll tell her straight to her face, while she's being banged, that I know what she's all about, and if she really wants to fuck with me, I'll make sure there'll be a constant supply of the photo that will haunt her for the rest of her life. I'll have thousands of them dropped from the sky over London like a World War II, airborne leaflet propaganda mission. I'll even have the photo printed so tiny that if she ever gets married, people will be throwing handfuls of it at the happy couple as they step from the church.

I know it's cuntish, but what else can I do?

Is she also not being a cunt for doing what she's doing?

No, fuck that comrade, I'm getting out when I get the chance, and I'm taking no prisoners.

I check down at my phone and as luck would have it, it's fucked again. This bastard just loves switching itself off when I need it most, which is pretty much all the time. We get to another coffeeshop and sit by the window.

It's snowing hard outside and with the canal frozen over, makes for a perfect Christmas card; a beautiful, peaceful image with a weeping willow by a bridge that seems to be the ideal photo opportunity for every passing tourist.

Amber's feeling horny, she wants to do her kink already; doesn't hang about this girl. You may laugh, but somehow I'm a little uncomfortable doing it.

Don't get me wrong, if she asked could one of her friends suck my cock while she had a peep, trust me, I'd be up for it, unless of course she was a horror. This though... this for some reason... I dunno.

I immediately order some temple ball hash, which after two joints, turns Amber a strange kinda yellowy green colour. She's not feeling too great, so we decide to head back to the hotel to spend the rest of the evening in our room, with Amber trying her best to puke up her pelvic bone; all fucking night long, I must add.

My phone cheers up and allows me to call Dubs.

"Dubs, mate, how's things in London?"

"All good, blud. I've been trying to call you. Have you spoken to Pippa?"

"No, mate. I think it's my phone's time of the month; it's been playing up non-stop. What does she want?"

"She dropped it on Ratboy, the thing about her brother living out in Africa. She kept tight to the plan, told him her bro sends her free flight tickets every now and then as a promo for his tour, that's how she and her friends normally get to visit their families back home."

"What and Ratboy fell for it?"

"She said he's proper loved-up, keeps calling her all the time wanting to see her. He's well up for it, dread; hook line and sinker."

"What a result. I'm gonna have to give the Fox a bell to find out when he's next over in Africa. Any news on the Old Bill plotted outside Pete's?"

"I've not seen them there, at least not when I've been past early morning and evening. It's been spooky quiet around the manor since you lot left. When are you thinking of coming back, anyway?"

"I'm not sure to be honest, Dubs."

"I can't hear ya, blud."

"I've gotta whisper, mate, Amber's in the khazi puking her ring up... I was saying, I'm not sure when I'll be back. I'm gonna be doing that photo thing pretty soon, so need to see how that goes first. If it comes on top over here, I might shoot straight to Prague. You still up for Africa though?"

"Can't wait for that, dread. I heard the Rat is setting up another one of those places like the one that mysteriously burnt down. The fool doesn't learn, blud. He needs to visit Africa and fuckin' soon, ya get me?"

"I sure do, for everyone's sake. Can you do me a little favour please Dubs?"

"Of course, Rasta."

"Can you speak to the Fox and find out if he can go to Kenya at a moment's notice? I'm gonna bell Pippa to find out the score her end."

"No problem, blud, and he better be able to go at a moment's notice because I want some of that African sunshine. You know there's always gonna be sunshine in Africa."

"Cheers, Dubs mate. I'll speak to you later."

The news from Pippa is that Ratboy is indeed rather loved-up. She reckons all it took to achieve was acting like a sweet, little, innocent thing around him with the odd kiss and cuddle thrown in for good measure. I personally reckon, from reading between the lines, that Ratboy has fucked her, but she's too embarrassed to say so. I could be wrong though, but I'm sure I'm not. He's already told her about his strange fascination with crocodiles, even showed her his pet caiman; probably not chowing down a kitten though. What Dubs told me was spot on too. The Rat does indeed wanna go to Africa. He's even bought himself a fancy camcorder for the occasion if it were ever to happen.

I arrange with Pippa to buy two separate tickets for the same flight. That way it looks like they're not travelling together, don't know each other and will be sitting as far apart as possible. If Ratboy questions it, Pip can simply tell him that's how the promo ticket thing works, always in single tickets, you don't get to choose where you sit; unfortunately it's a company thing. Knowing the Rat, he won't dwell on it anyway. He's a cheap cunt and the thought of a free holiday to Africa is all that'll matter to him. January is when I wanna do the deed, because I remember the Fox saying it's always quiet in January; tourist-free.

The person with the soft voice I just spoke to over the phone is a local girl called Tess. She's the knot girl Dutch was telling me about. Apparently, when she's not tying people up, her main job is a tattooist, just around the corner. I told her what needs to be done and was given directions to a place bang in the centre of the red-light district. Tess said to call her when we're on our way and everything will be ready and waiting for our arrival.

Amber has been in the bath for the past twenty minutes, and I'm now itching to get this over with. I told her I'd only do her thing if she does mine first or no deal; it worked too. I'm not in any way feeling nervous. I had one of those moments this morning lying in bed. The ones where you just stare up at the ceiling, with your mind racing around all over the shop, trying to find a solution for I don't know what. Then I had a spliff and things cleared up, almost like a little voice inside my head was reassuring me that I'll be alright.

As far as scandals go, the photo of Amber could also work for me on another level. If she is a copper, and I still get nicked after I threatened her with it, then I'll use it against her in court. What sort of credibility would she have after a photo of her getting plunged by a prostitute wearing a strap-on, in the red-light district of Amsterdam, gets passed about? I know I shouldn't, but I'm actually starting to enjoy this.

The call is made to Tess, and within no time at all a cab drops us in the red-light district, 9.30 p.m. sharp. Tess is expecting us within the hour, so we make the rest of the way on foot. I've already started taking photos, only the tourist type though. I've been using my Leica for that. The sneaky, little camera is hidden down me Niagaras. It's just a touch smaller than a packet of twenty cigarettes so isn't noticeable even slightly. The shots I've been taking of Amber along the way are of her surrounded by red-fringed window parlours in the falling snow, not quite Christmas material but still beautiful to my eyes.

"Spaniard would you mind if I have a drink first before we do this? I think I need it to be honest," asks Amber.

"Yeah, sure. What's up? You feeling OK?"

"I'm about to get fucked by a woman with a rubber cock, sweetie, of course I'm not OK."

"So what do you wanna do? Do you wanna leave it?"

"No, because you won't do my thing, will you? I need to have a drink or two for the sake of my nerves first. Come on, don't worry, I won't get drunk. Let's just get this over with shall we?"

"Hold on a second, Amber. I don't want you thinking I'm in any way forcing you to do this, do you understand?"

"I know, I know... Take no notice of me, sweetie. I'll be fine after a drink, but you better not tell anyone about this, Spaniard. I mean it, mister."

After three very quick double gin and tonics, Amber says she's ready.

I buzz on the intercom to a place where Tess greets us at the door. She's a pretty little rock chick with two full sleeves of ink that really suit her.

"Come in," she says with a smile. Tess picks up instantly that Amber is nervous and attempts to comfort her.

"Relax, you'll have fun."

Amber, in all fairness, actually seems slightly tipsy. She took no prisoners with those G & Ts. They were downed in cold blood, or even twenty minutes. Tess takes us into a front room which looks like it's been lifted straight from the Victorian era. The furniture is antique and very worn, but you can tell it's expensive. Amber has a couple of questions she wants to put to Tess.

"Is it you that's going to do it?"

"No, that will be Anna. She's waiting in another room. I will tie you... And when you feel comfortable, I will call her, and she will come in."

"What, right here in this room? I didn't expect it to look like this somehow."

"No, we need to go downstairs to another room. It's the bondage room. It's very beautiful."

"Excuse me? The bondage room?"

"Yes, we are very famous in Amsterdam for our bondage room, or how we like to say, our dungeon."

"Dungeon!"

Tess laughs and leads us downstairs to what I can only describe as a dungeon; a medieval-themed dungeon with stone walls draped in tapestries, and a torture rack taking pride of place in the centre of the room with various other contraptions of pain scattered about that I should imagine would really fuckin' hurt. It's a pretty authentic-looking environment though, that wouldn't look out of place tucked away at the bottom of an old castle. Even the walls look right. They've somehow made them look like they're made from big stone blocks. It's not in any way tacky; it all really does look on point. The slightly overpowering smell of disinfectant distracts a touch, but at least you know they clean up after they've tortured ya. Tess leads us over to what looks like a timber vaulting box, like what you used to jump over at school in PE. It's got wooden runners along both sides, where

I think the legs probably go, and a padded, black leather top. Tess gives Amber some simple instructions.

"So you'll be lying with your front on this padding, your legs to the side with your knees bent resting on these sections here. Kinda like you're on a motorcycle... a racing motorcycle."

"Like I'm on all fours you mean?"

"Exactly, but with your arms behind so I can tie from this point here. What is this called?"

"That's your elbow," I pipe in, because I'm feeling left out.

"So, from your elbow to your wrist, I will make beautiful art. I will tie both your arms together like this, OK? But don't worry. You will be comfortable, I promise."

"Bloody hell Spaniard, I can't believe I'm going to do this."

Tess instructs Amber to undress and get comfortable on the box so she can begin with her art. Amber, quite nervously, begins to slowly take off her clothes until she's left standing shyly in her underwear.

"Well that ain't gonna work is it? Come on, take them off," I tell her with gusto.

Amber quickly looks around checking whether the coast is clear, which makes me chuckle as the only other people about are me and Tess. Then she quickly steps out of her knickers, takes off her bra, and looking a touch embarrassed, stands there with her hands covering her modesty. Tess gives the padded leather a pat indicating for Amber to climb on.

I quietly stand to the side, observing Tess go to work on Amber. Her tanned, naked body getting bound up like that made me wanna tell Tess to leave us alone for a couple of minutes, because a quickie was definitely in order. Dutch was right about those knots too, it's fuckin' art, believe me. None of the rope crosses, it's all perfectly neat; side by side like little soldiers.

"I don't want to see this Anna woman, and please, I don't want her to see my face either."

"Relax. Anna will not see your face. She has no need to come to the front, her job is at the back and she knows this," says Tess leaving the room to get Anna.

Fifteen minutes later, Anna enters the room wearing a black basque, black fishnet stockings, black stilettos and a ten-inch, black rubber cock. I can't make out if she's wearing a wig or not; her hair is far too perfect. I'm not saying it looks bad though – blonde, all tidy up in a bun – just looks like it should have a price tag hanging off it. The glasses make her look adequately serious enough, or she's just a miserable bird. I've not seen her smile yet. Even when Tess introduces us she has a face like a Pharaoh's chin. Tess disappears, and the three of us are left alone. Anna stands behind Amber and begins to spread lube all over the rubber cock, plus its destination. Amber glances over her shoulder at me with a panic-eyed, lost look but says nothing. Anna, now looking even more serious than before, slips two fingers inside Amber like she means it, and if you can give me just a second, I wanna take a closer look.

I swear at this point I hear Anna whisper to Amber, "I love your shaved pussy."

Amber sure as hell heard her say something, as she looks more than slightly startled.

I'm enjoying it big time, can't stop smiling. Tess said it was OK for me to smoke a spliff because I knew Dutch, the man not the language, so I wrap one up for the show and put my feet up. I'm a bit gutted there's no popcorn and refreshments available, but I suppose I can't have everything.

Anna, still stone-faced, very slowly and gently eases the rubber cock into Amber and begins a bit of rhythm, speeding up until I can see slight ripples across the top of her backside. Amber is gritting her teeth, as I motion to Anna to go faster. She sees me and without any expression at all, speeds up a gear.

"OK, slowly! Slowly...! Jesus fucking Christ, how big is this thing?" Amber politely enquires.

"It's not that big. I think they're all a standard six inches here," I tell her.

She's the one that didn't wanna look at Anna, so it's her fault. She only had to give it a quick glance, and she would've seen it was a ten-incher.

"I can see what the problem is from here Amber, you need more lube girl. Where you've been so nervous it's made you dry. Here, let me help you out."

I rest my spliff on the ashtray and position myself alongside Amber, but facing Anna. I squirt a generous amount of lube onto the thrusting rubber cock and pull Amber's arse cheeks as wide as possible.

"How's that? Any better?"

"It still feels really big," she replies, with a very strained look on her face.

This Anna bird is like a fuckin' mannequin, still no expression from her. I bet she'd make a cracking poker player though. Amber has been getting well rumped now for fifteen minutes. Her tightly closed eyes and clenched teeth give me a feeling she could be close to throwing in the towel, so I take my chance.

I stand to the side, frame the shot perfectly, and it's done. Well not quite. For such a small camera it made such a loud

CLICK, CLICK sound.

Amber, as tipsy as she is, immediately turns her head to me and shouts, "SPANIARD, WHAT THE FUCK ARE YOU DOING!"

"Renewing my insurance. What does it look like?"

"What the fuck are you talking about insurance?"

"Amber, I don't know who you are or what you're playing at, but whatever you've got planned for me, or any one of my pals, you better rethink it. You've been followed numerous times, and you're always in and out of West End Central nick. Imagine what I can do with a picture of you in this state."

"Spaniard, listen to me, it's not like that! Are you fucking crazy? My father is the chief inspector there which I could never tell you about, could I? He doesn't know anything about the real me, or my social life. I'm his sweet, little girl, not the bloody police."

"Really? I don't believe you somehow. This little voice in my head is telling me you're lying, and I'm gonna listen to it and jet. But, just so you know, Amber, if you're telling me the truth then nothing should happen to me. Your investment is safe too; it's still buried with the rest of ours. If you're nothing to do with the law, and you're miraculously telling the truth, then it should remain being safe until we're ready to dig it up. Think about it hard when I walk out this door. Nobody needs to know what went on here. It's just me, you and chuckles that are the only witnesses in this room."

"Spaniard, you know I work as an estate agent in Mayfair, which is a five-minute walk to have lunch with my father at his place of work, which is the station. That's all it is. Now, will you tell this woman to stop FUCKING ME?"

"Until you prove it, this photo is gonna be on a feather trigger. Are you listening to me? Because if you mess with me,

242

I swear people will be sitting down in the morning to have their cornflakes and the photo will spill out of the box into the bowl, just like when you were a kid all excited to find a toy in your cereal."

"Spaniard, please listen."

"Nope, I'm not listening. Anna, faster, faster."

Anna's bum is a blur; she's sweating onto Amber's back and going like a train. Amber's toes curl as Anna thrusts all ten inches to the hilt.

"You bastard, Spaniard! Tell this fucking whore to stop, now!"

"I ain't finished with you yet, and nor is she by the look of that frown. How come, in all the time we've been together, you've never invited me to your place of work? Or any of your work parties? And let's face it, there's been a few. Don't you think that's a bit fuckin' weird?"

"No, I don't!"

"Really?"

"Yes fucking really!"

"Well you're a cunt then."

"Am I...? OK, if you must know Spaniard, it's your accent. There, feel better? Now tell her to stop."

"No... What about my accent?"

"Isn't it obvious? The people where I work sound like me. Do you understand what I'm saying... mate?"

"Oh, I see... That's how it is. Well, cor blimey Mary Poppins, if you need me I'll be up a chimney somewhere."

I motion to Anna that Amber wants her to continue and go upstairs to find Tess leaning out of the window. There's a commotion going on outside, and the police are already at the scene. Tess tells me that one of her friend's passing by said a working girl opposite got beaten up real bad by some pissed up tourist. As the ambulance leaves the scene, I hand Tess 800 guilders, thank her for the service, and tell her that she might wanna tell Anna to stop fucking Amber in half an hour or so, and I'm gone.

Chapter 28

I can't remember the last time it snowed this hard in Amsterdam; it's more like a blizzard. It's coming down so hard I'm having trouble seeing where the fuck I'm going in any direction. The twinkling streets of Leidseplein are just in sight. I make my way to Rembrandtplein Square, to the hotel me and Amber were staying, to collect my stuff and move to another hotel in Dam Square.

An awesome night's kip later, I head to a cafe for breakfast followed by a call to Terry Taxi.

"Tel, is there any possible way you could find out for sure the score with Amber?"

"Find out in what way? I mean, what more do you need to know? I've told you what I've seen. Even your pal Dubs has seen it. Are you having trouble letting go of her or something?"

"Mate, my head is all over the gaff. I thought I'd ask you as a shot in the dark. I've just been up to something slightly scandalous involving Amber over here in the Dam. I put it right on her, Tel. She told me her old man is the chief inspector at that nick she's been seen at. According to her, she just visits him for lunch. Apparently, that's the reason you've seen her there."

"That could explain the two times me and Dubs saw her at midday, I suppose. However Span, I also saw her in the

245

morning a couple of times giving papers to coppers in a motor. So does she go there for breakfast as well then?"

"Fuck, I forgot to ask her about that. What a cunt. Tel, mate, you're always up and down Savile Row, am I right?"

"So?"

"Well, I don't know anyone else that can stealthily blend in around there like you can. Do you know what I mean?"

"And where exactly are you going with this?"

"For fuck's sake Terrence, you drive a London cab. How many of those do you see up West End?"

"Personally? Quite a few."

"Exactly, quite a fuckin' few. I'm just asking if you can keep your eyes peeled, that's all."

"I'll drive around the area like I normally do, mate, because it's my patch. Other than that I don't know what else I can do for ya. Why don't you plot up and watch her yourself?"

"There's no way that's happening, Tel. She can't see me at all now."

"Why? What the fuck did you do to her anyway?"

"Mate, I went proper old-school fiendish on her. We're talking top hat and cloak stuff. I took a photo, and I don't mean of windmills or tulips."

"A photo of what? Don't tell me you've taken a photo of Amber with her tits out?"

"A bit worse than that."

"Cunt out?"

"A bit worse than that."

"Fuckin' hell, son, worse than that? What then?"

"I've taken a photo of her getting smashed by a woman. Do you follow?"

"Smashed? What, as in rumped?"

"Well rumped."

"No way, mate."

"Yes way, mate."

"Blimey… How the fuck…? With a woman?"

"Well yeah, plus a rubber cock was involved. The woman had it strapped to her."

"Span, I'm stunned. I don't know what to say to ya, mate."

"So now you see? I wanna be triple sure about her, Tel. We have a good crack, me and Amber, but I've got this mad, little conflict going on between my nut and gut that needs sorting before I can move on to whatever I'm gonna do next."

"Talk about complicate your life. So how have you left it with her?"

"I left her at the scene of the crime, tied up and slightly angry. I told her what'll happen to the photo if it turns out she is a copper that fancies causing me any grief, then pretty much fucked off to another hotel."

"You tied her up and left her?"

"Yes and no, but lean a touch more over to yes."

"Why do you put yourself in these situations, Span? Is it really necessary?"

That's a good question. Why have I got myself into this situation? I would strongly say survival is the reason on this one, but don't ask me why I'm about to put myself straight into another situation, because I certainly didn't see this one coming.

"Fuckin' hell, speak of the devil. You ain't gonna believe this, Tel, but I think she just walked past the coffeeshop I'm in."

"Who, Amber?"

"I think so. She was on the phone. I'm gonna need to have a look though."

"Careful, Span. If she is who she is, then she'll be able to pull a lot of strings."

"I'm not worried about that. The photo alone cuts all her strings. I'm gonna shoot off, mate. I'll talk to you later."

I don't even know if it was Amber I saw; could've been anyone. There's a lot of people about, what with it being New Year's Eve, but my gut buzzed when that woman walked by. The time it took me to throw on my coat and stand outside, she was gone; disappeared in broad daylight? Well, not exactly disappeared. I just can't see shit through all this fuckin' snow.

I spot another Christmas card scene as I turn out of an alley; children ice skating on the canal, with more having a snowball fight in the distance. What a cracking painting this would make with all the trees along the canal covered in a blanket of snow. A five-minute walk from there brings me to an even better view. In fact, I'm gonna have to take a photo of this one. Hang on a second… Photo taken.

Check this out for a corker… I'm standing right by the edge of the canal, which is frozen solid. Now picture this… Everywhere you look is completely covered with snow; the trees, the houses, boats, everything is completely white, even the sky is white. That's not what makes the scene so special though, it's the red Ducati 851 standing bang centre of the frozen canal that does the trick. All that white with just the right splash of red has produced a stunning piece of visual art. I can't see any footprints in the snow anywhere around the bike from where I'm standing, so I gather it must have been put there overnight, more than likely as a joke.

As the snow melts from the trees and drips down into the canal below, the ice doesn't set properly and there's water visible. I stand there for a while looking down at my reflection.

I don't recognise that face, it could be anybody. There's this big, old weeping willow on my side of the canal with a bench beneath it. I take a seat and spark up half a joint saved from earlier on. It's nice here, I'm out of the snow and out of sight, but the main thing is I'm outside. I get a bit stir-crazy if left cooped up for too long. I need to breathe some clean, fresh air. My mind drifts to Amber.

Was she looking for me when she walked past the coffeeshop?

Was she on the phone talking about me when she walked past the coffeeshop?

Was it really her?

Has she already fucked off back to London?

Am I walking around Holland like a cunt in this blizzard following nothing but my paranoia?

First thing I done this morning was call the hotel we stayed at, and was told by the receptionist that the woman checked out a couple of hours before my call. Then there's Pete. That poor sod's on my mind too. He can't even go back to his house until all this mess is sorted.

I decide to make my way back to Dam Square, stopping beneath another willow for a smoke. Fireworks are starting to liven things up with a crackle and a boom that's far too close for comfort. A rocket in the eye is very possible in Holland, because the Firework Code doesn't seem to exist; it's full-on street warfare. They fire rockets down the alleys, across roads, across the canal, at shops and people if you happen to be standing in the way; pretty much anywhere other than up in the sky where they're meant to go. Then fog joins the party, a thick, grey mist that consumes everything within an arm's length of me.

As I look up at the sky, I see nothing but grey. I can feel

the ice-cold snowflakes gently settling on my face. I'm fuckin' freezing and stoned, not a good combination. I put my head down, hands in pockets, and make my way along the canal to the next tree. A small, stray dog is huddled under the bench trembling, scared to death. Whenever a firework goes boom the poor thing presses itself closer to the leg of the bench. Fuckin' breaks my heart to see animals in distress.

I bend down to talk to the little fella.

"Hello, mate. You're alright. Come here boy, come on. That's it. Don't take any notice of those little bangs and booms."

The dog gets halfway out, from under the bench, and suddenly freezes like a fuckin' statue.

"You're alright boy. Come on."

Then he starts to growl at me.

"Oi, what's all that about? You can trust me."

A shadow on the floor cast by a lamp post makes the hairs on my neck stand to attention. There's someone behind me. I stand and turn to face a silent silhouette; a silhouette that has no business creeping up on me like that. I'm a bit angry, and so is the dog. Then I spot the blade in his hand, but he's nervous now, wondering about his next move. This guy is clearly out for some Christmas mugging. The only problem is he's made a big mistake choosing me as his first target, because if he makes the wrong move it's gonna cost him, and I'm not in the mood to play around.

"That's a fuckin' big blade you've got there, pal."

No answer.

"Is there anything I can do for ya?"

Still no answer, until, "You give me money."

Clearly a crackhead. As he moves towards me, his sunken, hollow eyes and gaunt face come into view. I was right; he's a crackhead all day long. These people don't value life, so I'm not gonna value his. His eyes are glazed over, almost lifeless. This freak will stab me and not have a clue he's doing it. I now feel a bit uneasy, as I've just had a proper look at the size of the knife in his hand. Looks like a kitchen knife about eleven inches long. Whatever happened to the good old days when someone would pull a pissy, little flick knife on ya? If it wasn't for the fact this cunt just asked for my money, I would've thought he was a serial killer with that kind of blade.

And then it all happens and is over in three seconds. The freak comes towards me, and I see an opportunity to kick him in the chest, really fuckin' hard. So hard that the blade flies out of his hand and lands by the bench. I know he's obviously gone over and onto the frozen canal, but I'd completely forgotten we are under a tree, in other words he isn't there. There's no ice under the trees, remember? He's gone in and under the ice.

I look to the left, no place to breathe, all solid ice. I look to the right, can't see fuck all through the mist and snow; same in front of me. I know there's trees right the way over on the other side of the canal that would have breathing holes for sure, but can he make that swim all the way under the ice? Certainly not, being a crackhead, and what about the undercurrent? That could drag him anywhere, especially being a crackhead. Should I look for him? Technically, yes, but I'm not gonna. I take a seat on the bench and build a spliff. The dog is still there, he's lying underneath kinda dozing. As I smoke I look around. Nobody has seen what went down, or the freak going down. The splash was drowned out by the fireworks and bangers going off everywhere. The heavy, non-stop snow makes it impossible to see fuck all anyway, especially with the fog.

The reality of what just happened hits me kinda hard. There's a very strong possibility I've taken someone's life, and let's not forget, that freak wasn't always a crackhead. Before that he could've been a nice fella, and with the right help could've once again become a nice fella. Does he have kids? Have I made a child fatherless? I need to process the moment a bit more for my comfort. I need to run through different scenarios of what could have happened. Some people would say I could of just handed over my money, but I'm not built that way. I'm built to defend myself, and that's what I done. I don't feel great about it, believe me, but the thought of an eleven inch kitchen knife not sticking through my heart definitely makes me feel a hell of a lot better about it.

I wait and smoke for ten more minutes, but still no sign of the freak. I look down at the dog who now has a friend, another stray by the look of it; no collar and absolutely filthy. The dog from under the bench crawls out, looks right in my eyes and runs off with the other mutt wagging his tail. I take that as a positive sign to make a move. As I stand to flick my joint butt into the canal, I notice the blade resting on the side. A slight kick and the knife disappears down and through a hole in the ice, making everything feel instantly calm again.

A slow stroll along the canal has me thinking about what Amber said to me, back at the dungeon, about my accent. And there's me, like an absolute plum, planning on giving her a diamond ring, which if I can find it, should be in my inside pocket. And here it is. A gentle cast sees it across to the centre of the canal where it settles on the ice. Would it make me sound less romantic if I told ya I popped the diamond out first before I threw it? Because if it does, forget I mentioned it.

I make a random choice and head for an alley across the street. I don't recognise this part of Amsterdam, but I'm hoping when I exit this alley that won't be the case. The fog seems angry now, dark and thick, limiting my vision to just past my nose. I'm walking like a blind person without a cane, feeling the walls of the alley as I try for some kind of guidance. It's eerily quiet, with just the solo sound of my leather soles trying to find their way. I don't know where the hell I am, as I reach a junction where the alley splits into three. All the alleys look identical in this fog, so I stop to give my choice some serious consideration. Two lots of 'ip dip dog shit you are not it' later, and I'm heading down the left alley, hoping to have better luck at the other end, but no, another damn junction.

A sound coming from straight ahead of me makes my ears twitch towards it; a metallic sound, like someone picking up a knife from the ground. Could be nothing, but my instinct is telling me to take this next right turn. I stand for a few seconds in the shadow of a doorway waiting, listening, but all is quiet. My footsteps are now picking up the pace, as my racing mind plays havoc with me.

Where the fuck is this alley taking me?

Am I even going in the right direction?

The faint sound of a woman's shoes clicks and clacks far behind me, speeding up with every second step. It's enough to stop me in my tracks; sounds familiar, like I've been in this situation before. I wonder where the hell she's going in such a rush? I continue onwards through the mist, then realise I'm being followed. Those footsteps have not only caught up to mine, but are now mirroring them about twenty yards behind. Whenever I stop walking, they stop walking. If I speed up or slow down, so does she. I say 'she' loosely, as it could always be a slightly damp crackhead freak in a pair of Cuban heels, you never know. Time for a slight trot I think. Surprise, surprise, I'm now being chased. How the fuck does a woman run in heels anyway? My leather soles on the icy pavement ain't doing me any favours either. My slight trot is now a slippery sprint, but blind. I feel like I'm running on the spot with my eyes closed, and she's really close. It's impossible to see, but I can hear her. I've got a feeling that any second now I'm gonna get a blade plunged into my back, but it doesn't come, the chasing shoes fade away into the mist.

The soft golden glow in the distance tells me my ordeal with the alleys is over. Two minutes later, I'm in a coffeeshop heading for the gents busting for a piss. As I stand there, cock in hand, I take the time to admire all the graffiti the place is well known for; they actually encourage you to have a scribble. There's even marker pens, in various colours, on the side. Every inch of wall is pretty much covered with language and drawings from all over the world. Some people have taken the time to express some serious talent in here. Like the drawing of a pensive Einstein taking a shit for instance. I only wanna leave 'Spaniard' but seem to be struggling to find an empty spot. Even the ceiling is covered, not that I can reach up there anyway, that's for tall cunts only. Looks like my best bet is gonna have to be that two-inch spot down there on the skirting, next to 'ZG forever baby'.

I make myself comfortable and order a three-gram Nepalese temple ball and a cup of hot chocolate. The place is busy because it's that time of the year, but it's a pleasant and surprisingly relaxed atmosphere all the same. I feel like a crafty chameleon slowly blending into the background, keeping one eye on the entrance all the time. I feel safe here, plus Bob Marley is on my side. His 'Three Little Birds' couldn't have come on at a better time. The smoke takes me far away to a place where I forget all about alleyways and canals... It takes me to Pete's land. You see, our buried cash is kinda bugging me now. How the fuck are we gonna know if badgers or foxes decide to have another crack at digging at it if Pete ain't there to keep an eye on the thing? And I don't know about him, but I somehow am not fancying the idea of my cut being covered in shit and piss plus half eaten by the local wildlife. I need some peace for my troubled mind, so I buzz Peter in Prague.

"Hello Pete, can you hear me? Hello? I'm in a coffeeshop, mate, in Amsterdam. Hang on; I'm going outside for a better signal... Pete, how do you know those forest animals ain't gonna have another dig at our dough, mate?"

"Bruv, your reception is shit, man. Speak up."

"I've got four bars, ya cunt, it's your phone not mine."

"Oh yeah, I've got one, no two now, but I can hear ya sweet as. What's up?"

"The fuckin' animals, Pete. What makes you think they won't dig again at the new place?"

"Because I know my land, innit."

"So what about the first time, you nutter? Didn't you know your land then?"

"Yeah, but I had to find somewhere at short notice, remember? To keep going backwards and forwards quick time you said. It was too short notice to find a safer than safe spot, but this time round you'll need the Land Rover to get to the new place. It's like the fuckin' *Lost World*, bruv, trust me. It's so dense, the only animals you see are things that fly... Like birds."

"And what else? Pterodactyls?"

"Trust me, I wouldn't be surprised, man. I had to leave a secret marker so that even I'll be able to find the exact location. Believe me, when I say it's all good, bruv."

"OK, I feel slightly better now, and I do believe ya, Pete. Take no notice of me. You know what my head's like. I done that thing, by the way, the Amber thing with the photo."

"No fucking way, Span. Really?"

"Yeah, and it was indeed quite a thing."

"I believe it. Fuck, that's epic shit. So you've got your 'Get out of jail' card you was talking about?"

"When I get it developed, yeah, I hope so. It's still in the camera at the moment."

"Bruv, don't be losing that camera."

"I won't, it's down me balls."

"Nice, keep it that way. Did you go with the strap-on idea?"

"Yep, sure did."

"Brother that is sick. I've gotta see the photo."

"If the situation goes a certain way then yeah, Pete, the whole world will see it, but she threw a dainty, little spanner in the works; said some stuff that made me think twice and three times."

"I hear ya, man. You gotta be sure about it. You could fuck her life up so easy if she's innocent."

"I know that, Pete. Trust me, mate, it's been doing my head in thinking about it. Changing the subject, how's Dutch doing anyway?"

"He's gone already. Said something about business in Berlin. He's a good bloke, Dutch. He's now one of the boys, you know?"

"Yeah, I know. He's a funny fucker as well, cracks me up sometimes. Was he alright though?"

"Sweet as, bruv, he fucking loves us lot, man. I've gotta tell ya though, Span, that boy can pull a bird. Dutch banged four wicked sorts the first week he got here. I ain't had me end away even once in all the time I've been here."

"Yeah, but that's normal for you Pete, you're slightly

mental-looking, mate. Dutch, however, probably gives it the full-on Sting impersonation to strike lucky with the girlies. I know I fuckin' would if I looked like the cunt."

"Bruv, it works, I'm telling ya."

"Of course it does. Why wouldn't it? What's the place like where you're staying at anyway? Any good?"

"It's a big old, dusty house that never gets used. My dad bought it for my mum as a gift when they were getting on many moons ago. After they split, me old dear wanted nothing to do with it. Don't know where the fuck she is anyway, bruv, probably still with the gardener. I ain't seen or heard from her in years, so I claimed it. I go here to chill whenever I need to; it's a handy retreat to have."

"I should imagine it is, although you kept it a bit of a secret, you sly old dog."

"Everyone's gotta have a secret retreat. Just like the hotel you stayed at before the Dam."

"True. Fair comment. Anyway listen, Pete, you're really boring and I don't wanna talk to you anymore. I'm gonna have to shoot, mate. Gotta bell Dubs about the Africa thing."

"Cool, bruv, and you're the most boring fucker I've ever met. Get off my line. Oh, by the way, before you go, I watched a documentary the other day on African killer bees."

"See ya later, Pete."

I've been using the coffeeshops in the area of the freaky crackhead incident for the past couple of days to see if any news wafts by, but nothing. Is that because he found a hole to climb out of? Or is he lodged under the ice somewhere waiting to be discovered in the spring?

It's a beautiful morning in sunny Amsterdam, still freezing but beautiful. I'm looking forward to flying back to London this afternoon. I've been here for two weeks and that most definitely feels like enough. I'm calling Dubs on the regular to make triple sure it's all quiet back home before my arrival. He reassures me all's safe. I sit outside a cafe and order a cappuccino with a Danish pastry. A forgotten German newspaper left on the table is my time-waster.

Then I have one of those scary film moments, like a Hitchcock movie. I'm holding the newspaper up with both hands as if I'm reading it. I lower the paper just as a tram goes by and for a split second, I swear Amber is standing across the road staring at me wearing shades and a Burberry mac. It makes me do a double take to be sure, but another tram goes by at that moment blocking my view. When it passes she's gone. It sends a chill up, down and sideways. She was just there, I fuckin' saw her with me own eyes. I finish my pastry and drain my coffee. As I look up, Amber is sitting at my table.

"Spaniard, we really need to talk."

"About what?"

"Give me that fucking camera."

"What's that? A new show on Channel 4?"

"You fucking well know what I'm talking about."

"And I've already told you, I need to see nothing happens to me. That's gonna take time. Oh, before I forget, why were you seen giving papers to coppers in a car outside the nick early morning? Twice in one week."

"Early morning?"

"Yeah, around 9 a.m. I think it was, if I'm not mistaken."

"Around nine?" Amber looks confused but continues. "The only thing I can think of would be the time I dropped off the spare keys to my father's house."

"Take off the sunglasses Amber, we ain't playing poker here."

"Oh for God's sake...! Better...? My father left his home in a hurry one morning and forgot his keys. I've always kept a spare set at my place, plus I work in the area, so dropping them off to him would be the logical thing to do, don't you think? As for handing papers to policemen in cars, I honestly have no idea what you're talking about."

"What an absolute load of bollocks. Not even once did you look into my eyes while spinning those lies."

Oh, come on... After that last line even you must think I should be a rapper.

"Give me the camera, Spaniard."

"Come and take it."

"I could have you fucking killed, you bastard."

"Blimey, whatever happened to sweetie?"

"I'm not joking."

"Really? Because I find it quite comical, and you know what else is funny? You look and act nothing like the Amber I know. I think you may have some kinda split personality thing going on there. You might wanna get that looked at."

And that's no joke, her face now looks nothing like the sweet, little buttercup that captivated me so much, it's now more of a Venus flytrap, but really fucking angry.

"You think I can't do it? You think I can't have you killed?"

"Well you'd better do it soon then, before I get the photo developed."

"I can have it done anytime, Spaniard. I just need to say the word."

"Yeah, but I can be pretty elusive if need be, Amber."

"I found you now, I'll find you again. You're not as smart as you think you are."

"Maybe so, and maybe I could be wrong about you. I'm

not saying I'm definitely in the right here, that's for sure. So let's just talk and get this nonsense sorted shall we, now that we're sitting out here in the open where no funny business can go on? I've still got a couple of hours to kill, anyway, until my flight back to London. Hang on for just one minute and let me grab another coffee before I give you my undivided attention. This place does the best cappuccino in Amsterdam. Do you want one?"

"No, thank you."

I walk into the cafe, out the side door, straight into a taxi and fuck right off.

Chapter 29

Pimlico is my bolthole, a drab B & B just down the road from my brother's place in Battersea. Nicely out the way for distance but close enough for the grapevine. I dropped the mini camera off on my way through from the airport to have the photo developed and ready for collection sometime tonight.

Fast forward to sometime tonight when my brother calls me to confirm that the shot is fucking awesome, and he's not wrong, it's fucking awesome; a full-length, crystal clear side shot of both the girls in all their glory. Amber's eyes are closed tight, her teeth clenched, but you can see it's her, without any shadow of a doubt it's her alright. The strap-on is also in full view, and there's a slight blur around Anna's backside indicating rapid thrusting. I leave the photo with my bro for safekeeping and head back to Pimlico for a hot bath, spliff and bed. I'm exhausted, mentally and physically drained. I felt great an hour ago, but I suppose it had to catch up with me at some point.

I slept well that night, woke up in the morning with an urge to take on the day. A couple of hours later, me and Dubs are pulling up at the Fox's pub. He tells us he can be out in Africa waiting for me and Dubs whenever we're ready to show us the croc site. The plan is for us to get out there a day early, on Friday, before Pippa and the Rat. The Fox will take us straight to the croc spot to check out the area then drop me and Dubs off at a local hotel back on Watamu Beach. We'll meet up with the guy who's gonna be driving Pip and Ratboy around on Saturday morning in Hemingways' bar. He's the fella that's acting as Pippa's brother, so I hope there's at least some likeness to her.

The Fox leads us around the back of the pub to an empty beer garden out of earshot of his nosey missus.

"Fuckin' hell fellas, my wife is getting well suspicious with all the shady phone calls. She asked me the other day if I was slipping it to some tart behind her back. What's the apple with Pippa, Span? Are we moving forward with this thing or not?"

"Yeah definitely, mate, it's gonna happen. Pip is doing us proud, brother Fox, but she needs to be a touch delicate, you know?"

"Yeah well, you don't know my missus like I do."

"You'd be surprised."

"Fuck off Span, I'm being serious, mate. I just want this thing out the way so I can get back to running me pub in peace, that's all I want. You know what I'm like. I'm not cut out for anything else but running my pub."

"It sounds very much like your missus wears the strides out of you two. What do you reckon Dubs?"

"Of course she does, dread. The Fox is well under manners."

"I'm not under manners, Dubs. I value my marriage, mate. There's nothing wrong with that, is there? When you get married you'll know what it's like. Spaniard when is this gonna be done?"

"Soon, Foxy, in about three weeks' time if all goes well. Pippa is probably sorting out the tickets as we speak. I'm waiting to hear from her anytime now. I'll give you the date the second I know. Relax."

"I am relaxed. I just wanna get back to my life, that's all I'm asking, a bit of normality."

"I hear ya loud and clear, and really appreciate what you're doing, but some things need delicate planning first. You can't casually just take some cunt out to Africa and feed him to a crocodile, my friend; it takes a bit of preparation. You're only gonna be showing us the spot anyway, then you're off. You won't exactly be getting your hands dirty, so what are you worried about?"

"I know, I know... It's just that... Well, the thing is."

"You're under manners?"

"No, Dubs."

"You're a shit trousers?"

"No, Span."

"What then, brother Fox? For fuck's sake speak up, fella."

"I'm gonna be a dad, boys. Found out last Tuesday."

"Blimey, that's great news. Congratulations, mate. Fair play to ya... Still gives ya nine months' legroom to play with though, don't it?"

"You're a heartless cunt, Span."

"I'm joking, Foxy. Honestly, that's wicked news. I bet you're chuffed to bits."

"Over the fuckin' moon is more like it. We've been trying for nearly three years."

"Yeah, but you're still under manners, dread."

"Fuck off, Dubs, I'm not."

"So anyway, Foxy, who's this geezer we're meeting up with over there? The bloke meant to be Pippa's brother. Is he a poacher?"

"Who Eddie? No, he ain't a poacher. Eddie's one of me South African fishing pals. He's sweet as a nut, Span. You can trust him all day long."

"Blinding, but how much does Eddie know?"

"Fuck all, mate. He'll pick you up from Hemingways and take you to where you wanna be. Then he'll drive back to the airport for Pippa and the Rat when the time comes."

"Beautiful. And we'll be all set ready for their arrival. What about the bod cooking the steaks and serving? Who's gonna be doing that?"

"That'll be Ayo. He helps out on the boat whenever I go fishing. He's a bit dim but will do anything for a pound note. He'll be dropped off with you and Dubs on the day."

"Nice. I bet that's gonna be fun. Did you tell Eddie about the table for two and candles?"

"Yeah, he knows, don't worry. He'll have all the bits you need on board when he picks you up; table, two chairs, barbecue stuff and tent, the works, mate."

"Sweet, because I wanna try and make it look proper romantic out there, it's all in the presentation, Foxy."

Driving back home, we take a detour by Pete's house and immediately pick up on an unmarked police car parked in the usual place being nosey. Time we had a little giggle, so we take three left turns and park a couple of hundred yards behind, watching them while they watch Pete's.

Half hour's worth of observation goes by when we spot another motor slowly drive past Pete's house then stop by the unmarked police car. Nobody gets out of either vehicle, but we can see there's communication going on. The mystery car moves off, after three minutes, up the road towards us. We both duck down as the car very slowly approaches, engine humming, creeping closer and closer. It stops alongside us for a couple of minutes, but nobody gets out.

We know it's there, we can hear the engine ticking over. Whoever they are, they seem to know my motor.

Very slowly, we chance a peep as the car moves off. It's a rather familiar blue VW Golf that I last saw in my rear-view mirror one rainy, early morning. The driver is Ratboy, you probably could see that coming, but this is the bit you're gonna love the most. Have a guess who the passenger half ducking down is? Go on, have a guess? Did you say Amber? Because you're bang on, I kid you not. I know this for a scientific fact, because the soppy cow sits up too quick as they pull away giving me and Dubs a clear look at her face. There's a word you've heard me use before that neatly sums up this kind of scenario that I've been trying ages for the folks up at the Oxford Dictionary to recognise, and that word is 'cuntish'.

So now it's all coming together. Ratboy must be Amber's snitch. I bet he had bods posted all over our rave buying pills and whatnot as evidence. They probably passed him all the info that he then dropped on Amber. Knowing Ratboy, he's doing his bit purely to get me out the way so he can move in, it's as simple as that, and I should have seen it coming, but could I have? I mean, you've been with me all the way here. You can't tell me you saw a connection with Amber and the Rat? That's what I thought. Me and you are on the same page.

So let's look at this from a few angles.

Ambitious Amber, the renegade copper, could be looking at the bigger picture as a whole. She could've had her sights set on Dutch before I even met her, and I was just a stepping stone to the other side, our side. I wonder if Amber is in cahoots with Ratboy's old man? I mean, if she's that crooked why not be part of the firm? She could tell them where and what dealers to rob. Here's another juicy side thought for ya to rattle around. What if she gets her lot, the Old Bill, to raid dealers because she has access to where the seized drugs are held when they get back to police land? Amber could then help herself to the stockroom and pass drugs over to Ratboy to sell, slipping her a cut along the way. Now let's look at another scenario. Imagine for a second you're a copper. You're not quite where you wanna be in the force, so you get an opportunity to change that in a rather spectacular way. What you start to plan, completely off the record of course, you're no mug, is to clean up big time. Imagine if you could not only have me and Dutch banged up, but also Ratboy and his dad's complete empire all wrapped up in one quick swoop. Don't get me wrong, I'm not trying to large it, I know I ain't big time here, but if we were talking food, I'd be a half decent appetiser. Imagine what all that could do for your career?

Me and Dubs make the difficult decision to get really fuckin' stoned and head for his place.

Four hours later, I'm still there, rooted to the sofa wondering what the fuck the world is coming to. We've already solved the planet's problems, discussed global warming and sussed out the meaning of life; that only took three joints. We filter through all the current affairs that's been going on around us when the conversation turns to Amsterdam.

"I fancy getting out there, blud. It's been ages since I hit the Dam."

"Oh, mate, I was meaning to tell ya. Some cunt tried to mug me when I was out there."

"Mug you? Why would he wanna do that?"

"Dunno Dubs. I kicked him into the canal."

"You kicked him into the canal?"

"Yeah, mate."

"Seriously, blud?"

"He came at me with a huge, fuck off blade and a look in his crackhead eyes like he was gonna do me some damage. I was crouched down petting a stray dog when he crept up behind me like the fuckin' Grim Reaper. Even the dog was freaked out."

"A crackhead you say? I guarantee he was gonna stab and rob ya, no doubt about it."

"That's what I thought, and nobody would've seen if he had done. Mate, it was foggy, snowing like fuck and ridiculously freezing. I was plotted under one of those weeping willow trees to get a break from the bastard wind freezing me fuckin' ears off. My hands were in my pockets when he came at me, so I kicked him in the chest."

"What? Bruce Lee-style?"

"No, more like kicking-a-door-in-style."

"Sweet."

"Yeah, the thing is though, Dubs, the canal was frozen over, and he went through and disappeared."

"So he's dead?"

"Don't know for sure. I stayed another week just to find out. Never heard a thing. The canal was still frozen when I left."

"Dread, if he was coming at ya and you feared for your life, technically what you done is self-defence, am I right?"

"I'd like to think so, mate."

"Trust me, Span, don't let that shit haunt you, blud. I would've done the same thing. Your life meant nothing to that guy, believe me."

"To be honest with ya, Dubs, I've played it over a few times since and always come back to the bottom line, and that's the fact I'd do exactly the same every time. I mean my hands were in my pockets, had no choice but to kick him."

"Exactly... Fuck him. And what about Amber? Have you thought about your next move with her?"

"Yeah, I've been thinking about that since we saw her and Ratboy in that Golf. Amber knows we've got cash buried, but strangely the police haven't started digging all over Pete's acres, so is this a waiting game to catch me bang to rights? Is she feeding the Rat info about me so he knows exactly the right moment to have his dad's squad of murderous robbers come and turn me over again? On the other hand, has Amber done this a few times before? Tucking a small fortune away every now and then until she's got enough to call it a day. Think about it Dubs, we made a shitload in just one weekender. What would've happened if we'd continued with a two-day rave at the end of every week? It would've been a massive thing, mate, and Amber could've been getting a very tidy half a million quid every couple of months easy. Another thing that's been bouncing around my nut is whether the police parked outside Pete's house are there because they think he's the man serving up. I've had no Old Bill parked up outside my place while I was in the Dam, according to everybody, including yourself, Dubs."

"True, true, I see your point. Plus, no Old Bill round my place either."

"That's what I mean. There's always the possibility that untold, spaced out idiots got pulled over on their way home from our rave and simply said they got the drugs at the venue. That's why the police are now watching Pete's house, thinking he's a dealer, or even Mr Big."

"Pete the drugs baron, dread."

"Exactly Dubs. Funny enough, if you squint he does look like a young Pablo Escobar. Try it next time you see him."

"Yeah man, Pablo Escobar, I can see it already, blud.

What's he doing for his birthday next week? Have you spoken to him?"

"Who, Pablo Escobar? I ain't got his number, Dubs."

"Pete, ya bumbaclart."

"Yeah, a few days back. He's still in Prague lying low. I'll give him a bell now, as it goes."

Since the Amber episode, my phone is switched off until I need to use it. Changing my number might be the sensible thing to do, but I can't really do that at the moment. Too many valuable contacts out there have my digits but me not theirs. I mostly count on calls coming in for business, and it's always worked out well for me that way, so I'm not gonna go changing anytime soon. I switch my phone on and can see a missed call from Dutch, two from Amber, two from Pete and four from Pippa.

"Hello Pablo, I mean Pete, how ya doing, fella?"

"Bored as hell, man. Everyone's gone and deserted me. I'm just getting stoned here on me jacks, bruv, chillin' out watching MTV. Have you spoken to Dutch? He said he was trying to call ya."

"I had a missed call, I'll bell him later. What does he want, anyway?"

"Span man, you know what next week is, don't ya? Yep, my birthday, innit. Dutch called to say he was gonna be over in Ibiza next week and that we should all go over there to get proper messed up for my special day and ting."

"And ting?"

"Exactly. Personally, I think it's a fucking quality idea, bruv."

"Not a bad one, Pete. I take it you'd be flying there straight from Prague then?"

"Sure would. I'm already looking at flights. We gotta get

all the boys to go, Span man, it'd be sick as fuck... And guess what? I was chatting to my bro Dingo yesterday all the way in Australia; he's well up for it too. Can you believe that? He's coming over."

Pete's brother Dingo is one of those characters you never forget; a huge stoner, to him it's a religion. He's your stereotypical surfer dude with blonde dreadlocks and a golden suntan.

Dingo moved to Australia six years ago to follow his dream of becoming a pro surfer, but realised after a couple of years he was actually shit at it and instead hitched up with some surfer girl and started cultivating weed for a living. He's a super cool, laid-back guy that's always a pleasure to have around.

The name Dingo came about simply because he was a bit of a dog when he first touched down in Australia. Dingo the dog fucked his way around Oz for the entire first year he was there. The man couldn't stop fucking, so inevitably ended up catching a dose nine times.

"That's brilliant news, Pete. I ain't seen Dingo for years, mate. He's gonna have a blast in Ibiza. It's gonna get messy now though."

"Sure is... So you and Dubs up for it, or what?"

"Of course we are you sigh, plus being out the way can only be a positive move my end. Also, you know what else I was gonna say to ya?"

"What?"

"When we get back from Ibiza we should dig that dough up. It's been long enough don't you think? I reckon if something was gonna happen, it would have by now."

"I'm up for that all day long, bruv. It's gonna be sweet,

trust me. How are you gonna be in Ibiza and Africa at the same time though?"

"I won't be in Africa until the end of the month. That's what I told Pippa, to sort the tickets out for around that time."

"Yeah, which is now, it's the end of the month, bruv, and Pippa has the tickets. Ain't you spoken to her?"

"Fuckin' hell, Pete, are you joking?"

"No, man. You should check your phone more often, innit."

"I'm gonna have to bell you back, mate, I need to speak to her lively."

"Sweet. Laters, bruv."

Fucking unbelievable. Talk about time flies by and me being an absent-minded cunt.

"Pippa, I've just spoken to Pete."

"Why the hell do you have a cell phone but never answer it? I've been trying to call you. I have the tickets, man."

"My phone's fucked. When for?"

"This Saturday, Spaniard."

"This Saturday? You mean this Saturday coming? Like in five days' time Saturday?"

"That's the Saturday I'm talking about, yes."

"Why the fuck didn't you tell me sooner, Pip?"

"You told me to call you when I had the tickets. Two separate tickets for the same flight, which I got, and have been trying to call you to bloody tell you. You also told me not to worry because you would be ready at any time, so what's the problem?"

"The problem is I just told Pete I'd be in Ibiza for his birthday, which is next week. Untold people will be there Pip. For fuck's sake, even Pete's brother Dingo is gonna be there, and he's coming all the way from Australia."

"So what do you want me to do? I'd rather not be doing this shit at all. I need the money yes, but this fucking guy, man, I don't like him. I'm starting to see his nasty temper, because I don't let him touch me whenever he wants. I told him things will be different when we get to Africa. I think that promise is stopping me from getting seriously beaten up. I'm telling you, Spaniard, this is not fun, man, and very dangerous; he's a fucking psycho."

"Why don't you just wank him off every now and then to keep him sweet? At least it'll calm him down a touch."

"Excuse me?"

"OK, look Pip, we're gonna stick with the plan. I'll bell Pete back and give him the heads-up on what's going on, he'll understand. I'll tell him me and Dubs will be joining him in Ibiza straight from Africa."

"So everything is good then?"

"Sort of, I just need a big favour."

"Am I not already doing you a big favour?"

"If you were doing it for free yeah, it would be a favour, but favours don't cost six large, Pip. Let's face it, you're not exactly giving him any skin to make life easier are ya? Seems like you're doing the bare minimum, if you don't mind me saying so."

"Because he creeps me out, man. What do you want me to say?"

"Pippa, no disrespect, mate, but you're a working girl. Since when the fuck did appearances ever come into play?"

"When I can pick and choose my clients, Spaniard. When I make the rules. I spend an hour with them, not entire days and nights at a time. Believe me when I tell you that the thought of having sex with Rathead really fucking bothers me."

"It's Ratboy."

"Whatever. I sit round his flat almost every evening while he plays poker with his stupid, fucking friends. I just want to be anywhere else but there."

"And that's exactly what I'm talking about, Pip. Maybe if you gave him something other than a kiss and a cuddle, he'd be different. You've got him all frustrated. Take it from me, he's getting bored. You, of all people, should know how a man works; no offence."

"He's disgusting to look at."

"So don't look at him. It's work, remember? If his appearance bothers you that much just look the other way. At his next poker night do us all a favour and join in. When it's your turn to deal you could shuffle the cards with his cock under your arm."

"What?"

"Problem solved, Pip. Get him to stand behind ya with it tucked under your armpit."

"Ag sies, man! What's the favour, Spaniard?"

"Can you get me and Dubs tickets to fly for this coming Friday?"

Chapter 30

"How long have we been trying to get hold of Posh Mark, Dubs?"

"Fuckin' months, dread."

"That's what I thought, and I've left, what? Thirty messages on his answer machine?"

"I'm telling ya, he's hiding, Rasta. He knows the deal about Amber, trust me. That's why you ain't heard or seen him. Track that fucker down, blud, Comanche-style. It'll be easy, just go to where he plays golf. Guaranteed he'll be there."

"Yeah, I thought of that already, mate. Only thing bugging me is you get a lot of coppers that also play there. Don't really wanna show my face if I can help it, you know?"

"What about his drum? You know where he lives, Span."

"Thought of that too, but his wife and kids will be there, and if he says the wrong thing there's a strong possibility I'm gonna have to chin him and end up getting nicked."

"Yeah, I can understand that... Shall we go then?"

"Sweet. Let's go."

The thing about Posh Mark is he's not like us. He'll call the police in a second if he thinks violence, of any sort, is coming his way, so obviously that's not the way to play it. Subtlety is definitely the way to go with Mark if he's to spill the beans on

Amber. Then, as me and Dubs are heading towards Mark's place up in Richmond, the perfect person I could ever wish to see steps in front of my car while I'm stopped at a zebra crossing.

"Dubs have a look who it is. It's only Shirty Bertie from number thirty."

"Fuckin' hell, blud. Check out the walk... That's a bit over the top. I think even gay people would be offended by that."

Don't get me or Dubs wrong, we've got absolutely nothing against gay people whatsoever. The way we see it is whatever makes you happy, keep doing that, no matter what any cunt says to ya.

Shirty Bertie from number thirty is a gayer than gay character who runs 'Pump', the nightclub in Streatham, that just so happens to be located at number thirty on the high street. Part of the attractions he puts on at the club are dancing midgets dressed in all black, leather freaky gear, like harnesses and cowboy chaps.

Everybody knows about those midgets, even Mark, so the second I saw Bertie the idea came to me in a flash.

"Hello Mark, fancy seeing you here."

"Spaniard... What...? How...? How did you get into my garden?"

"Just climbed over the wall. Tried knocking, didn't you hear?"

"No... No I didn't. Who's that over there by the roses?"

"Oh, that's Dubs. He's just having a piss, mate."

"Mark, you little bumbaclart, wagwan...? Shake my hand then, don't leave me hanging, dread."

"Er... Yes, I'm sorry... Hi Dubs, it's good to see you."

"Where's the missus, Mark?" I ask.

"Helen's gone to collect Spencer and Sasha from school. She'll be back soon."

"Maybe it's a good time to get to the point then."

"Perfect time I reckon, blud."

"Mark, why so invisible, mate? I've known you for ages haven't I? You know you can talk to me about anything. You've ignored all my calls, and I'm sure you've listened to your answer machine. What did you think would eventually happen by blanking me? I'm obviously gonna start getting suspicious, don't you think?"

"Double suspicious, Rasta."

"So what's the deal with Amber then Mark?"

"Who?"

"Amber... The number you gave me over the phone that time."

"Amber? I really don't remember, Spaniard. I'm sorry."

"OK. Well, do you by any chance remember Shirty Bertie... the owner of Pump the nightclub in Streatham?"

"Bertie the gay guy?"

"That's the fella. Well, he's agreed to let me and Dubs take you to his club tonight, where you'll volunteer to go up on stage while eight midgets, with Freddie Mercury moustaches, do unspeakable things to your ring-piece, and rather vigorously I must add. Oh, and while all that's going on, I'll be on the sidelines taking a shitload of photos to share with your friends and family, as I seem to have quite an eye for it. Your arsehole will look like a baggy polo neck by the time they've finished with ya, like a peeled banana skin flapping in the wind. So... Ephialtes, do you remember giving me Amber's number now?"

My little bit of bullshit seems to be working, I can tell by his eyes, and the fear in them he's about to spill everything I wanna know. On this occasion, I'm more than happy to burn a bridge. However you look at it, Mark has betrayed me, and there's no possible return from that as far as being an associate goes; business or whatever.

"Spaniard, I honestly don't know anything about her... Only..."

"Only what?"

"Yo Mark, before you carry on, what's that in the jug? Looks kinda fruity."

"That's sangria, Dubs, help yourself."

"That's very kind of you. Don't mind if I do. Do you want some Span?"

"No thanks, mate."

"I'd rather you use a glass please Dubs... Dubs...? Could you...? Is he going to drink the whole jug, Spaniard?"

"It certainly looks like it."

"Ah... that hit the spot, man."

"So carry on Mark, where were we now? Oh yeah, that's right, we were talking about Pandora's box and why you gave it to me."

"OK listen, Spaniard... Swear to me."

"You're a cunt."

"No, swear to me it won't go any further than us three."

"OK, no problem, Scout's honour."

"I was told to give you the number or my life would become very difficult."

"In what way?"

"In a way that a specific thing I do would be exposed to everyone that knows me."

"I take it you're talking about your powder habit?"

"Precisely... He told me to make sure you got the number and everything would be alright."

"And who's 'he'?"

"The chap I score from. You know him. He drives a blue VW Golf."

"Yeah, that'll be Ratboy."

"Yes well, I once overheard him bragging to one of his friends, while completely off his head on coke, about a woman police officer that's been supplying him with a certain merchandise, which I gather must be this Amber person. That's all I really know of her. I've never seen or spoken to the woman. Ratboy's exact words to me were: 'Make sure Spaniard gets this number. Tell him her name is Amber, and she's looking to do business'."

Talk about the plot thickens. It makes perfect sense when you think about it though. Like I said earlier on, Amber the rogue cop obviously has access to seized drugs that are destined for the police furnace. She then simply drops the drugs on Ratboy to sell, discreetly picking up her cut along the way as it's sold, then repeat the process. Ratboy passes information to Amber regarding the whereabouts of other dealers who are then promptly raided, eliminating all competition for the Rat. I bet that's how I came into the picture in the first place. Ratboy must have told her I was serving up and was probably on the radar to get spun. Amber, being ambitious though, would have got a whiff of Dutch that changed her plan. Snaring Dutch could've been a jackpot win for her, with me thrown in as a bonus. Also, for all we know, there could be other crooked cops involved; cops that know about our hidden money because they're in on Amber's thing. The cash she put up probably came from the same place she gets the charlie anyway, so it's dirty money, drug dealers' money.

As me and Dubs set off, I remind Mark not to mention anything about our conversation to absolutely anybody, or else it's midget time.

"So what are you gonna do about Amber, blud?"

"Fuck all at the moment, mate, just wanna see how it pans out. I'm sure at some point she'll be wanting to contact me about the photo or her money. Africa is around the corner, so I'll put my mind to it when we get back."

"What if she wants to do a deal with the photo? Would you be up for it? I mean supposing she asks for the photo and money, and you could walk away from any grief. Would you do it?"

"No, mate. But if she said I could keep the money and walk away scot-free then yeah, she can have the photo, as long as I keep the negative."

Even with all the shit going on with Amber I still kinda miss her. I miss going round her place and experiencing her experimental cooking, the laughs we shared and the drug-fuelled nights; it's a real fucking shame. I thought I'd found 'mi media naranja'.

"Hello Span, can you hear me?"

"Just about. How's things, Tel?"

"Blinding, but listen, I'm coming up to a tunnel and we'll get cut off. That address you gave me over in Battersea to check out is a show home, mate. No cunt lives there."

Forget what I said about missing Amber, I take it all back.

Chapter 31

Surprise, surprise, turns out the crafty Fox can't be in Africa this Friday as planned. Apparently, he all of a sudden needs to be at an important family christening on Saturday, which doesn't do our original plan any favours. All's not lost though, as the sly old Fox had a backup plan; probably all along knowing him.

Me and Dubs will now meet Eddie at Hemingways' bar on Watamu Beach sometime this Friday to go through what needs to be done. Eddie will then take us straight to the site on Saturday morning, picking up this Yo-yo geezer, or whatever the fuck he's called, en route. He'll then wait for a call from Pippa telling him they've arrived so he can bring them to the spot.

I've got a feeling the Fox would've already shown Eddie where to go, because he had no intention of being anywhere near the vicinity with us in the first place; reason being he's a shit trousers. I look over at Dubs who's rocking in his chair with excitement.

"So we're really going, blud?"

"Yeah, and pretty soon, by the look of things."

"And we're gonna be cool with no animals giving us problems?"

"What do you mean Dubs?"

"When you was in the Dam, me and Pete were chatting on the blower one night. He was telling me about a documentary he watched called 'The Laughing Killers'. It was about hyenas in Africa."

"Pete smokes far too much weed, mate. He was trying to freak me out as well with all that bollocks."

"He also said mosquitoes fuck you up too, so we need to get jabs for malaria."

"Pete's paranoia again, Dubs. I've been to Africa before and never bothered with jabs. I was fine and so was every other cunt with me."

"Man, I should know all this shit anyway, dread, my parents are African for fuck's sake. Can you believe I've never been? It's fuckin' embarrassing."

"I know Dubs, you told me ages ago. I wouldn't worry about it. Honestly, it's gonna be fine. Before you know it, we'll be in Ibiza getting on one, matey."

I lay as low as possible the days leading up to Friday. Dubs checked on Pete's house a couple of times during the week for me and all was quiet. Terry Taxi has gone and done the unthinkable at the ripe old age of thirty-two. He's only gone out to Ibiza to try his very first Ecstasy tablet, bless him. Pete and Dutch will look after him, but I've a strong feeling it will get mad pronto. Terry's mind may explode, turning him into an instant raver overnight, possibly even buying a smiley T-shirt.

All I've got to go on when we touch down at Malindi Airport is to make our way to Watamu Beach and look out for a fella sitting in Hemingways' bar with blonde hair called Eddie, who's got an unusually big head. Apparently that's how he got the name Eddie, his real name is Steve.

We arrive in Kenya at three in the afternoon and make

our way straight to Hemingways. The place is like a ghost town, not a big-headed person in sight.

"I fuckin' knew it Dubs. The Fox said Eddie would be here and guess what? He ain't."

"Chill, blud. We're still a bit early, man. Let's build a spliff on the beach, he'll soon come. I'll get us drinks and ask the barman if Eddie has been in yet."

"You got weed Dubs?"

"Of course, man. I ballsed a quarter."

Considering we are in sunny Africa, the barman is the second whitest man in the world. Pete is still campeón del mundo.

"Yo, Rasta, where the fuck is Eddie, man?" says Dubs to the startled barman.

"I'm sorry, sir, I don't know anybody called Eddie. Was he meant to meet you here?"

"Yeah, it's cool though, brother, we're early anyway. We'll wait on the beach for him and take in some African sunshine."

"That sounds marvellous, sir. Can I get you something?"

"You certainly can, my friend. Let me have a dark rum and Coke with plenty of ice in that bad boy, and can you make up some wicked fruit drink for ma bredren? No alcohol though, and put the biggest umbrella you've got in it."

"Of course, sir."

"If you see Eddie, tell him we're just over there on the loungers."

"I'll look out for him, sir. What does he look like?"

"He's a white man with a big, fuck off head, and cheers, brother."

We take a plot outside the bar and relax on some nice plush loungers, surrounded by sand you could fry an egg on. People are slowly emerging with hangovers from nearby hotels dotted along the beach. I'm feeling apprehensive for some reason. I know we're early, but I wanted Eddie to be early too. I wanna get to the site already.

"Is that him, Dubs?"

"Where?"

"Over there by the tree."

"That's a signpost, man. Are you stoned that much?"

"Mate, the sun is proper caning my eyes. I forgot me shades... Can't see fuck all here."

"Relax yourself, Span, he's coming, trust me. I've got a good feeling. Here, blaze this spliff, man, it'll do ya good."

Two hours and three spliffs later, still no Eddie. I'm now getting restless, hot and bothered. My jeans are soaked through with sweat, and sand has found its way up my arse. I'll give Pete a bell and wish him happy birthday to take my mind off the heat and going insane. As my phone is no use to me out here, I make my way into the bar and get comfortable by a payphone, and pretty much feed thirty quid in change to it.

"Hello Pete, can you hear me? How's things going your end, fella?"

"Safe, bruv. It's mad here already, man. Dutch is giving me tips, boy. I'm gonna be fucking some honeys tonight."

"Glad to hear it. How is Sting by the way?"

"He's epic. Walked straight through customs with a thousand Ecstasy like a boss."

"Fuck off."

"I'm telling ya. Maybe they thought he really was Sting and let him swerve a frisk. The rest of us got proper searched."

"At least you're there now, mate. I still say you should've come out here with us though. I'm telling ya, it's ridiculously hot. Me and Dubs are just plotted on the beach having a pleasant little smoke waiting for this Eddie bod to turn up. The cunt's late, to be honest, but other than that it's beautiful here, you'd fuckin' love it."

"Trust me, that's never happening, bruv. One word; hyenas, the laughing killers."

"That's four words, Pete."

"I don't care, it still ain't happening."

"I'm telling ya there's no hyenas here, or lions, or leopards."

"There's always hyenas in Africa, man, and they're always laughing, which means they love killing. I'm perfectly happy here in Ibiza, bruv. I think you and Dubs are just jealous, innit, that I'm out here kicking it with the boys in fanny central."

"Yeah whatever, ya clown. Is Dingo there yet?"

"No, he arrives sometime tomorrow now, his flight was delayed."

"That's a fuckin' surprise."

"Yeah, tell me about it. You boys ready? For Ratboy I mean."

"We're ready, or should I say will be when Eddie turns up."

"Then what's next? What the fuck is that noise, man? Can you hear it? Every five seconds?"

"That's me feeding this fuckin' payphone... Anyway, then we kip at his place for the night, then off to the site first thing in the morning to set up. I just hope Eddie's got all the stuff we need; can't afford a setback, you know what I mean? Me and Dubs are sitting here with hand luggage only for a couple of days, so this Eddie better liven up."

"Span, just come over here if he don't turn up soon, it's as easy as that. Me and Dutch will warm a couple of birds up for ya, sorted innit."

"Nice, I appreciate that Don Juan. You clubbing it later or taking it easy?"

"You know we're gonna be smashing it, Span man. My birthday started the second I touched down. I'm taking no prisoners. It's already getting mucho messy."

"Pete the party monster ready to paint the town red."

"You know that. I fuckin' love it here, man. I'm gonna use my stashed cash to buy an apartment here, I'm telling ya."

"Now is that before you crack the music business or the cannabis oil business?"

"Forget that, I want a place out here, innit bruv."

"You probably could quite easily I should imagine. I'm itching to dig that dough up to see how much we actually made. I'd like to treat myself to a nice little studio flat in the Dam; been thinking about it all week."

"Wicked Span, we could visit each other and shit."

"I don't need you visiting me to shit if I'm being completely honest, Pete."

"Funny. And what about Amber? Any news on her?"

"Yeah, a bit. Me and Dubs managed to bump into Posh Mark in his back garden, of all places. Anyway, he told us some stuff about her that we'll fill you in on when we see ya. Basically, I'm still gonna wait to see how it pans out now she knows about the photo."

"Safe. So in case it goes tits up your end, do you wanna know where I moved the cash? You never know, bruv, you might need that money fast before I get back, man."

"You're kidding, right? You really wanna tell me over the phone the location to our dough knowing how hot things are at the moment? And I'm not talking about this sunshine here that's melting my fuckin' forehead into me eyes."

"OK, but don't be calling me for the location if it comes on top for ya tomorrow and you need to grab your cut to disappear overnight. I'll be well and truly off my face, bruv, missing in action. This is the last sensible conversation I'm having until next week."

"You don't know the meaning of the word sensible, Pete, but anyway listen, I'm out of change and have to fuck off. You have a blinder of a time, mate, and happy birthday to ya. Hold on... Dubs is here now and says happy birthday, bumbaclart."

"Tell him cheers."

"He heard ya. He's right next to me."

"Also tell him, when he gets here, he needs to teach me how to dance. When I can dance like Dubs, combined with my tips from Dutch, I'm gonna be an unstoppable sex machine, Span man, you wait and see."

"I can believe it. You take care, Pete. We'll catch up with you on Sunday. See ya soon, mate."

"Safe, bruv."

Eddie is now really taking the piss, he's three hours late and knows I have no way of contacting him. The soppy cunt's probably gone fishing or is sitting in the wrong bar pissed out of his mind waiting for us.

"Dubs, there he is."

"Who?"

"Eddie."

"Where?"

"There... With the head."

"Where, man? You talking about him over there? With the blue shirt?"

"Yeah, with the big head."

"Blud... That's a geezer carrying a TV on his shoulder."

It's getting late, we are both now thinking of the awkward situation facing us when Pippa arrives with the Rat, and we're also hit with a serious case of the munchies, so pop into Hemingways for the best fuckin' burger in the world.

"Jambo, gentleman. You must be Dabs and you must be Spanish," says a fella sitting at the bar with the biggest head I've ever laid eyes on. Christ almighty I've never seen anything like it. How the fuck he got into the building with it is a mystery on its own. It reminds me of a hot-air balloon.

"He's Dubs, I'm Spaniard. You must be Eddie. How long have you been sitting here?"

"Only about fifteen minutes. Sorry I'm late; the fucking Land Cruiser wouldn't start."

"Nice... Is it gonna start tomorrow Ed when we need it?"

"Of course, Spanish, it's not a problem. I put a new battery in her this afternoon. She purrs like a cat now."

"That's reassuring to hear, and it's Spaniard, Eddie."

"You guys will be coming back to my house, yes? Then we leave first thing in the morning, yes?"

"What do you reckon Dubs? Are you ready, mate?"

"I reckon this burger is fuckin' incredible, blud."

Chapter 32

Eddie is alright really. People are always late, so what. Dubs is right, I need to chill out more. At the end of the day, he managed to get the right gear together and that's the main thing, although I had to have words with him about the deckchairs which are absolute bastards. I had a decent four-hour kip on Eddie's sofa, and judging by Dubs snoring away on a hammock outside so did he. Before we set off on our mission, it's back to Hemingways for a spot of breakfast.

"I'm gonna give Pete another bell Dubs; guaranteed he's still raving."

"Safe blud. You want me to order you some breakfast?"

"Yeah, please mate; eggs and bacon."

Back by the payphone, the air conditioning feels far too fuckin' cold, honestly I'm freezing. It's too early to have it on anyway. The sun's only just now having a stretch and rubbing its eyes. I make the call to Pete, and get greeted by Terry Taxi.

"Tel, you raver, how's things? Where's Pete?"

"Span? Fuckin' hell."

"I hope so, because I certainly ain't going to heaven."

"Mate... It's Pete."

"What's he done? You sound hyper, Tel. Slow down you first-timer."

"It's Pete, Span... He's gone."

"What do you mean he's gone? Gone where?"

"He's gone, mate."

"What are you telling me, Tel? He's dead?"

"Yeah, I can't believe it."

"For fuck's sake... How the fuck?"

"We'd been out clubbing and ended up at an after-party at some DJ's fancy apartment in San Antonio. Pete was out of it, Span, proper rotten. Coke, Ecstasy, booze; he wasn't holding back. Me and Dutch tried to get him to calm down but it's his birthday, what are we gonna do? He told us he was going to get some fresh air over by a window. We heard screams and was told by some sort, he sat on the window ledge thinking the window was closed and leant back against it. He rolled straight out and down four floors. The paramedic said he died on impact."

"Fuckin' hell, Tel."

"I know, Span. We're all over the place out here. What a fuckin' thing to happen."

"Tel, I'm on a payphone, and about to run out of..."

Pete's dead? That's gotta be a joke, but Terry doesn't do jokes... so fucking hell.

Dubs can see by the expression on my face something is up.

"What's up, blud?"

"Pete's dead."

"What?"

"He's gone, Dubs... Fell out of a fuckin' window."

"How the hell did he manage that?"

"According to Terry, he took coke, pills, booze and lost the plot. Went to sit over on a window ledge for some fresh air and fell out of it, or something like that. Me money ran out, and we got cut off."

Eddie has no clue what we're talking about. He knows it's a personal thing and pretty serious, but fair play to the man for giving us some space and not questioning it. Me and Dubs agree we've come too far; we can't let it get in the way of our mission. Gotta stay focused, gotta put Pete to the back of our minds, at least until the Ratboy situation is mission complete. Easier said than done I know, but there's nothing we can do anyway... I feel fuckin' sad... I miss my crazy pal already and it ain't even sunk in yet.

The place we're heading for is the Tana River. According to Eddie, it's a four-hour drive from Watamu.

"So Ed, did Foxy give you the message about another car?" I ask.

"For you guys? Yes, of course. Ayo will bring a car for you. How else would you leave when we go, eh?"

"Exactly, mate."

"So Spanish."

"Oh, for fuck's sake."

"If you don't mind me asking, why the hell do these people want a romantic dinner on the Tana River? That's very dangerous business."

"Dangerous in what way, Ed?"

"Well, let's just say they better not go swimming. Look, there's Ayo now. He will follow us."

"What the fuck is that?"

"That's a Datsun Cherry, blud."

"Yeah, I know Dubs, but of all the motors you could pick to go where we're going, this clown brings a Datsun Cherry."

"Span, get on that paint job though."

"Ed, are you sure about that car, mate? It looks like it's been painted with a roller."

"That's because it has. Ayo done it himself."

290

"He's used three different shades of green, with a painter's roller and brush. Is that normal behaviour to you, Ed?"

"I did ask him about that. He said it's paint he had left over that was sitting in his shed doing nothing."

"So he thought it'd be a cracking idea to paint a car with it? Me and Dubs are gonna look like a right pair of cunts in that."

If you're wondering about this marvel, the car is a 1972 Datsun Cherry in three shades of green that definitely wasn't an optional extra at the time. The body of the car has been hand-painted with a decorator's brush and a roller, in pistachio green. The bonnet is apple green, and the roof is olive. All done without the need of any masking whatsoever; we are talking strictly freehand here. Speaking of hands, I've just noticed green handprints on the tyres too, like a fuckin' cave painting. Believe me, the car is a sight to behold.

The conversation regarding the Datsun Cherry pretty much lasted the four-hour drive to the Tana River. On arrival, an executive decision was made.

"Ed, you're taking the fuckin' Datsun, we'll have the Land Cruiser."

"You can't guys, I need it."

"Not as much as us though, you know where the fuck you're going. You ain't gonna get lost, so you can take the bastard Cherry. If we get lost, four-wheel drive is what could save us out here. Have a look around, Eddie; do we really look like we're meant to be here? We're a couple of bods from Stockwell, mate. I'm wearing Chelsea boots and a Ben Sherman shirt, and you're dressed as a fuckin' explorer. Who out of me and you looks like they know this sort of land?"

"Really guys, I can't do it. Trust me, if I could I would."

"Do you want Dubs to punch you in the head?"

"No, I don't want that."

"And let's face it, he's got some fuckin' target, he ain't exactly gonna miss is he?"

"I'm gonna punch him anyway Span, his head annoys me. Eddie, come here."

If my calculations are right, Pippa should be at Watamu Beach in around five hours. Eddie sets off to pick them up, leaving Ayo with us to crack on with our cunning illusion.

The spot we're at is surprising beautiful considering our intentions. We're on a grassy bank with a five-foot, gentle slope to the water's edge. Dunes, lined with dense plant growth, conceal us from anyone this side of the river; not that there's anyone about, it's completely deserted. Flying insects of every sort zigzag and dart over the water's surface, as the early morning sun jump-starts the river's ecosystem; Mother Nature's rise and shine. Can't see any crocodiles though, which is a bit of a downer. As nice as this place is, we're meant to be here for the crocs, not sightseeing. It's half six in the morning, surely at least one croc would be around? Nope.

"Ayo, where's all the crocodiles, mate?"

"Sleeping now. It is too cold for them, they like the sun when it is hot."

"Sleeping where?"

"Across river, there. Plenty crocodiles sleeping, hiding, waiting for the sun. They not wake up now. Later when the sun is high in the sky you will see crocodile."

We decide to build the campsite twenty metres from the water's edge, up on the lush green part of the bank away from the mud. There's a horseshoe of bushes and trees surrounding the site giving me and Dubs ample hiding places to observe from when Pip and Ratboy arrive.

I cross my fingers, as I double-check to see what Eddie has

left us. A small, foldaway, wooden table, one cooler filled to the brim with ice containing two steaks, a six-pack of beer, bottle of white wine, a shit, throwaway barbecue with a couple of paper plates, for fuck's sake, some plastic cutlery, and not forgetting the two bastard deckchairs; oh, and a camouflage tent for two.

Ayo goes off to gather wood so he can build a campfire, while me and Dubs doss on a fallen tree to smoke weed and be lazy. Ayo comes back, minutes later, carrying enough wood to build a Trojan Horse. How the bloody hell somebody so tiny can carry that amount of wood is beyond me. He reminds me of an ant that can lift untold times its body weight. Ayo's about five foot or just under, but with a never-ending supply of energy. It's like he's on some kind of Duracell high; he ain't stopped for a break since we got here. It's obvious to us Ayo's a good bloke with a heart of gold; the fella can't do enough and always with a smile. I had to pull a cuntish move on him earlier though, that I genuinely feel pretty rough about, but it had to be done because it was fuckin' with me retinas. I got him to park the Datsun far away behind a bush, out of sight. It hurt his feelings and was the only time Ayo lost his smile. He motions for us to come over, like he wants us to follow him. He disappears behind a row of small trees, as we stumble after him. Ayo hushes us as he points down to a thin, sandy stretch of the river, a bottleneck no more than twenty yards from our position.

"There's elephants, Span, look, and zebra. Wicked, blud."

"Now that's what I call a savannah view. I knew I should have brought my camera."

Ayo points lower, then lower still, towards a huge log resting on the muddy bank down below.

"Span, are you seeing what's next to that log down

there...? It's a crocodile, dread."

"That is the General," whispers Ayo.

"The General?" asks Dubs, not even slightly whispering.

"Yes, my people call him the General. He is the number two boss of the river. Look carefully, he has only one eye. King Bolo took the other eye."

"Slow down, Ayo. King Bolo?" Now I'm interested.

"Yes, that is King Bolo, with the General."

He points towards the log lying next to the General. I'm squinting but can't see fuck all.

"All I can see is one croc, Ayo, the General. Can you see what he's on about Dubs?"

"Nah, blud, I only see one as well, and he looks fuckin' evil. Ayo, what are you going on about King Bolo? I see only the General and a big-arse log."

"That is no log. That is King Bolo."

From what I can make out, that log right over in the distance has gotta be around seventeen feet long. It's hard to tell, as it's the same colour as the mud; a dark brown, almost black, definitely not the normal look for a croc. He's a massive beast, broad and chunky, with a head as long as a Mini Cooper. Never saw anything like it on Pete's nature videos. He's like a cross between an alligator and a crocodile, a crocogator. The General, on the other hand, looks like a textbook crocodile; around thirteen feet with various shades of green and black markings. He's also rocking a much narrower build, streamlined for speed. King Bolo is wide, really fuckin' wide, like an aircraft carrier.

"What kind of size is he Ayo?" asks Dubs.

"He is over five metres, a very big boy. The General is four metres but very fast."

Ayo tells us that King Bolo and the General are the reason

there aren't any other crocs in this small section of the river, they've all fucked off out the way of these two troublemakers. The King has claimed these waters, and all bow to the King. The General is his partner in crime. They hunt together, grabbing the prey at opposite ends and death rolling the fuck out of it into manageable chunks of flesh to be swallowed. To survive a harsh environment, teaming up is always gonna do you a favour. King Bolo has the power, the General has speed; a deadly combination.

If I had Ratboy here now asleep, we could simply carry him down and just leave him snoring at the water's edge in full view of King Bolo; job done. That's only a distance of twenty yards from Rat to croc, but more importantly, there's an easy escape route for us in case the scaly rascal fancies afters.

Ayo slowly descends to see if he gets a reaction, but nothing, he's still too far. The reptiles lie motionless on the riverbank, mouths open, eyes watching. Ayo approaches the water's edge and throws a small pebble just to the side of the General. Still no reaction from either croc, so Ayo moves closer. He's now on the bank where I thought would be an ideal spot to lay Ratboy if he was here. King Bolo is the first to take interest. He shifts his massive bulk round to face Ayo, mouth closed, observing what's on the menu. Ayo seems to be having fun.

"You see me King Bolo, I am here. Come and say hello to Ayo."

The King is waiting, he ain't stupid. He's not gonna burn precious energy to cross a stretch of river and onto land for a disappointment, he knows he's been seen. Crocodiles are ambush predators; he wants you in his world where you haven't noticed him. Ayo kicks off his boots and stands ankle-deep at the river's edge, pounding the surface with a stick.

King Bolo launches into the water with astonishing speed.

Ayo must have some kind of sly teleportation device, because he's now standing behind me, and his boots are somehow back on his feet; incredible. The King cruises off, his massive back glinting in the sun, closely followed by the General in his wake. The two crocs are now closer to the campsite, with more closing in, but still keeping their distance from the dynamic duo. Ayo's presence has sparked activity, as scores of smaller crocs quickly invade the area left by the King.

We decide to head back to the campsite in preparation for Ratboy and Pippa. It's all looking good. The tent is up, the fire is blazing, table for two set; all is cosy. I'm keeping a mental time of their arrival, and I reckon around two hours until they get here. We're ready and waiting. I want them to hurry up; King Bolo and the General are right where we need them.

A parade of elephants, with thirsty calves, approach the edge of the river, eyeing the shallows with caution. Years of experience, handed down by the elders, have given them everything they need to know about the dangers of a watering hole. The calves are still too young though; babies that see water as a happy place. The General sees an opportunity and moves into position. King Bolo stays within sight of the herd as they cautiously approach, always visible, a classic strategy unfolding. Two calves innocently enter the murky water, the overwhelming need to drink blinding them to the imminent danger lurking a metre beneath the surface. The General inches closer, pausing to get his bearings. King Bolo senses the General's position and makes his move to flank one of the babies; diving like a stealth submarine, he moves in. The calves are in shallow water, and the King needs to be careful with his approach. He can't afford to blow his cover, so he waits. Breaking the surface without a ripple the King's eyes scan the horizon, the babies are playing. A slight flick of his tail and the trap is set, he's in position; the General on the right, King Bolo on the left, baby in the middle. Ayo tells me the target is a two-week-old female calf, who at the moment, is rolling about and having a splash, doing what baby elephants do in water, going slightly nuts. She's not shy, probably never even seen a croc. A glimpse of the General's back, breaking the surface a couple of feet away, looks like an old log to her, but not to the experienced. The matriarch charges into the shallows with its tusks lowered, almost knocking over the calf, stabbing and thrashing at the water. The General vanishes with lightning speed into the safety of the deep, surfacing slowly behind the King. Two more elephants enter the river. The three form a defensive line in front of the calves who have no idea what all the fuss is about. Bolo eyes up the competition, twelve tons of trumpeting madness is not exactly his idea of a pleasant day, especially when he can see in the distance a couple of parched-looking zebras approaching on the other side of the riverbank, where the General is already heading, right next to the campsite.

Chapter 33

As much as I've been trying to not think about Pete, he still keeps creeping into my thoughts. I'm only human, not a machine you can just switch off like that. A very good pal of mine has just died and not a thing can be done about it. I feel like I should be doing something, but what? The boys over in Ibiza will be sorting whatever needs to be sorted, I'm sure, but I feel like I shouldn't be here. I feel like I'm the one that should be over there doing the sorting, and it's haunting me. Is it because I wasn't in Ibiza to stop Pete from getting so out of it? No, I can't blame myself for anything that went on out there. Truth be told, I wouldn't have stopped Pete from getting so caned. He always gets out of it, and always handles it. What happened was an accident; a very fuckin' unfortunate one but still an accident. The same thing would have happened either way. Knowing Pete, he would definitely want us to see this mission through. He knows how dangerous Ratboy is, and so do I... I also feel a bit better after processing all that.

"Dubs can you hear anything?"

"That's a motor... Definitely a motor."

The faint sound of a car approaching has us on alert. Are we ready? Of course we are. What am I even thinking? We've been ready for hours. A quick jog to the river's edge confirms the General and King Bolo are still waiting for those two zebras to go for a paddle; perfect.

In the distance, a speeding Land Cruiser is kicking up more dust than it should be. I mean, is he fuckin' sure? We're trying to be a touch sneaky here, and he's swerving all over the shop like there's a wasp in the cabin.

"That's Eddie, Dubs... driving like a cunt."

"Is he pissed or something?"

"Definitely something, mate... OK, so when they get here Ayo, you're gonna be like a waiter, yeah?"

"Yes, I will cook steaks. Ayo cooks the best steaks."

"It might be worth waiting to see if they want them first before you fire them up, Ayo. Besides, I'm starving and would rather us eat them steaks."

"You know that, blud."

A quick glance up at the dirt road and we're seconds away from contact. Me and Dubs blend into the bushes like we're really fuckin' good at it. The Land Cruiser comes to an irate stop. Doors fly open followed by an angry Eddie, followed immediately by an even angrier Pippa, absolutely dripping with puke. No sign of Ratboy though. What the hell is going on?

"Spaniard! Where the fuck are you, man? It's OK, he's sleeping already," shouts Pip.

"This is not cool, Spanish, not fucking cool! Look at the state of me... Jesus Christ!" says Eddie.

We tiptoe over to find out some news. It's not as bad as I thought. Ratboy got absolutely smashed on the plane; ridiculously drunk. Pip says he kept coming over to her seat hassling her and there was major grief when they touched down too. He was non-stop, aggressively groping her all the way through the airport and into Eddie's waiting Toyota Land Cruiser. Within ten minutes, she styles it out to Eddie that she's busting for a piss and to pull over at a bar, where she quickly jumps out to buy a bottle of Tusker beer, dropping a 30 mg temazepam inside. We peep inside the Land Cruiser, and there's puke everywhere. It's on the windows, roof, floor, seats, not a dry spot to be seen. Ratboy is slumped on the back seat, with the side of his face pressed against the window, head-to-toe in vomit.

"This bastard puked all over my car. That's not good Spanish."

"He was drunk, Ed, it happens. The important thing is you're here now."

"Where's the Datsun, Spanish?"

"You don't need to know where the Datsun is, Eddie boy."

"Come on, man, I'm taking the fucking Datsun."

"No way, Ed, it ain't happening, mate. We're going from here straight to the airport in the multi-green Cherry. I'm not gonna be sitting on a plane reeking of puke. Now if you don't mind, can we lie this cunt on the ground?"

Just as I say that I open the back door, and Ratboy rolls straight out, face first, onto the grass. We freeze; is he gonna wake up? Doesn't look like it, thank fuck. He's lying on his back, smiling and snoring.

"Ed remember, I'm sorry about the puke, mate, but stick to the plan, yeah? If he wakes up at some point, don't leave without Pippa and Ayo because it'll fuck us up big time."

"I'm not leaving, Spanish, I'll be here cleaning my fucking car."

"You've done well Pip, I'm proud of ya. Even more so now you're covered in his puke."

"Yes, thank you Spaniard, that makes me feel wonderful right now."

Just as she says that, Pippa gives the sleeping Rat the lightest of kicks that makes him twitch.

"Oh fuck!" I think I say. I might have thought it while diving into a nearby bush. Ratboy rolls onto his front and starts coughing and swearing. He's still clearly pissed, but the sleeper also still has hold of him, and as he stumbles to his feet it could go either way. He could turn aggressive, chilled, or fall back to sleep.

The Rat stands there, swaying, with his face pointing to the sky but eyes closed. He's got no idea where he is, and I'm thinking if he were to walk in a straight line for about twelve yards to the water, it would be goodnight from him, and a thank you from us.

Eddie is taking no notice whatsoever of what's going on around him, he's too busy standing there with his hands on his hips looking at his Land Cruiser while swearing loudly in Afrikaans. I stick my arm out of the bush and point to the table for two.

"Pip, sit him down at the table," I whisper… obviously loud enough so she can hear.

Pip slowly tries to guide the Rat towards one of the chairs, speaking to him with a happy tone. Not far to go, about four more steps should do it, but he stops. Come on you fucker, just four more steps and you can sit down… Not sure if I just said that out loud, but if I did, he didn't hear it. Ratboy begins to shuffle towards the river, it's as though the sleeper is trying its best to shut him down but the amount of booze in him is somehow fighting to keep him upright. Either that or he puked up the sleeper before it had time to fully dissolve into his system.

The Rat is standing motionless, just feet away from the water's edge. A slight ripple dances across the surface, followed by an eerie stillness. The General is interested, those zebras can wait. He's already in position, as Ratboy takes a half step forward. Do I really want this to happen in front of Pip, Ed and Ayo? Mind you, accidents happen, but the original plan leaves no witnesses, and my gut is telling me the same thing. I chance a move and slip out of the bush, sneaking within earshot of Pippa on my hands and knees, hidden from the swaying Rat by the tent.

"Pip... Psst, Pip... Pippa... Oi!" Now she hears me. "Come here."

Pip sidesteps towards the tent.

"Listen Pip, drop another sleeper in one of those beers in the cooler, and hand it to him. He'll drink it. Fuck the original plan about getting him to sit at the table, just get him to take another kipper and leave the rest to us."

"OK... Man, I'm shitting myself."

"You're doing well Pip. Relax, mate."

Pip pops open a bottle of beer and drops in a 30 mg temazepam. Ratboy immediately turns and walks straight towards the tent. I drop to my belly and slip off backwards with a wriggle, like a cheeky salamander.

"What the fuck are you doing, slag?" Is what I think he just said to Pippa.

"Just getting you a beer. I thought you might like one."

That's my girl. Relax. Gently does it now.

Ratboy snatches the bottle from Pip and begins to funnel it down like it's the last beer in the world. Technically, if all goes well, it will be.

"You said you was gonna suck my cock when we got out here, so there it is. Suck it then."

Can't really call what he's just pulled out a cock, more like a three-inch, limp, veiny vein. Pip does a stellar job at swerving it by suggesting they get comfy on the grass and drink some more.

"Here... Let's sit by the fire, but I'm going to ask Eddie and the other guy to give us some privacy."

"Who the fuck is Eddie?"

"My brother, the driver that brought us here, remember? He's over there cleaning his car. Wait here, I'll be two minutes."

"Fuckin' hurry up."

Ratboy lies back on the soft grass and closes his eyes. Pippa stands over him, with a look of complete disgust on her face. I honestly think if nobody was about there'd be a strong chance she'd plunge a knife in him and roll him into the water. That's the sort of look we're talking about.

"What do you reckon Dubs? I think he's out, mate."

"I think the same, blud. Shall we sling him in then?"

That's what I'm talking about, enthusiasm.

"Soon... Let's wait a second. I'll get Pip to check him."

After checking him, we let ten minutes go by without any movement from the Rat, then show ourselves.

"Ed, Pip, Ayo, you've all been amazing, but now it's time for you to split. There's not a lot of time for goodbyes, so goodbye."

We leave Pippa, Eddie and Ayo arguing over who sits where in the Land Cruiser and head back over to the sleeping Rat. I look at him snoozing away, with the sun glinting off the dry bits of vomit plastered all over his face. I remember when he was different; I remember when we were friends. I don't hear Eddie leave, but can tell by the lack of noise behind me we're now alone, and a quick turn confirms it. Dubs grabs hold of Ratboy's ankles and me the wrists, followed by a cursory look around; all is clear.

"How are we gonna do this Span?"

"Let's just drop him over there near those reeds, on the bank, where Bolo can see him."

"The General's there, dread. I can see his nostrils just out of the water. Look, see him? He'll snatch us instead of Ratboy. I'm not going near there, blud, trust me."

"Let me go have a quick look."

I very slowly edge my way down the bank towards the reeds. The mud is baked rock hard by the sun making progress swift and easy. There's a small branch at my feet begging to be thrown at the General. I do and he disappears underwater.

This is our chance to place the Rat. Another look; still clear. King Bolo must be on the bottom of the river chillin' with the General. I sprint back to Dubs and get hold of the Rat's arms, Dubs grabs his ankles. Three metres from the water and we're looking good. Two metres, I can see bubbles but no crocs. One metre and that'll do for me.

"Here will do, Dubs. We don't want Ratboy getting wet or he might wake up."

Ratboy is still in our hands, as the King rockets from the water clamping his massive jaws around the Rat's waist. Ratboy's eyes spring open, he doesn't scream or make a sound, just stares right at me, into my soul, as he's dragged to the bottom of the river.

I look at Dubs, who's still holding on to the Rat's shoes.

"Did you see that, blud! Did you see his fucking eyes open? Jesus Christ, man, that was awesome!"

"Fuckin' hell Dubs, did you see him look at me...? That shit is gonna haunt me for the rest of my life, mate."

"Nah, man, you'll forget that shit in time. It's done, he's gone, dread. Shame we never got to see him suffer though."

The timing of Dubs saying that couldn't have been better. The second we turn to walk away, Ratboy shoots to the surface screaming and gasping for air, arms outstretched, hoping to grab hold of something that clearly isn't there.

"HELP ME PLEASE!"

"Now that's interesting Dubs."

"What's that then, blud?"

"FUCKIN' HELP MEEE!"

"Well, we might get to see him suffer after all. He does look pretty scared at the moment."

"SOMEBODY, PLEASE HELP ME!"

"He looks double scared, dread, but I wanna see blood and gore. We came all this way, you know? Kinda feels like an anticlimax what with all the planning it took."

"SPANIARD, YOU CUNT, HELP ME!

"OK, GIVE ME A SECOND… Sling him his shoes Dubs."

King Bolo's jaws clamp down on the Rat once again, as he frantically tries to swim to shore. Bolo lifts his head high out of the water and crunches down hard, a now limp Ratboy hanging between his teeth. It's like he's showing all the other crocs watching from a distance why he's the king. Bolo smashes the lifeless Rat down onto the surface, as a signal for the General to get in on the snack. The second Ratboy hits the water, the General rips in and takes hold of his head, shaking it once then twisting it clean off. King Bolo only has to gulp twice and the Rat is gone. The General, however, seems to wanna savour the moment. He's proudly cruising close to the bank with Ratboy's head still in his mouth. He's showing it off to us, it's his trophy. The panic in Ratboy's eyes staring back at me between those jaws, frozen at the point of death, makes me wonder about all those girls he put through hell. They probably had that same look of terror every single day while they were imprisoned at his hole.

"Now that's more like it. BRAVO GENTLEMEN! BRAVO."

"That was amazing, blud. I feel like I got my money's worth now."

A standing ovation had to be done. I mean, come on, you've gotta admit, twisting the Rat's head off and cruising past us with it in his mouth was flash as fuck from the General. He was smiling too, the General that is, not Ratboy. I'm trying to think of a way to describe the expression on the Rat's face, and I think I've nailed it. Picture someone about to blow a smoke ring, now open their eyes as wide as they can fuckin' go. Have you got that visual? Good, now open the eyes even wider and that's exactly how he looked. And do you wanna know something else? I don't feel bad for what I've done. I know it's only just happened, and maybe it's too fresh to sink in yet, but a world without Ratboy is now a better place for everyone. That's how I see it anyway. Don't get me wrong, I also don't feel amazing for what I've done, believe me, but if I didn't get rid of Ratboy, he would've got rid of me one way or the other, whether that's by grassing me up, or having me killed... like he already tried before. What's just happened goes further than revenge though, it's about those girls' souls too. You heard Dubs say Ratboy was already setting up another place to continue that business, so in other words, he'd never stop until he's stopped. I'm listening to myself while telling you that, wondering in a way if I'm the real monster. Let's not forget something here, and that's the crackhead I kicked into the canal over in the Dam, who's more than likely dead. That makes two people I've killed, and my feelings are blunt to both of them. I look at my hands and don't see any blood, but I'm fully aware that don't make it right, I still did it. Only time will tell if it affects me later on in life and if my conscience can

306

handle it.

The campsite looks spot on as it is; just needs a couple of empty beer cans here and there for the final touch.

"Dread, the steaks are still in the cooler. I'm cooking them up, do you want?"

"Yeah, sweet. The same as you, medium rare."

"Safe. Do you want some wine?"

"As it happens, on this occasion, I will Dubs... Cheers and good health to ya."

We sit at the table and look out on to the savannah. Grazing animals in the distance go about their business, while dark clouds threaten a heavy downpour.

"We better fuck off after these steaks. It's gonna piss down, mate."

"Span, you know it ain't over yet. Remember the Datsun Cherry? We've still gotta drive that bastard cuntmobile back to Hemingways."

"The nightmare continues, Dubs. Let's skin one up for the road and fuck off from here."

"Sounds good to me."

We leave the campsite exactly as it is and make our way to where Ayo parked the car. I'm feeling relieved to be going, it's been an adventure and a half I'll never forget.

"Where the fuck is the motor, Dubs?"

"It was here, blud, I know for sure it was here. I saw Ayo park it here."

We both do a three-sixty; no Datsun Cherry on the horizon. Quite a few giraffes but definitely no Datsun Cherry.

"What the hell do we do now?" asks Dubs.

"I can't believe Ayo took the car. It was only him and us that knew where it was. It's gotta be him. What a little cunt."

"Man, let's hit the road and hope for a lift. It's getting

dark, Span. What time is it anyway?"

"Coming up to half six. Mate, check out that storm in the distance."

We trot back to the campsite and take the road Eddie took. His tyre tracks are fresh giving us at least some idea of a direction. We walk for an hour soaked through to the skin, miserable, tired and maybe too stoned for these conditions.

"Do you know what Dubs?"

"What's that, dread?"

"With everything that's just gone on, I completely forgot about Pete."

"Fuck, yeah man, me too. Poor Pete."

"I'm gonna miss that crazy bod."

"Definitely."

"The funeral is gonna be double grim, I'm not looking forward to it."

"I was thinking something back at the camp, blud. I know this might be a bad time, but what about the buried money?"

"It's not a bad time, I've been thinking about it too. We're fucked, I think, as only Pete knew the spot."

"Maybe he told Dingo? You and him get on well, so all could still be sweet. You gotta look on the bright side."

"Dubs, have you noticed anything?"

"Like what?"

"We don't seem to be walking on the road anymore. We're in the fuckin' bush, mate. We could've been walking hours across the savannah in the wrong direction. I think we need to go back that way."

"Span, I swear it's this way."

"Are you sure, Dubs? Your sense of direction is better than mine, so I'm going with yours."

"Yeah, let's go, man, it's almost dark. The road's gonna be

this way, trust me."

Two more hours and still no road. It's now night and very fuckin' dark. The light cast by the moon is all we have to go by. We're lost, very lost, and our adrenalin has now kicked in, the various growls and indescribable noises in the darkness make sure of that.

"Span, do you hear laughing?"

"I was hoping it was in my head Dubs, but yeah, to the left of me. I can hear it."

"Blud, I can hear it behind and to the right of me."

"Fuckin' hell, now it's all around us. I bet Pete's looking down shaking his head saying he told us so."

"Span, the laughing's close, man! WHAT THE FUCK! We're surrounded!"

A flash of lightning turns night into day for a split second.

"Dubs, did you see that tree? Just up ahead in front of us?"

"What that skinny thing over there? That ain't gonna hold the two of us, no way."

"It's our only hope, mate. We jump on either side and climb up; balance it out. Come on it's twenty yards away, we can make it. Are you ready?"

"FUCK! Something just touched my leg! There's untold, Span. They're too fast, there's too many of them!"

"Dubs, are you ready?"

"I'm ready, blud! I'm ready!"

"On the count of three, I'm gonna go for the left-hand side."

"Let's fuckin' do it, Span!"

"One... Two... Three..."

GLOSSARY

Apple / apple core: *score*

Boat / boat race: *face*
Bod / bods: *a person / people*
Bottle / bottle and glass: *arse*
Brass / brass flute: *prostitute*
Brown gear: *heroin*

Canister: *head*

Dairy: *heat / pressure*
Drum / drum & bass: *place / home / house*

Ghosted: *killed / murdered*
Gregory / Gregory Peck: *neck*

Hampton / Hampton Wick: *prick / dick / penis*

Jacks / Jack Jones: *alone*
Jekyll and Hyde: *snide / fake*

Keep dog / keeping dog: *a lookout*

Lemon / lemon barley: *charlie / cocaine*
Little fellas: *Ecstasy tablets*

Niagaras / Niagara Falls: *balls*
Nish: *nothing*

On top:	*rumbled / discovered*
Percy:	*a small amount of drugs for personal use*
Plate / plated:	*oral sex on a female*
Pony / pony and trap:	*crap*
Radio Rental:	*mental*
Sherbet / Sherbet Dab:	*cab*
Shit trousers:	*a coward*
Sigh:	*an idiot*
Sky / sky rocket:	*pocket*
Syrup / syrup of figs:	*wig*
Tackled up:	*stockings and suspenders*
Wizard / Wizard of Oz:	*an ounce*

ACKNOWLEDGMENTS

Before I forget, I've gotta thank a few people for making my life that much easier, while embarking on this little experiment (adventure).

Kasia Krasuska.
A rock seems too weak a word.

Juan Luis Arias Gutierrez.
What can I say mate? A massive thank you.

Ron Mayne.
For being an encyclopaedia on weaponry
(which is pretty fuckin' scary).

Dean 'Binsy' Cook.
For keeping it old school.

And a big thanks to **SpiffingCovers** for putting it all together. I can't wait to see what you guys come up with for my next cover.

Printed in Great Britain
by Amazon